P9-DEV-358

THE TRUSTEES OF THE PUBLIC LIBRARY
OF THE CITY OF BOSTON
EMR

# The Great Movies

A Ridge Press Book

Grosset & Dunlap, Inc.

Publishers, New York

A National General Company

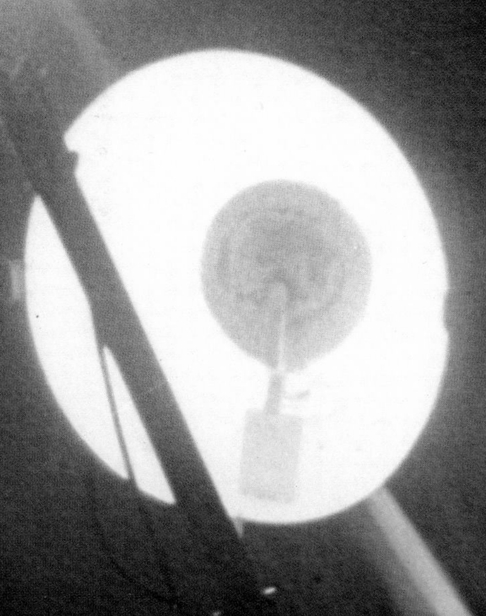

by William Bayer

Picture research by Marion Geisinger

Editor-in-Chief: Jerry Mason
Editor: Adolph Suehsdorf
Art Director: Albert Squillace
Associate Editor: Moira Duggan
Associate Editor: Barbara Hoffbeck
Art Associate: Mark Liebergall
Art Associate: David Namias
Art Production: Doris Mullane

The Great Movies
by William Bayer

A Madison Square Press Book.®
Prepared and produced by The Ridge Press, Inc.
Published in 1973 by Grosset & Dunlap, Inc.
Published simultaneously in Canada.
Library of Congress Catalog Card Number: 73-75614
Printed and bound in Italy by Mondadori Editore, Verona.
ISBN: 0-448-2217-6

FOR ELEANOR PERRY

## Contents

HOTEL
CALUMET
THEATRE TICKET
SERVICE
OUGHNUTS
15¢
ASTOR
GRETA GARBO-JOAN C
GRAND
JOHN AND LIONEL
1531
TYSON
NEWARK - JERSEYCITY - NEW YORK

# Choosing the Great Movies

The decision to publish a book on "The Great Movies"
was easy. Picking and choosing the contents was difficult. Pleasantly difficult — for there is no child of the twentieth century who is not an instant expert on movies — but difficult.

Once the task was begun, perplexing problems arose. For instance: What are "The Great Movies"? Are they the inevitable warhorse classics (INTOLERANCE, GREED, CITIZEN KANE, THE SEVENTH SEAL), which turn up again and again in all serious literature on film? Or should they include the great entertainment films (GONE WITH THE WIND, THE GRADUATE, THE GODFATHER, even THE SOUND OF MUSIC), whose popular appeal is undeniable and overwhelming? Can the collective list of the all-time best films chosen by the most important international critics, as reported in the British film magazine, *Sight and Sound*, be reconciled with the list of all-time box-office champs, as reported in the American show-business weekly, *Variety*? Can GONE WITH THE WIND be spoken of in the same breath with HIROSHIMA, MON AMOUR? There was no simple answer, for many plebeian movies have had as long a life span, and are as deeply cherished, as those of the highest artistic accomplishment.

There were other questions. Among the many thousands of films produced in the seventy-year history of movies, how many are really "great"? One thousand? Five hundred? A little research discloses that film history, as written by experts and critics, focuses on less than two hundred and fifty titles. Yet even these are far too many to deal with in a single volume, certainly if anything interesting or sensible is to be said about them.

Should a film by every important director be included? What about important screenwriters and stars? How should the various national schools of cinema be balanced off, and should equal space be given to each of the seven decades of the movies' existence? What, when it came to that, were our premises about film as film? Is the cinema a fine art, or merely a vulgarian form that has replaced the coliseum and the circus as the principal source of spectacle in modern life? Can there be such a thing as a "great masterpiece of entertainment," or even a "great piece of cinema trash"?

Finding an acceptable set of answers, and establishing the criteria for them, we decided, should be the

Preceding pages: Marquee of long-gone Astor Theater in New York for premiere of MGM's GRAND HOTEL, a multistarred big picture in Depression year of 1932. Based on Vicki Baum's novel, it was directed by Edmund Goulding and photographed by William Daniels, Garbo's favorite cameraman.

1939'S GREATEST SCREEN ADVENTURE!
CARY GRANT ★ JEAN ARTHUR
in
ONLY ANGELS HAVE WINGS
with
THOMAS MITCHELL ★ RITA HAYWORTH ★ RICHARD BARTHELMESS
Screen play by Jules Furthman
A HOWARD HAWKS PRODUCTION
A COLUMBIA PICTURE

EDW. G. ROBINSON IN "Little Caesar"
A WARNER BROS. RE-RELEASE

KING KONG
A Monster of Creation's Dawn Breaks Loose in Our World Today!
with
FAY WRAY
ROBT ARMSTRONG
BRUCE CABOT
MERIAN C. COOPER-ERNEST B. SCHOEDSACK PRODUCTION
FROM THE STORY BY EDGAR WALLACE
AND MERIAN C. COOPER
Chief Technician
WILLIS J. O'BRIEN

BOMBSHELL!
KIRK DOUGLAS
"PATHS OF GLORY"

TOGETHER for the first time!
MAE WEST W.C. FIELDS
My Little Chickadee
with
Joseph CALLEIA • Dick FORAN • Donald MEEK
Anne NAGEL • Fuzzy KNIGHT
Margaret HAMILTON • Ruth DONNELLY

THE STORY OF THE STRANGEST VENGEANCE EVER PLANNED!
CHARLTON HESTON • JANET LEIGH • ORSON WELLES
in
"TOUCH OF EVIL"
JOSEPH CALLEIA • AKIM TAMIROFF
MARLENE DIETRICH • ZSA ZSA GABOR
Directed by ORSON WELLES • Screenplay by ORSON WELLES • Produced by ALBERT ZUGSMITH

There never was a man like
SHANE
There never was a picture like
SHANE
The greatest story of the West ever filmed
From the master producer director GEORGE STEVENS
ALAN LADD • JEAN ARTHUR • VAN HEFLIN
GEORGE STEVENS'
SHANE
BRANDON DE WILDE • JACK PALANCE
TECHNICOLOR

Greta Charles
GARBO • BOYER
in Clarence BROWNS PRODUCTION of
CONQUEST
Directed by CLARENCE BROWN
with
REGINALD OWEN
ALAN MARSHAL
HENRY STEPHENSON
LEIF ERIKSON
DAME MAY WHITTY
C. HENRY GORDON
Metro Goldwyn Mayer PICTURE
Screen Play by Samuel Hoffenstein, Salka Viertel and S.N. Behrman
Produced by Bernard H. Hyman

AS EXCITING AS THE LANDING AT CASABLANCA!
WARNER BROS.'
Sensational Story of the City that Rocked the World!
HUMPHREY BOGART • INGRID BERGMAN • PAUL (Now, Voyager) HENREID
A SURPRISING CAST TO TELL A SUPER-SURPRISING STORY!
"CASABLANCA"
HAL B. WALLIS PROD'N.
CLAUDE RAINS • CONRAD VEIDT • SYDNEY GREENSTREET • PETER LORRE • Directed by MICHAEL CURTIZ

WHAT A GLORIOUS FEELING
SINGIN' IN THE RAIN
GENE KELLY
DONALD O'CONNOR
DEBBIE REYNOLDS
M-G-M's TECHNICOLOR Musical Treasure!
JEAN HAGEN • MILLARD MITCHELL • CYD CHARISSE
BETTY COMDEN • ADOLPH GREEN
GENE KELLY • STANLEY DONEN • ARTHUR FREED

responsibility of an author committed to movies as a joyful experience, a matter of cultural importance, and even as a way of life. We wanted him to be partisan, but not doctrinaire. We wanted acute observation, fresh insights, and independent judgment.

William Bayer has brought all of these qualities to this book. Although young, he is well versed in the history of the cinema; he has seen the several thousand important films, and each of the key two hundred and fifty many times. He also has an understanding of and sympathy for the filmmaker's plight, for he has made films himself and has written a lively and incisive book on the incredible process by which films are produced today. He is intimately aware of the clash between money and art in the world of film.

Rudolph Valentino

In all, he has chosen sixty movies. They qualify as great, he says, because "they create a fictional world and give you access to it. They are films in whose presence you feel exaltation, whose images you find memorable, whose elements — whether a scene, a character, a performance, an idea, a way of looking at the world — move you and stamp themselves upon your memory. In short, they are pictures which resolve some segment of experience in some irrevocable way."

Ultimately, Bayer constructed his list in terms of genres — twelve categories broad enough to accommodate practically any film ever made, yet specific enough to permit meaningful comparisons and some judgments on greatness. Eight of the genres are familiar storytelling forms which have preoccupied movie makers — and captivated

Garbo and John Barrymore



Garbo as Anna Karenina (1935)

Jeanette MacDonald and Nelson Eddy

Betty Grable

Hedy Lamarr

Cary Grant

Bette Davis

Errol Flynn

D. W. Griffith
directing WAY DOWN EAST (1920)

audiences — since THE (less than great) GREAT TRAIN ROBBERY first showed the way: Westerns, Comedies, War films, Musicals, films of Intrigue and Suspense, of Fantasy and Horror, Period films, and films of Adventure. Several — Manners, Morals and Society, Personal Expression, and the Cinema of Concern — were devised to organize the unique and intensely personal visions of great directors. And one — Films about Films — pays tribute to the movie industry's eternal narcissism and occasional unblinking self-revelation.

The categories make no pretense of precision. War, or its side effects and aftermath, shows up in four genres besides War. A number of films in various categories could be construed as Period pieces. In the end, however, each movie was assigned its place on the basis of its prevailing mood and intent. Despite its Civil War setting, THE GENERAL is innocent fun. The warlike DR. STRANGELOVE, by taking contemporary militarism to an extreme limit, is really black comedy. And M*A*S*H, while essentially funny, is breathtaking by being horribly funny about war.

The principal advantage of the system of genres is that it permits full and fair consideration of deserving films that usually are ignored when all-time-anything selections are being made. Even as the man picking literature for a desert-island sojourn feels constrained to take Shakespeare over his favorite junk novel, so movie-list compilers are likely to dismiss Musicals and Westerns and Adventure films as inconsequential in their search for the greatest of the great. Well, maybe SINGIN' IN THE RAIN doesn't rate with PERSONA, and maybe SHANE isn't KANE. But within the lively, lovely little world of Musicals, SINGIN' IN THE RAIN is worthy of some kind of immortality. In the incredibly vast array of Westerns, SHANE must stand among the top five. And if PERSONA is to be chosen, it should survive the competition of the finest, most sensitive films of Personal Expression.

Useful as it was, classification by genre did not solve all problems. Certain decisions had to be made, almost arbitrarily, along the way. "Underground films," shorts, animated films, and documentaries are excluded, without apology. They are out of the mainstream of movie history.

As for the silents, THE GENERAL, METROPOLIS, and CITY LIGHTS are in. Nothing else. (THE BIRTH OF A NATION, probably the greatest single accomplishment in film history,

Al Jolson

Joan Crawford and Neil Hamilton

Margaret Livingston and George O'Brien
in Murnau's SUNRISE (1927)

Douglas Fairbanks and Julanne Johnston in THE THIEF OF BAGDAD (1924)

Marlene Dietrich in THE DEVIL IS A WOMAN (1935)

Rouben Mamoulian directs Sylvia Sidney and Gary Cooper in CITY STREETS (1931)

Jean Hersholt, Gibson Gowland, and ZaSu Pitts in GREED (1923)

When double features cost 10¢

Barbara Stanwyck

Lana Turner

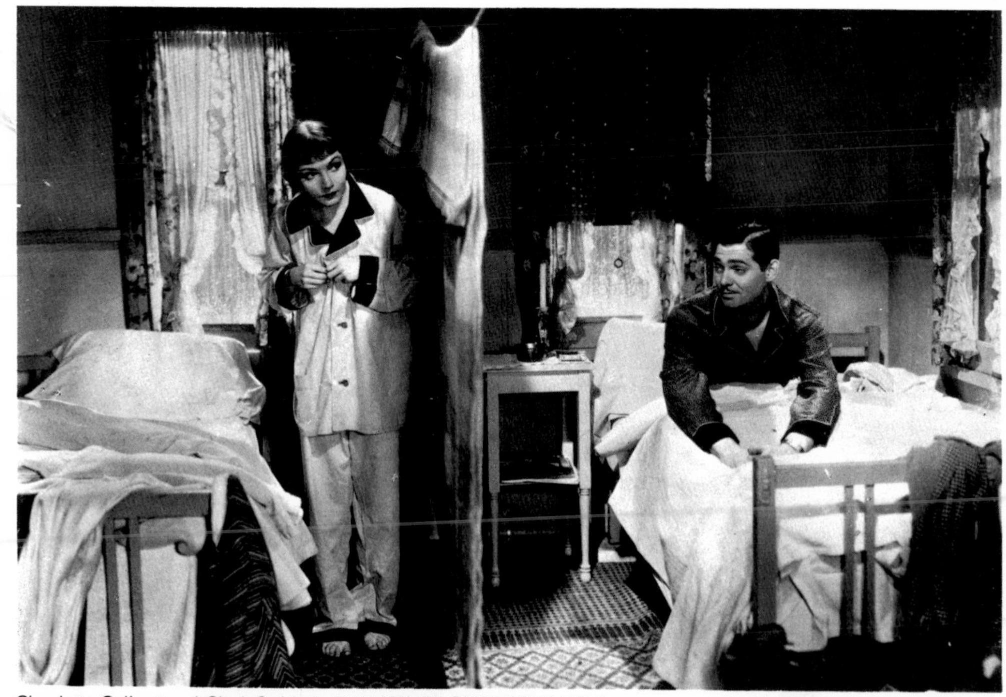

Claudette Colbert and Clark Gable in IT HAPPENED ONE NIGHT (1934)

Spencer Tracy

Jean Harlow

Robert Taylor

Katharine Hepburn

Floodlit opening at Grauman's Chinese

Laurel and Hardy in BRATS (1930)

Filming W. C. Fields in THE OLD-FASHIONED WAY (1934)

Eddie Woods and James Cagney in PUBLIC ENEMY (1931)

Mickey Rooney and Judy Garland

Mae West in I'M NO ANGEL (1933)

is not in only because Bayer felt there was nothing new worth saying about it.) No disrespect intended. The silents were the glorious sunlit springtime of the movies. Prodigious things were done, stars were born, Hollywood make-believe enchanted the world — not only through the pictures themselves, but by the splendid magic by which they were made. Through the stunts, the make-up, the cardboard castles, and the "special effects," we discovered that the visual possibilities of movies were limitless, that we not only had a new form of entertainment, but a whole new way of seeing. Before our eyes, Doug Fairbanks could ride a flying horse, Tom Mix could shoot a villain, and John Gilbert could make love to Vilma Banky. We never got over it.

Still, despite the marvels of the era, the silents — with rare exceptions, mostly comedies — have become antiques, valuable but quaint, like a butter churn. Their mechanics show too easily and their crudities afflict us, particularly those designed to compensate for the absence of sound. We bring different expectations into movie theaters today.

Inevitably, much is missing from our book. There is, for example, no film starring Greta Garbo or, for that matter, Marlene Dietrich or Joan Crawford. Garbo certainly was greater than Janet Leigh, who appears in three of Bayer's choices, but PSYCHO, TOUCH OF EVIL, and THE MANCHURIAN CANDIDATE are far superior films to ANNA CHRISTIE, CAMILLE, or NINOTCHKA.

The same principle applies to Douglas Fairbanks, Mae West, W. C. Fields, Lon Chaney, Errol Flynn, and Katharine Hepburn, all of whom are absent, while Humphrey Bogart, John Wayne, and William Holden join Miss Leigh with three selections each. To include the first group would have meant settling for trivial films, which would be self-defeating since movies, not stars or directors, are the subject of the book.

And this fact turned out to be another virtue of the genre system. Strong films survived. Lesser films by famous names, historic names, critics' pets, and cult favorites

George Raft

# Westerns

1

The western, along with the musical and the thriller, is one of the three great escapist genres invented in America. The "spaghetti westerns" of Sergio Leone notwithstanding, Americans can rightly claim that the western belongs to them, that American filmmakers are the only ones capable of exalting the genre to heights of sublimity, and that American audiences are the only ones qualified to judge the greatness of their works. When we hear that Jean-Paul Sartre considers himself a connoisseur of westerns, we must smile slightly at his presumption. We knew more about them when we were sixteen than he can ever hope to comprehend.

More than any other genre, the western is enveloped by rituals and conventions. We are at home in any frontier town. The main street, the cemetery (often called "boot hill"), the saloon, the general store, the stable, the bank, the railway terminal, and the sheriff's office enclosing a jail are all immediately recognizable places. We also know the people who inhabit these towns: the sheriff, the doctor, the prostitute, the telegrapher, the saloon keeper, and the quiet, mysterious stranger who wanders in and may be the fastest gun alive. We recognize the hired killer, the ranching baron, the cardsharp, and the itinerant notion-vender. We know the role of women in this society and we understand the rituals of the posse, the hanging party, the cavalry rescue, the Indian attack (and massacre), the poker game, the cattle roundup, the cattle drive, and the shoot-out on the main street. Whether the story is about law and order, crossing a dangerous territory, an Indian war, ranchers versus homesteaders, cattlemen versus sheepmen, the construction of a railway, the threat of a marauding outlaw band, a stagecoach heist, an Easterner's initiation, a man torn between public duty and private desire, or a hundred other basic situations, we know the parameters and we know what to expect. Because of this knowledge, bred into us since we saw our first movies, we are all connoisseurs of the western, on the lookout for the brilliant variation, the unexpected twist, the expert crossbreeding of themes, the novel vision, the fine points and stylistic ingenuities that will make one western stand out from the herd.

The huge backlog of westerns from which we formulate our expectations and draw our standards is the result of a discovery made quite early by producers that westerns are infinitely marketable, that stories set in the West can be told over and over again without people tiring of the rituals, the characters, and the settings. Thus, there has been an endless stream of works, beginning with THE GREAT TRAIN ROBBERY of 1903, through the pictures starring William S. Hart, Tom Mix, and William Boyd, into the subgenres of the singing westerns of Gene Autry and Roy Rogers (the true horse operas?), the message westerns (THE OX-BOW INCIDENT, 3:10 TO YUMA), the psychological westerns (DUEL IN THE SUN, THE HANGING TREE), the historical westerns (GUNFIGHT AT THE O.K. CORRAL, LITTLE BIG MAN), the comedy westerns (DESTRY RIDES AGAIN, BUTCH CASSIDY AND THE SUNDANCE KID), and the numerous other types represented by such works as RANCHO NOTORIOUS, JOHNNY GUITAR, THE UNFORGIVEN, HIGH NOON, THE SCALPHUNTERS, THE VIRGINIAN, APACHE, WINCHESTER .73, THE COVERED WAGON, THE BIG COUNTRY, THE LEFT-HANDED GUN, and all the stories about the James brothers, Billy the Kid, Wyatt Earp and Doc Holliday, Tombstone, Dodge City, Virginia City, the California Gold Rush, the Alamo, and the other combinations of guns, horses, Indians, cavalry, cattle, frontier towns, and vast and magnificent landscapes which are the threads that bind these many types together into a genre.

Many people have intellectualized the western, studying the mythical and romantic elements that make it so popular. One school of thought maintains that the western provides a moral universe in which violence, supposedly so dear to Americans, can be vicariously experienced without harm. Others believe that the western is an everchanging mirror in which one may read a particular era's perception of itself as reflected in its view of the American past. (The danger of this theory is that it encourages filmmakers to make allegories, almost always self-conscious and deeply flawed.) Still other theorists view it as the terrain of alienation, a peculiarly American syndrome, derived, one is told, from the paradox that the world's greatest democracy was founded on genocide and slaughter, that the settlers who expanded the frontier were disguised imperialists, and that lawmen who lived by the gun were murderers even when they killed on behalf of right. And there is the view that Americans love westerns because of nostalgia for a time when life, which has become so maddeningly complex in urban society, was simple and values were clear. All of these things and many more have been discerned in the western, and though some of them have more merit than others, none of them is relevant to the question of what makes certain westerns great, to such things as filmmaking craft, story, acting, action, the personal vision of a director, his feeling for people and for land, and the dimensions of his spirit which determine his ability to create art.

Because of the richness of the genre it is impossible to pick five great westerns without leaving out works of importance and quality. John Ford is unavoidable (as is John Wayne; he appears in three of the five films dis-



Preceding pages: John Ford's STAGECOACH (top, l. to r.) – Andy Devine (Buck), George Bancroft (Wilcox), Donald Meek (Peacock), Claire Trevor (Dallas); (bottom, l. to r.), – John Carradine (Hatfield), Chris Martin (Chris), Louise Platt (Lucy), John Wayne (the Ringo Kid), Thomas Mitchell (Doc).

cussed). Ford not only reinvented the western with STAGECOACH, but he is responsible for THE SEARCHERS, easily the most perfect western ever made. Howard Hawks, master of so many genres, made at least two great westerns, RIO BRAVO and RED RIVER, one of which, at the very least, has to be included. George Stevens made only one western in his career, but SHANE is so exemplary that to leave it out is to ignore the *ne plus ultra* of the mythologizing branch of the genre. And Sam Peckinpah, who, along with Stanley Kubrick, is the most distinguished of the younger American filmmakers, made a western called THE WILD BUNCH which, along with 2001: A SPACE ODYSSEY, may be one of the great films of our time.

But what about Samuel Fuller, Robert Aldrich, Anthony Mann, Henry Hathaway, and Arthur Penn? It is a pity that a picture of each could not be included here. As for the two very popular and defective hits, HIGH NOON and BUTCH CASSIDY AND THE SUNDANCE KID, their exclusion is somewhat less of a pity. But it is with regret that Robert Altman's MCCABE AND MRS. MILLER and Marlon Brando's ONE-EYED JACKS are absent here; though these pictures are, perhaps, outside the western mainstream, there is no doubt that in their unique and sometimes perverse ways they are both masterpieces.

## John Ford's **Stagecoach** 1939

Prior to STAGECOACH, the western was in grievous decline. For a decade it had been a genre unfulfilled. But with STAGECOACH a renaissance occurred. The genre was reinvented, its possibilities as spectacle were reaffirmed, and a new classicism was born. Since 1939, STAGECOACH has been a reference point for anyone who has worked within the genre, as a picture either to be emulated or reacted against, as a treasury of themes and motifs to be worked out in new variations. For John Ford, STAGECOACH was the starting point of that portion of his career most likely to be remembered, and though it may not be true, as some have claimed, that Ford *is* the western, there can be no doubt that his influence upon it has been unprecedented and dominating.

STAGECOACH was the western in which the public first saw Monument Valley, Utah, on film—a place that Ford would revisit again and again, and that became his favorite location for the exterior sequences of his westerns. The rocks and plains of Monument Valley have become a signature on Ford's pictures, immediately identifying a place that plays as meaningful a part in his vision of the West as a certain remote Swedish island plays in the universe of Ingmar Bergman.

STAGECOACH was also the first western to feature John Wayne, the picture that made him a star. Wayne is as deeply merged with the western in the public's consciousness as Humphrey Bogart was with the private-eye film. The amazing thing about Wayne as an actor is the same thing that is so amazing about Bogart: the way he can play a variety of roles maintaining the rough outlines of a single persona, yet transcend those outlines so that each character is individual and unique.

STAGECOACH is so rich it has become a treasury of western characters and motifs. It exemplifies, first of all, a technique especially amenable to the cinema form, the Grand Hotel or Ship of Fools device, whereby characters representing various types are closely confined for a period of time and act out in their relationships with one another the social structure of their era and place. On the stagecoach to Lordsburg, one finds a drunkard doctor, a whiskey drummer, an aristocratic gambler, a woman of quality, a "good" prostitute, a compassionate sheriff, a grizzled driver, a crooked banker, and in the person of the Ringo Kid (Wayne) a good-guy gunslinger.

As for motifs, there is, first, one of Ford's favorite types of scene, a life-ceremony. Sometimes a wedding, sometimes a funeral, in STAGECOACH it is the birth of a child. There are, in addition, cut telegraph lines, an attack by Indians, a chase (with much acrobatics on horses), a cavalry rescue (announced, of course, by a bugle call), a poker game (Luke Plummer holds aces and eights, "the dead man's hand"), a three-against-one gunfight on the streets of a town (the Ringo Kid kills all three Plummer brothers and settles an old score), and a happy ending (the Ringo Kid and the heart-of-gold prostitute, Claire Trevor, ride off to Mexico with Sheriff Wilcox's blessing).

Ford in STAGECOACH thus sets the form for a particular type of folk art, and by his unique ability to use characters both as individual personalities and as social types he singlehandedly gives birth to a mythology that no American can ever escape. The remarkable thing about Ford's westerns, and one sees this process expanded in his later films, is his gift for simultaneously contemplating people as individuals and as representatives of virtues,

did not. Among directors the casualty rate was high. Jean Cocteau, Satyajit Ray, Joseph Losey, Luchino Visconti, and Max Ophuls — all missing. Also, and regrettably, Sternberg, Cukor, Lubitsch, Rossellini, Vigo, and Bertolucci.

In? Ingmar Bergman, of course; Truffaut, Godard, and Renoir; Bresson and Buñuel, a couple of specialists; and then a rather wide range of Hollywood offspring — Ford, Hawks, Welles, Kubrick, and the inevitable Mr. Alfred Hitchcock. But, as noted, this is not a director's book.

Marilyn Monroe

Elizabeth Taylor

Soviet cinema is out. A surprise perhaps, considering the impact Eisenstein and others presumably have had, but Bayer said no. He dismissed THE BATTLESHIP POTEMKIN as a cul-de-sac, EARTH, MOTHER, and STRIKE as overrated, and the spectacles, ALEXANDER NEVSKY, IVAN THE TERRIBLE, and WAR AND PEACE, as appalling.

In the end, an amazingly eclectic sixty films were selected. Though weighted in favor of the American cinema of the past thirty years, they reflect the developing cinema everywhere. Included are films that no one can ignore (CITIZEN KANE, RULES OF THE GAME, LES ENFANTS DU PARADIS, THE GENERAL, for instance). These are supplemented by popular pictures which some will scorn (THE WILD BUNCH, EASY RIDER, CABARET, M*A*S*H, FROM HERE TO ETERNITY), marginal pictures which many people have forgotten (ONLY ANGELS HAVE WINGS, THE MANCHURIAN CANDIDATE, THE BAD AND THE BEAUTIFUL, THE BIG SLEEP), pictures which now are difficult to see on a full-size screen (THE SEARCHERS, PATHS OF GLORY, TOUCH OF EVIL), and some pictures which few people have seen at all (CONTEMPT; AU HASARD, BALTHAZAR).

Altogether, they represent a coherent vision of the movies, internally logical, extremely solid and energetic in its arguments — and fun to disagree with. As Bayer himself says: "Exactly what these films indicate about my needs for fantasy, how they fulfill my desires for romance, melancholy, music, laughter, diversion, and escape, or why it is my wish to see again and again movies that are inexhaustibly rich and that reflect the most perverse, grotesque, and selfish aspects of man, as well as his warmth and humanity and the glories of comradeship, I cannot begin to explain. That I cannot explain it is, to me, one of the wondrous mysteries of film, a medium of which — even when one tries to write authoritatively — one finds oneself in a state of awe." THE EDITORS

Marlon Brando and Maria Schneider
in LAST TANGO IN PARIS (1973)

Sophia Loren PHOTOGRAPH BY DOUGLAS KIRKLAND

S. MAI

Grandeur of Monument Valley, Utah, became part of the signature on a John Ford western. Ford loved this particular piece of American turf and returned to it again and again. Another Ford trademark was appearance of familiar faces from his "repertory company," chief among them, John Wayne's. With his first scene in STAGECOACH (top), Wayne became a major star. Above: Cavalry rescue, pursuing Indians pursuing stage.

vices, and other abstract qualities.

For those familiar with STAGECOACH, perhaps the greatest surprise on seeing it again is how small a role the Monument Valley scenes actually play in the whole design. It is a credit to the intensity of these scenes that they expand in one's memory until they seem to dominate the film. Actually, most of STAGECOACH was shot on sound stages with rear-screen process projection, and on sets constructed on a studio back lot. Ford, who in his old age seems to relish the role of the curmudgeon, "Pappy," "the Admiral," or the just plain "guy who made a few westerns," recalls that STAGECOACH cost about $220,000, came in $8,000 under budget, that the chase took two days to shoot, that Wyatt Earp had once personally advised him on how to stage a gunfight, and that the picture was more or less "cut in the camera."

This man, who created STAGECOACH, MY DARLING CLEMENTINE, FORT APACHE, SHE WORE A YELLOW RIBBON, WAGON MASTER, THE HORSE SOLDIERS, THE MAN WHO SHOT LIBERTY VALANCE, and the incomparable THE SEARCHERS, is in no danger of being underrated, thanks to the many who now place him, along with Alfred Hitchcock and Howard Hawks, in a triumvirate of American filmmaker immortals. Two of his most famous pictures, THE INFORMER and THE GRAPES OF WRATH, labeled by some as art films, will in time be forgotten, while his westerns will be screened forever.

There is some irony in the fact that though Ford's STAGECOACH rescued the western from decadence in 1939, its remake in 1966 (starring Ann-Margret and Bing Crosby, and directed by Gordon Douglas) evidenced the descent of a new decadence upon the genre. Twentieth Century-Fox, which released the remake, threatened with unparalleled arrogance to prosecute anyone who dared to exhibit Ford's original version. What further proof is needed that the cultural heritage of Americans is in constant jeopardy, that a new breed of barbarians exists willing to ban the showing of a film so great that Orson Welles viewed it (he claims) some forty times while "in training" for CITIZEN KANE?

Opposite: Ringo — "Looks like I got the plague, don't it?" Dallas — "No . . . it's not you." (Berton Churchill, as pompous banker on run with embezzled funds, is at right.) Pair's mutual isolation leads to romance, culminating in love scene (r.), when they walk past the whorehouses of Lordsburg just before shoot-out with three Plummers. Above & left: John Ford, in black coat and beret, supervising setups on location. Though movie is closely associated with Monument Valley, Ford shot much of STAGECOACH on studio sets.

# John Ford's **The Searchers** 1956

It is unfortunate that John Ford's THE SEARCHERS is not widely known, for it surpasses many famous westerns and is among the few pictures in the genre that one can safely label a work of art. Ford would most likely sneer at such a statement, but then it is his very lack of self-conscious artiness, his utter absence of pretension, his singular desire to tell a good story, and his equally fervent wish to avoid delivering a message that ennobles so much of his work and enables him to subliminally transcend the genre. THE SEARCHERS is a picture of such economy of expression and such purity of line that it puts to shame the self-important works of filmmakers who treat the western form as if it were a vessel that anyone who has the nerve to call himself an artist is qualified to fill.

Just as General de Gaulle held "a certain conception of France," so John Ford holds a certain conception of the West. He is not a realist or a buff steeped in the details of western lore, but a fantasist and a stylist who has meditated on the West for a long period of years and has painstakingly, picture by picture, created an imaginary West that is uniquely his own. While other directors sought new locations for westerns, Ford has stayed in Monument Valley, a fact that does not, as some would claim, demonstrate the limits of his imagination, but rather certifies his concern for the refinement of an ideal. One has the feeling that without knowing it, Ford for years was working toward some ultimate western; his continuing reuse of a location and of a company of actors and technicians suggests a quest for a perfect expression. That quest, it seems, was resolved in the film THE SEARCHERS. The pictures that follow, including the fine THE MAN WHO SHOT LIBERTY VALANCE, suggest a cooling off, the beginning of a trek downward from dizzying heights.

There are striking differences between STAGECOACH and THE SEARCHERS, reflecting a change more important than the mere passage of seventeen years. STAGECOACH is a sprawling spectacle; THE SEARCHERS is a confined epic. In STAGECOACH the characters express themselves in speech; in THE SEARCHERS they say more by gestures and glances. STAGECOACH is literary and theatrical; THE SEARCHERS is visual and cinematic. In STAGECOACH the actors come alive while on the screen; in THE SEARCHERS they radiate, from their first appearances, an understanding of who they are that reaches far back into the past. In STAGECOACH the types overshadow the personalities; in THE SEARCHERS the personalities transcend the types. STAGECOACH is a picture that excites the senses; THE SEARCHERS is a film that moves the heart. And STAGECOACH holds our attention because its story is in constant flux, while THE SEARCHERS entrances us because its story is so single-minded and intense.

For those who know and admire THE SEARCHERS, its opening and ending encourage interminable speculation. A door opens out from the screen while a woman waits in darkness for a solitary man who dismounts his horse and moves slowly from brilliant sunlight toward comforting interior warmth. And when the picture ends that man is again outside, and that same door closes upon him. He is Ethan Edwards, played by John Wayne, the outsider, the wanderer, the quintessential Ford protagonist. He returns to his family from the Civil War, nourishes himself in their domestic warmth, goes on an obsessive five-year rampage of revenge when they are slaughtered and his favorite niece is kidnapped by Comanche Indians, and when he returns, somehow changed and mellowed by the madness of that search, he is still an outsider, still a man alone, shut out from domesticity, destined to wander even more. But that famous door, that opens to beckon him in and then closes at the end to shut him out, is also a door Ford opens for us onto history. It is a means by which he formalizes the distancing that turns the story of THE SEARCHERS into a myth, and the way, too, by which he gives us a glimpse at the enigma of a man's soul.

The five-year search by Ethan Edwards and Martin Pawley (Jeffrey Hunter) for Debbie Edwards (Natalie Wood) is an adventure story encompassing violence, subterfuge, and terror. It is also a story of a strange man, torn between such brutishness that at times he rivals in savagery the very Indians he hates, and such gentleness that at times his "civilization" surpasses that of the family for whom his presence causes such unease. He is admirable for the way he despises money (in contrast to his brother who secretes it), and at the same time he is a man so obsessed with racial hatred that he prefers to kill his own niece rather than allow her to live as a Comanche squaw. He and his brother's wife are unspokenly in love, and this strange, superbly gentle side of his character is revealed in one of the great moments in the western when he embraces Natalie Wood instead of killing her—a moment that Godard has described as so moving that it filled him with love for John Wayne, a man whom he despised politically.

THE SEARCHERS is rich film. Its uses of color, its



John Wayne, badly underestimated as an actor for many years, gives a towering performance as Ethan Edwards in Ford's THE SEARCHERS. Projecting complete conviction and deep inner torment, he exceeds himself and becomes a great screen presence.

THE SEARCHERS: Flanking bands of Comanches (top) close for the kill – again in Monument Valley. Above, left: Wayne grasps Natalie Wood in culminating scene, when we and she are certain he will kill her. Above: In one of the final frames, Wayne stands outside the house. In a moment the door will shut him out once more. Left: The funeral sequence, a favorite motif in many John Ford pictures.

feeling for the passages of time and the changing of the seasons, the funeral sequence, the recurring use of figures silhouetted against brilliant backgrounds of white and red, its lack of reliance on dialogue, its many moods echoed in landscapes, the supreme eloquence of the gestures of its characters, its strange combination of warmth and hardness, its evocations of terror, and, above all, the sensibility of the unseen man behind it, a man both meditative and wise, are the things that raise it from the level of a fine adventure story into the realm of art.

## Howard Hawks' **Red River** 1948

RED RIVER is not a work of art, but it is an extremely good adventure western, justifiably admired despite its controversial ending. A classic series of comparisons have been made between Howard Hawks and John Ford, and though sometimes valuable they often turn out to be less interesting than they seem. For example, there is a theory that while Ford distances his material and places it in an historical perspective, Hawks tends to become directly involved with his and to endow it with a sense of immediacy. As an example of this, one critic contrasts the river crossings in Ford's WAGON MASTER and Hawks' RED RIVER, pointing out that Ford transforms this western ritual into a scene of epic grandeur by shooting it from a distance, while Hawks gets right into it with rapid cutting and close shots, and emphasizes its excitement. This is a valid analysis as far as it goes, but if one recalls the river crossing in Ford's STAGECOACH, quite close in spirit to the one in RED RIVER, one is forced to admit that directors are less consistent than critics might wish.

Hawks and Ford are of the same generation and are both master filmmakers of the American cinema, but while Ford's contribution has been more or less exclusive to the historical film, particularly the western, Hawks has ranged widely over many genres. While Ford has been deeply committed to the western and has treated it as a way of life, Hawks has viewed it as merely one of several modes in which he can work out variations on his long-standing interest in action, adventure, and men in groups. This difference in their commitments shows, for Hawks, good as he is with the western (RED RIVER, RIO BRAVO, THE BIG SKY), has never come close to the intensity of THE SEARCHERS, or ever made anything quite so moving and profound.

Ford's heroes tend to be quiet men. Hawks' tend to be violent. This difference shows in their respective uses of John Wayne. (Ford even made Wayne the hero of a nonwestern, set in Ireland, entitled THE QUIET MAN.) In Ford's westerns Wayne becomes less verbally articulate and more eloquent and more gentle in his strength, while in Hawks' films (Wayne appears in four of them) he plays roles that sometimes border on the unsympathetic, roles in which he is either sloppy or monstrous and nearly always unsubtle.

RED RIVER, the story of a cattle drive up the Chisholm Trail, involves such rituals as the river crossing, the funeral, the cattle stampede, the Indian attack, and that favorite motif of Howard Hawks, the proper role of a leader of men. (See ONLY ANGELS HAVE WINGS.) In RED RIVER we observe the hardening of Tom Dunstan (Wayne) as he carries ruthlessness too far, and we simultaneously observe the personal growth of Matthew Garth (Montgomery Clift), who wrests leadership from Wayne and takes control of the drive. This conflict between Wayne and Clift, father and adopted son, is one of the fascinations of RED RIVER, complicated by the fact that it was Wayne's ruthlessness and implacability years before that led to the death of the woman he had loved and whom Clift symbolizes in his mind. Though we start the film admiring Wayne, we eventually reject him and transfer our sympathy to Montgomery Clift. For this reason, and the fact that their "father-son" struggle is not properly resolved, the ending of RED RIVER is less than satisfactory.

In an interview with Jim Kitses, Borden Chase, who wrote the screenplay and the original story upon which it was based, complains bitterly of Hawks' refusal to use his ending. Wayne was supposed to arrive in Abilene, get badly wounded in a gunfight with John Ireland, proceed to a showdown with Clift, fire half a dozen shots at him, and collapse in a way that makes it clear he is a dying man. He was then to be taken by Clift and Joanne Dru across the Red River, so he could die in his beloved Texas. Hawks, however, did not want Wayne to die, and the result is an artificial ending in which Clift refuses to fire at Wayne, and Joanne Dru intrudes on the showdown, saying something like, "Now, you two boys please stop fighting," which, sheepishly, they do.

RED RIVER, fortunately, is a strong film. The first two hours are so good they cannot be ruined by a bad

Hard, tough, vast in scale, and beautiful in images, RED RIVER is one of the great westerns and among the finest accomplishments of Howard Hawks. Again, John Wayne dominated the screen, but in RED RIVER a major new talent appeared – Montgomery Clift (far right). The love-hate battles of Wayne and Clift, as father and surrogate son, told in the context of a tale of the first cattle drive on the Chisholm Trail, give movie its interesting blend of character conflict and epic sweep. But resolution is badly bungled and the final minutes are disappointing. It took all of Hawks' great feeling for terrain and understanding of men in groups to make RED RIVER work.

final five minutes. However much one may wish to do so, one simply cannot justify Wayne's final actions in this movie in terms of the sort of magical character transformation that occurs in THE SEARCHERS, when he recognizes that he loves Natalie Wood and cannot kill her. His recognition of his love and admiration for Montgomery Clift in RED RIVER is bungled and comes close to being silly.

(In the same interview Borden Chase tells an amusing anecdote about how Wayne, rehearsing the way he will enter Abilene and pass obliviously through the cattle herd, wrecked much of Chase's living-room furniture.)

The aftermath of the stampede is a perfect expression of Hawks' continuing concern with the behavior of men in groups. Bunk Kenneally has caused a stampede by sneaking into the chuckwagon at night and knocking over a pile of pots and pans while in search of sugar. The spooked cattle erupt, and in the ensuing commotion Dan Latimer is overrun and killed. After Wayne has buried Latimer he turns to the business of punishing Kenneally, whom he proposes to tie to a wagon wheel and whip, a perfectly justifiable use of power to Hawks, since in his world a man becomes a pariah and deserves to be punished when he lets his companions down.

RED RIVER, among other things, was the film that made Montgomery Clift a star. More than five thousand head of cattle (at $10 per day per head) were used in the filming, some of which had their faces painted white. Rainstorms held up shooting and the budget doubled from the original estimate to something close to $3.5 million.

RED RIVER is characterized by Howard Hawks' famous eye-level shooting, and is one of the most beautiful of all black-and-white westerns. Its stupendous shots of the cattle drive, particularly the scene on the morning of the departure from Texas, are spectacular and memorable, and the funeral scene, surprisingly close to similar ceremonial scenes in John Ford films, is embellished by the miraculous effect of a cloud passing the sun and casting a shadow on the background. (This same effect is equally moving in a scene in BONNIE AND CLYDE.) When asked how he achieved it, Hawks admitted that, of course, it was a fortuitous accident. While shooting the funeral he saw the cloud coming, indicated to Wayne that he should hurry up with his speech, and the mountains behind were darkened at just the right moment.

## George Stevens' **Shane** 1953

There can be little doubt that if George Stevens had wanted that cloud-shadow effect in SHANE, he would not have achieved it accidentally but by design, even if that meant setting up the scene and waiting days on end for the proper sun-clouds-mountains conjunction to take place. This is the very thing that annoys some people about SHANE: the aestheticizing, the contrived beauty, the calculated precision, the perfection which, annoying or not, is the picture's major strength.

SHANE is no rough-and-ready western like RED RIVER, nor a meditation on history and character like THE SEARCHERS. It is the most self-conscious attempt ever made to use the western form to create a myth. SHANE is a willed legend, an invented artifact, and as such it represents at one extreme the furthest possibilities of the film as instant mythology—and, at the other, a decadence paralleled in such aspects of contemporary culture as the tattered and patched-up poorboy jacket that costs $600 and is designed by a Parisian couturier. Only a most sophisticated filmmaker could have achieved the studied simplicity of SHANE. Only a man in total control of his medium could have created so perfect a primitive folktale. These things are mentioned not to put George Stevens down, but, on the contrary, to say that even when one understands exactly what SHANE is, one may still be moved by it, and one most certainly must admire Stevens' mastery of technique.

The dualism between right and wrong in SHANE is central to this technique. Alan Ladd as Shane, the good-guy gunfighter who chooses his cause on principle, is a golden prince, a blond-haired superman in fringed buckskin. His antithesis and enemy, Jack Palance, the bad-guy gunfighter for hire, is dark, dresses in black, and even drinks black coffee from a blackened pot. Ladd radiates spirituality; Palance radiates evil and menace. Ladd is a knight-errant who shoots to kill only when reason fails and after the exhaustion of all other less deadly means of settlement. Palance is a black knight who enjoys killing and has no compunction about shooting an opponent who is clearly unequal to him in fighting skill.

In addition to using dualism, Stevens creates his myth by heightening certain standard western rituals. In SHANE the fistfight, the gun duel, the funeral, and even idealized love are pushed to extremes and then placed in an allegory about the settlement and civilization of the

George Stevens' SHANE is very much an exercise in instant myth-making. Every one of its images is composed with extreme care: The deer (below, l.) will raise its head and frame the oncoming rider perfectly between the branches of its antlers.

SHANE is the story of a duel between good and evil. Good is represented by Alan Ladd (l.), the golden-haired prince in buckskin. Evil is Jack Palance, merciless, black-clad hit-man for the cattle interests. Above: He kills Elisha Cook, Jr.

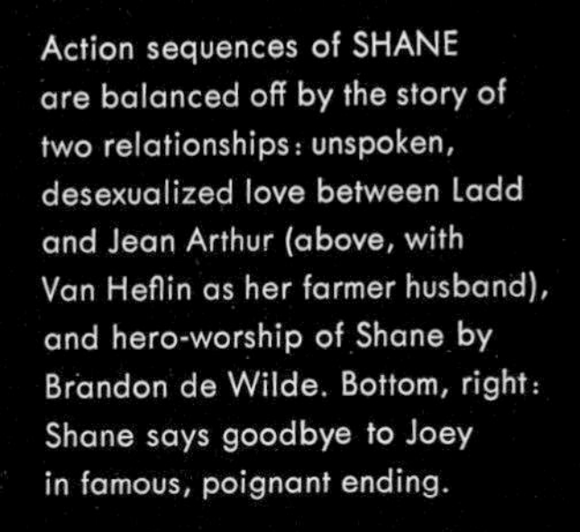

Action sequences of SHANE are balanced off by the story of two relationships: unspoken, desexualized love between Ladd and Jean Arthur (above, with Van Heflin as her farmer husband), and hero-worship of Shane by Brandon de Wilde. Bottom, right: Shane says goodbye to Joey in famous, poignant ending.

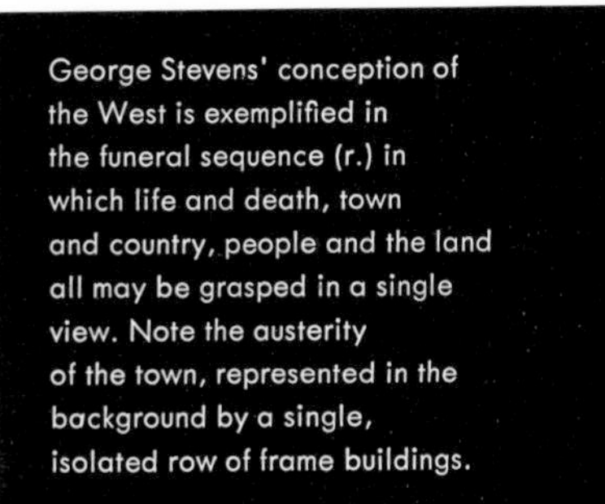

George Stevens' conception of the West is exemplified in the funeral sequence (r.) in which life and death, town and country, people and the land all may be grasped in a single view. Note the austerity of the town, represented in the background by a single, isolated row of frame buildings.

West. The fistfight in SHANE is a Big Fistfight. The gun duel involves some of the fastest gunplay one is likely to see. The funeral in SHANE is much more studied than the funerals in THE SEARCHERS and RED RIVER. The people are grouped more artfully; their buckboards and the covered wagon of the mourning family are positioned with perfection; the reactions of the children and the domestic animals are purified to the point that the dead man's dog actually scratches mournfully at his grave. Cattle graze here and there. The tiny settlement that is the setting of the allegory is lonely on the plain behind, and in the background stands the powerful wall of the Grand Teton mountains of Wyoming, magnificently luminous, captured in perfect light. According to Stevens, this arrangement symbolizes what the West was all about: a continuity between life and death, a positioning of elements, so that all of existence could be grasped at a single glance.

It may be instructive to compare the idealized love between Alan Ladd and Jean Arthur in SHANE with the unspoken love between John Wayne and Dorothy Jordan in THE SEARCHERS. In the latter film, the scene in which Dorothy Jordan caresses John Wayne's army cape and is observed by Ward Bond, who simply notices her gesture and looks away, is typical of the throwaway enrichment of the story. As far as John Ford is concerned, if you pick up on it that's fine, and if you don't then that's all right, too. But in SHANE Stevens makes certain that everything that is unspoken between Ladd and Jean Arthur, every gesture and every glance in every scene, tells us of their impossible and unrealizable love. To make sure we get all the implications, he has the boy, Joey (Brandon de Wilde), make naïve utterances that demonstrate that he senses what has been going on, too. Though one may prefer Ford's subtlety, one must give Stevens credit for having ingeniously inserted a love story into a western—a love story that tantalizes adults and yet does not turn children off the adventure.

The special rhythms of the dialogue of SHANE reinforce all its other myth-making effects. For instance: "Yes, he was fast—he was fast on the draw"; "A man's got to be what he is—you can't break the mold"; and the cadence with which Shane says to Ryker, "I'm a friend of Starrett."

Shane is the ultimate example of that classic character of the western, the melancholic and mysterious stranger who is the fastest gun alive. Take his control, the way he sidesteps a fight until he sees that it is inevitable, and then goes into it without fear. We have seen this kind of man before, the gunfighter with the implied violent past, who will do everything in his power to avoid a showdown and whose avoidance is often misconstrued as cowardice. We want Shane to show Joey how brave and fast he is, and then when Shane does fight, we feel ashamed because we know that the glow of hero-worship in Joey's eyes is there for the wrong reasons, and that Shane knew better than we that once he killed he would be tainted and would have to leave the valley. What is admirable about Shane is not his skill with his gun, but his restraint in using it—something that Joey will understand in time. Joey's famous cry at the end of the picture ("Come back, Shane....") is the cry of all of us for a mythical West that never was, and for a mythical hero so perfect he would not allow himself to be admired by a boy for living by the gun. SHANE is a movie that not only presents its story as a myth, but that evokes nostalgia for itself before it even ends.

## Sam Peckinpah's **The Wild Bunch** 1969

If SHANE makes a myth of the West, THE WILD BUNCH demythologizes it. If SHANE draws sharp moral distinctions that are, literally, black and white, THE WILD BUNCH blurs all moral distinctions, offering us only choices between various modes of immorality. If in SHANE violence is viewed as a necessary evil only to be employed as a last resort, and killing is depicted as swift and clean, in THE WILD BUNCH violence is viewed with exaltation, and killing is prolonged, tormented, and bloody. In short, within the genre of the western, THE WILD BUNCH is the precise opposite of SHANE. Each film may be considered an artifact of a view of the American frontier. SHANE, made during the quietude of 1953, romanticizes and idealizes. THE WILD BUNCH, made fifteen years later in a turbulent time, tells us that the American Dream is dead.

The opening sequence of THE WILD BUNCH stakes out the moral territory. A band of outlaws masquerading as soldiers rides into a town, passing children torturing a scorpion and adults attending a temperance meeting. The band robs a railway office, then finds itself ambushed by a gang of bounty hunters working for the railroad. A ferocious gunfight erupts, many innocent bystanders are killed, and the children afterward wander among the bodies mimicking the dying with glee. We know at once that we are in a terrain that is beyond good or evil, a world of arbitrary violence where the only morality consists of such distinctions as Pike's (William Holden's) pronouncement that "when you side with a man, you stick with him; otherwise you might as well be some kind of animal...."

This moral confusion continues throughout the story as the U. S. Cavalry (the *deus ex machina* in Ford's westerns) is revealed as a mob of bungling fools, the management of the Pacific Railroad (so often the pioneering force in westerns) is depicted as a ruthless enterprise that employs scum as henchmen, children (so often used as symbols of innocence) are shown to be amoral, and the entire myth of the frontier is debunked. If there are any myths left unexploded in the film, they take place on the Mexican side of the border, where the bandits' departure from a village is staged as it might have been in SHANE. (This scene has been criticized as being overly sentimental, but that's just the point. The time of the film is 1913, when the American frontier was closing fast. Mexico, on the other hand, was still in a romantic era, the time of Pancho Villa and the Mexican Revolution.)

The credit title for Sam Peckinpah, who directed THE WILD BUNCH, comes on the screen directly after William Holden snarls at his men: "If they move, kill 'em!" This juxtaposition is in keeping with Peckinpah's reputation as a connoisseur of violence. In THE WILD BUNCH he presents the violent scenes passionately, even excessively, and it is his passion and excess that make the picture great. When a man is killed we see blood gush from his body. In THE WILD BUNCH we even see a full frontal view of a man's throat being cut. There are at least two hundred violent deaths in the picture, and Peckinpah often aestheticizes this violence by showing it in slow motion, as Kurosawa did in the early reels of THE SEVEN SAMURAI.

THE WILD BUNCH probably was influenced by the SEVEN SAMURAI, not only stylistically and in terms of its virtuoso sequences of violent action, but also in theme.

Robert Ryan (top, c.) and his cutthroat bounty hunters pose for a publicity shot for THE WILD BUNCH. (Strother Martin and L. Q. Jones are top, extreme l. & r.). In Peckinpah's original version, relationship between Ryan and William Holden, the hard-bitten leader of the bunch, was clear, but later studio cuts obscured it.

Right: Chaos in the streets, as innocent bystanders get slaughtered in crossfire during attempted robbery of railroad office in opening reels of THE WILD BUNCH. Below: William Holden, flanked by Ernest Borgnine and Warren Oates, leads remnants of the wild bunch against troops of the Mexican despot in an orgy of blood, destruction, and death. Bottom: Scummy bounty hunters crawl over bodies searching for loot at picture's end.

The bigger-than-life characters are killed off in both films. If there is a winner at the end of THE WILD BUNCH it is the Mexican peasants who are at last rid of their oppressors, just as the Japanese peasants are said to be the only winners at the end of THE SEVEN SAMURAI.

This "aesthetic of violence," this use of slow motion to prolong dying and turn it into a ballet, has been attributed to a love of violence that Peckinpah is supposed to possess. Actually, it has to do with a legitimate desire to show us what it feels like to kill, sensualizing the killer's pleasure by subjectifying and then prolonging the death of his adversaries. In these terms, the "ballets of death" can be understood as condemnations of violence. Still, one senses an ambiguous attitude in Peckinpah. He, too, seems to be savoring the gyrations of men who have been killed but have not yet bitten the dust.

Another parallel between THE WILD BUNCH and THE SEVEN SAMURAI is in the excellence of the acting. Like Kurosawa, Peckinpah creates his characters in depth, a rare feat in an action movie. Even the smallest parts in THE WILD BUNCH are superbly played. William Holden has never been better than as the aging outlaw, Pike. The sequence in which he decides to rescue Angel is brilliant. In the hands of most actors and directors, a scene such as this, in which a character is shown making up his mind, is usually embarrassing, especially when actor and director think they can bring it off without dialogue. Holden and Peckinpah have no such difficulty. All the relationships in THE WILD BUNCH are convincing, especially the scenes between Robert Ryan and Albert Dekker, when they argue about the scummy bounty hunters.

The final sequence in the Mexican courtyard is extraordinary. After Holden has shot Mapache, he and his companions stand with drawn guns facing hundreds of surprised Mexicans for several seconds of calm. It is clear that the wild bunch is condemned. They are surrounded, outgunned, as good as dead. They realize it, we realize it. At that point, it is simply a question of how many men they will take with them. The moment passes. Holden shoots Mapache's German advisor between the eyes, and we find ourselves in the greatest scene of bloodshed and slaughter ever filmed, with Peckinpah's excesses carrying us to ever higher plateaus of exaltation (while Lucien Ballard provides brilliant cinematography).

If the story of THE WILD BUNCH is against the classic western, the imagery is in its best tradition. Peckinpah may be the only one of the younger American directors to have the feeling for the grandeur of the West and for the look of men in its landscapes that one finds in the westerns of John Ford. There is a scene in THE WILD BUNCH, when Pike's band holds up and captures an ammunition train, that is staged and shot with the precision and suspense of a great action sequence. There are many directors (e.g., Jules Dassin) who would use such a scene as a culminating sequence. It is as good a heist as one is likely to see on the screen. But Peckinpah does not linger over it. He has many great scenes, such as the long-lens, slow-motion shot of Ryan and the bounty hunters as the bridge explodes, a shot that classicizes a violent moment, prolonging it for eternity. Such is the richness of texture of his film that he can afford to dazzle us for a few moments with the train heist and then move on, more or less throwing a great scene away.

THE WILD BUNCH is a picture that dares to be excessive. Peckinpah courts condemnation and risks disaster by putting so personal and unorthodox a conception upon the screen. Because he is successful, a case can be made that THE WILD BUNCH is not only great within the genre of the western, but may be among the very greatest films of the 1960s.

Sam Peckinpah is considered difficult and intransigent when up against ignorant studio personnel and uncooperative crews. Though THE WILD BUNCH was badly mutilated by Warner Brothers, it gained Peckinpah his reputation as connoisseur of violence and reinterpreter of the western.

# Credits

## Stagecoach

U.S.A.; 1939; 105 minutes;
released by United Artists.

**Directed by** John Ford.
**Produced by** Walter Wanger.
**Screenplay by** Dudley Nichols, based on the story "Stage to Lordsburg" by Ernest Haycox.
**Photographed by** Bert Glennon.
**Art direction by** Alexander Toluboff.
**Edited by** Dorothy Spencer and Walter Reynolds.
**Music by** Richard Hageman, W. Franke Harling, John Leipold, Leo Shuken, Louis Gruenberg (adapted from 17 American folktunes of the early 1880s).
**Cast:** John Wayne; Claire Trevor; Thomas Mitchell; Andy Devine; George Bancroft; Donald Meek; Louise Platt; John Carradine; Berton Churchill; Tim Holt; Joseph Rickson.

## The Searchers

U.S.A.; 1956; 119 minutes;
released by Warner Bros.

**Directed by** John Ford.
**Produced by** Merian C. Cooper.
**Screenplay by** Frank S. Nugent, from the novel by Alan LeMay.
**Photographed by** Winton C. Hoch.
**Art direction by** Frank Hotaling and James Basevi.
**Edited by** Jack Murray.
**Music by** Max Steiner.
**Cast:** John Wayne; Jeffrey Hunter; Vera Miles; Ward Bond; Natalie Wood; John Qualen; Olive Carey; Henry Brandon; Ken Curtis; Harry Carey, Jr.; Dorothy Jordan; Pippa Scott; Antonio Moreno; Pat Wayne; Hank Worden; Lana Wood; Walter Coy; Beulah Archuletta.

## Red River

U.S.A.; 1948; 125 minutes;
released by United Artists.

**Directed by** Howard Hawks.
**Produced by** Howard Hawks.
**Screenplay by** Borden Chase and Charles Schnee, from the story "The Blazing Guns on the Chisholm Trail" by Borden Chase.
**Photographed by** Russell Harlan.
**Art direction by** John Datu Arensma.
**Edited by** Christian Nyby.
**Music by** Dimitri Tiomkin.
**Cast:** John Wayne; Montgomery Clift; Joanne Dru; Walter Brennan; Coleen Gray; John Ireland; Noah Beery, Jr.; Chief Yowlachie; Harry Carey, Sr.; Harry Carey, Jr.

## Shane

U.S.A.; 1953; 116 minutes;
released by Paramount.

**Directed by** George Stevens.
**Produced by** George Stevens.
**Screenplay by** A. B. Guthrie, Jr., from the novel by Jack Schaefer (additional dialogue by Jack Sher).
**Photographed by** Loyal Griggs.
**Art direction by** Hal Pereira and Walter Tyler.
**Edited by** William Hornbeck and Tom McAdoo.
**Music by** Victor Young.
**Cast:** Alan Ladd; Jean Arthur; Van Heflin; Brandon de Wilde; Jack Palance; Ben Johnson; Edgar Buchanan; Emile Meyer; Elisha Cook, Jr.; Douglas Spencer; John Dierkes; Ellen Corby; Paul McVey; John Miller; Edith Evanson; Leonard Strong; Ray Spiker.

## The Wild Bunch

U.S.A.; 1969; 143 minutes;
released by Warner Bros.

**Directed by** Sam Peckinpah.
**Produced by** Phil Feldman.
**Screenplay by** Walon Green and Sam Peckinpah, based on a story by Walon Green and Roy N. Sickner.
**Photographed by** Lucien Ballard.
**Art direction by** Edward Carrere.
**Edited by** Louis Lombardo.
**Music by** Jerry Fielding.
**Cast:** William Holden; Ernest Borgnine; Robert Ryan; Edmond O'Brien; Warren Oates; Jaime Sanchez; Ben Johnson; Emilio Fernandez; Strother Martin; L. Q. Jones; Albert Dekker; Bo Hopkins; Bob Taylor.

# Intrigue & Suspense

2

Call them films of intrigue and suspense, or crime and punishment, include the subgenres of the gangster flick, the private-eye flick, the spy and espionage story, the *policier* and the thriller—in the end one is talking about the same thing: a certain kind of action picture characterized by certain specific ingredients, criteria, if you will, for greatness within the genre.

1. A great film of intrigue and suspense must be entertaining. Nothing falls so flat as the suspense picture with weak suspense, or the crime-and-punishment film in which the crime is ordinary and the punishment is feeble. Films in this genre must move inexorably, remorselessly. They must take hold of the attention of the audience and not let go. No message is necessary, though it's all right if the director wants to throw one in; the important thing is that he remember always that the raison d'être of his picture is its ability to entertain.

2. A great film of intrigue and suspense must be complex. Nothing simple-minded will do. The more twists and turns the better. Often the story is about a spider web of entrapment, or the double or triple cross. At times it is so complex that the motivations and subplots become impenetrable. It does not matter, because complexity in this genre is an end in itself. The pictures are made for chess players and problem-solvers, who will return a second or third time if necessary in order to unscramble the infernal internal logic of the story.

3. A great film of intrigue and suspense must be strongly visual. Each shot must make a point. Each must be stunning to the eye. Each must move a character or the story forward. Each, above all, must be designed. Intrigue and suspense is a B-picture genre; the object is entertainment, not art. Production budgets are medium or low, and the form is restrictive in that certain conventions must be observed, i.e., police procedures, the chase, the final confrontation, etc. The filmmaker, then, must work under pressure, expressing himself more in visual terms than in terms of message, theme, or meaning. All the great directors who have worked within this genre—Hitchcock, Reed, Lang, Welles, Hawks, Fuller, Siegel, Huston, Walsh—are men whose work has visual distinction. The way in which they stage and shoot what is basically a standard type of event—the way, in short, that they impose themselves on their material—is the way we measure their achievement.

4. A great film of intrigue and suspense takes place in a special sort of urban world. These pictures are often called *films noirs* because they take place in a fictional landscape which might be called the "night city." This is an environment of bars, and back streets, peopled by whores, junkies, psychopaths, henchmen, gunslingers, gamblers, and private eyes. The night city is a world beyond good and evil, estranged from the values of the middle class, a demimonde. The way the night city—the terrain—of a film of intrigue and suspense is depicted is very much to the point in judging its success.

## Fritz Lang's M 1932

M is an inevitable choice, a masterpiece in its own right, and in many respects the grandfather of the genre. Unlike other early pictures, it does not seem quaint on account of primitivism. It is as strong and gripping an entertainment as it was the day it opened, and although it is one of the earliest German sound films, it contains some uses of sound which have yet to be surpassed. M is as visually strong a picture as has ever been made, and its depiction of the night city is exceptional.

The screenplay, written by Fritz Lang's wife, Thea von Harbou, was based on the true story of the famous Düsseldorf child-murderer, Kürten. His crimes so upset the underworld that it organized an independent attempt to identify him and track him down. This, basically, is the story. M, the first letter of the word "murderer," is chalked on Hans Beckert's (Peter Lorre's) jacket to identify him when he is being shadowed by members of the "Beggars Union."

While law-enforcement officials, who are mercilessly satirized, use modern police methods to identify the psychotic Beckert, the underworld employs its own skills and personnel, and succeeds in catching him first. It tries him before a kangaroo court, sentences him to death, and is about to render punishment, despite pleas that "I can't help myself" (shouted, screamed, and whimpered with all the force at Peter Lorre's command), when the police suddenly arrive and take him away to a fair trial.

There is some sort of message here, typical of Lang at the time, probably a result of his thoughts about Nazism, that "the Law" is the only thing that stands between civilization and anarchy. Thus, the battle between the underworld and the police over the destiny of

Opening pages: Torment and claustrophobia in the final moments of Fritz Lang's M, as Peter Lorre pleads for mercy before underworld tribunal. Gustaf Gründgens (wearing derby) plays master criminal Schränker in this famous scene set in deserted brewery. This page: Police aide with Detective "Fatty" Lohmann (Otto Wernicke) in sleepless search for clues; Lorre finds he is marked as "M"; symbol shot of child victim, murderer's shadow, and reward poster. Lang's "night city" is embellished with geometric compositions, draws viewer into an oppressive world of terror.

a murderer, who is himself a split personality, half psychotic, half law-abiding, must be resolved in favor of a merciful court, not the jungle court of the underworld. As in so many films of this genre, the message tends to be simplistic, and comes close to being undercut by the satire. What is important in M is the expression of the story. The visual ideas and formal elements are supreme.

Lang is not a humanist director; he could not be further from Jean Renoir. He is a manipulator, a master puppeteer, and, as a matter of fact, he belongs among the filmmakers who delight in using human beings to make designs. (See METROPOLIS. Busby Berkeley had this obsession, and so did Leni Riefenstahl.) M is full of designs, high shots in which people, along with architectural elements, are used to make geometric patterns. Note the high shot of the children, watching the organ grinder; the shot of Lorre in front of the shop window surrounded by the reflection of geometrically displayed knives, surely a portent of evil; and the configuration of underworld characters in the low-ceilinged basement of the deserted distillery. Lang's choice of certain shop windows that contain a rotating spiral and a sort of jumping-jack puppet echo another of his curious concerns: an obsession with human mechanicalism, automatic and compulsive movements, which is taken in his METROPOLIS to the fringes of madness.

In M the people are puppets, fools, hysterics. The only real exception is Peter Lorre, whose final, heart-rending cries for pity break through Lang's barrier of misanthropy and make the murderer human. No, Lang is not concerned with people, but with designs, traps, visual geometry, and structural irony.

Lang pushes the idea that the underworld and the law are after the same man as far as it will go, cutting back and forth, making ironic comparisons as the lawmen and the outlaws come up with parallel schemes. As the double trap closes tighter around Peter Lorre, the audience is drawn into the frantic hunt, a passionate pursuit carried out by men who swarm like insects. The camera angles become increasingly portentous, suggesting a constant closing-in, and the atmosphere of the night city becomes more and more nightmarish, more and more claustrophobic. An example of the tensions Lang can generate is the famous bouncing-ball sequence. We hear Mrs. Beckmann calling frantically for her lost daughter; then her cries are intercut with shots of Elsie's ball coming to rest and her balloon being caught in telephone wires. The effect is fateful and powerful. We hear the rough nasal whistling of the theme from Grieg's "Peer Gynt" whenever Peter Lorre is hanging around. The effect is ominous and frightening. Such riches, visual and oral, seem less like primitive experiments than contemporary usages. Many of these effects, the use of a child's ball, the use of music, montages of police evidence, and the construction of a trap, turn up in basically the same form, seventeen years later, in Carol Reed's THE THIRD MAN.

## Alfred Hitchcock's **Rear Window** 1954

We come now to the man whose name is synonymous with the genre, the towering presence, the supreme champion of intrigue and suspense. We are speaking, of course, of Alfred Hitchcock, who has built a career on films of this sort, and has made nearly fifty of them. If we wished, we could quite easily find five great intrigue-and-suspense films among his works: THE MAN WHO KNEW TOO MUCH (1934 version), THE 39 STEPS, and THE LADY VANISHES from his early English period, and NOTORIOUS, STRANGERS ON A TRAIN, and the very great VERTIGO from his Hollywood years, with SUSPICION, SHADOW OF A DOUBT, SPELLBOUND, and NORTH BY NORTHWEST coming in very strong. Why then choose REAR WINDOW? Simply because it comes very close to being the perfect Hitchcock film, the one that illustrates nearly all his major strengths.

In the first place, Hitchcock is a voyeur, and God knows REAR WINDOW is a film about voyeurism. Hitchcock loves to spy on his characters through windows—this is a recurring motif in his films—and REAR WINDOW comes to grips with the problem once and for all: James Stewart, forced to stay in his apartment because of a broken leg, spies on people through windows in an orgy of voyeurism one hundred and twelve minutes long.

Secondly, REAR WINDOW is an archetypal Hitchcock film for the way it rises to meet a difficult technical challenge. Ninety-nine percent of REAR WINDOW is shot from within James Stewart's apartment, and more than half of the shots simulate his point of view. Hitchcock imposes limitations on himself, as he did in LIFEBOAT, where he used a single location, and in ROPE, where he shot in real continuous time, as though in one unbroken scene. Having boxed himself in, Hitchcock is required to be ingenious,

Great master Alfred Hitchcock presides over single set of REAR WINDOW. James Stewart and Grace Kelly play the leads in this orgy of voyeurism. Behind them, on the other side of the "window," are apertures into the miniature world that reflects their personal problems in many variations.

to construct a set and people it in such a way that the restriction becomes a strength, that the solution becomes an example of what he likes to call "pure cinema." He has never been more successful in meeting a technical challenge than in REAR WINDOW, which is constantly energized by his imaginative solutions to his problems.

Thirdly, REAR WINDOW represents Hitchcock at his best for the way it works on many levels, yet conceals its own complexity. Many Hitchcock films seem to be light entertainments, but often, particularly in his American period, there is a dark side to them, a psychological probing, an inner exploration that parallels in some way the exterior events. In REAR WINDOW, Stewart is not only restricted to his apartment by his broken leg, but is boxed in, too, by pressure from Grace Kelly, who wants to marry him. Everything he sees out of the rear window of his apartment is related to this problem, though he himself does not seem to realize it. All the people he spies on represent different facets of married life, or the miseries of being single: the older, childless couple who have invested their emotions in a pet dog; the newlywed and ultracarnal lovers; "Miss Lonelyhearts" and her fantasies of entertaining gentlemen callers; and, most important, the couple across the backyard, the bedridden woman and the husband who murders her because he can no longer abide the tyranny of her illness. The murderer and his wife parody Stewart's problem with Grace Kelly on a nightmare scale. While looking out, Stewart is forced to look subconsciously within himself. His backyard view reflects a miniature universe of stories relating to love and marriage, and they relate to his problems, too. The urban backyard setting is the night city terrain of REAR WINDOW, a night city of the soul reflecting the mysterious, unfathomable darkness that lurks inside an ordinary man in an ordinary situation tyrannized by a sick, complaining, difficult wife.

Fourth, REAR WINDOW is visually very strong, reflecting that precise use of designed shots that has made Hitchcock famous. Hitchcock is not a director who arrives on his set and says: "I don't know what to do today. Let's improvise." He knows precisely what he wants to do. His film is completed in his head and in his sketches before he ever steps onto his set. Shooting and editing are for him simply mechanical phases. The creativity has all taken place before.

The first shot of REAR WINDOW is a perfect example of this, and typical of many Hitchcock first shots for the way it visually conveys exposition to the audience. The camera pans from Stewart's face to the cast on his leg to a broken camera on a table to photographs on the wall, including photographs of smashed-up racing cars. We know without a word of dialogue that Stewart has a broken leg, that he is a photographer, that he specializes in action photography, and that he probably broke his leg taking a photo of an auto race.

Hitchcock is a master at using his camera to create suspense. In REAR WINDOW we see Grace Kelly rummaging inside the murderer's apartment, when the murderer appears suddenly in the hall outside his front door. Stewart can see all this from his rear window, and we can see it, too, though neither of the characters under observation is yet aware of the other's presence. Like Stewart in his chair, we are helpless. We cannot warn Grace Kelly. We want to scream out: "Watch out! Escape! Hide!" This is what suspense is all about—not surprise, but helplessness in the face of knowledge that we possess but the characters do not. In this particular scene the suspense is amplified by the fact that we are in the same position as Stewart, restricted inside his apartment. And, of course, this strong suspense is created by purely visual means.

In REAR WINDOW, we find two other Hitchcock specialties: the use of an object as a major clue, and the use of major motion-picture stars. The object is the wedding ring. Grace Kelly says the murderer's wife would not have left town without her wedding ring, so if the ring can be found there is strong reason to believe a murder has been committed. The ring, then, is the giveaway, as was the cut-off finger in THE 39 STEPS, the cigarette lighter in STRANGERS ON A TRAIN, the reversely rotating windmill in FOREIGN CORRESPONDENT, etc., through twenty or thirty pictures. Truffaut points out that the wedding ring in REAR WINDOW has double significance, since Grace Kelly wants to marry Stewart. When she indicates to him that she has found it, the smile on her face constitutes a double victory—another example of complexity and layered meaning in Hitchcock.

As for the use of major film stars, this is something for which Hitchcock is often criticized. He has used Cary Grant, Gregory Peck, James Stewart, Laurence Olivier, Robert Montgomery, Joseph Cotten, Montgomery Clift, Farley Granger, Paul Newman, Anthony Perkins, Grace Kelly, Kim Novak, Doris Day, Janet Leigh, Marlene Dietrich, Ingrid Bergman, Joan Fontaine, and many, many more. The sin here is supposed to be that Hitchcock is dependent on stars because he is weak with actors, a snobbish myth. The fact is that James Stewart in REAR WINDOW, as well as in VERTIGO, ROPE, and THE MAN WHO KNEW TOO MUCH (1955 version), gives the performances of his life, behaving with a naturalness of which more "actorish" actors are not capable. Stewart is the perfect

Hitchcock character, an ordinary-looking, unpretentious man who becomes enmeshed in extraordinary, nightmarish events. An extraordinary thing happening in an everyday situation to an average person is one of the continuing motifs in Hitchcock's films.

Alfred Hitchcock is in fashion now, thanks to his idolization by French critics whose views have been reimported and have finally made him respectable in his adopted country. For years he was not taken seriously in America. He was the funny little fat man who liked to appear in his own movies, a put-on artist guilty of the worst of all sins, making pictures the public liked, which meant, of course, that his pictures were bad. The incredible thing is that, as late as 1967, Bosley Crowther could write a book entitled *The Great Films* and not discuss a single picture of Alfred Hitchcock in his text.

# Carol Reed's **The Third Man** 1949

THE THIRD MAN is a flawless film of intrigue and suspense, a summit of perfection within the genre. It is one of the most literate thrillers ever made. (The original screenplay was by the great British writer, Graham Greene, who lated adapted his screenplay into a novel.) It is superbly acted by an ensemble working in an understated, effortless style (Joseph Cotten, Orson Welles, Trevor Howard). Its cinematography includes some of the best black-and-white work ever done. (Robert Krasker won the Academy Award against SUNSET BOULEVARD, ALL ABOUT EVE, and THE ASPHALT JUNGLE!) Its score of haunting zither music by Anton Karas is still remembered, instantly familiar to anyone who ever saw the film, and now thoroughly identified with most people's impressions of Vienna. Finally, the producing of Alexander Korda (known for having "saved" the British film industry on account of his "quality" productions) and the direction by Carol Reed are exemplary. Rarely has a motion picture represented the collaboration of so many exceptional talents. THE THIRD MAN may be the greatest film made in Britain since World War II.

The night city terrain of THE THIRD MAN is unique: occupied postwar Vienna, baroque, bombed-out, decadent, patrolled by Jeeps containing representatives of the four occupying powers, an American, an Englishman, a Frenchman, and a Russian. Corrupt, world-weary people hang about its fringes: the overly suave Rumanian, Popescu; the frayed violinist, Baron Kurtz; the atheistic collector of Catholic antiquities, Dr. Winkel; Crabbit, the tired head of the Anglo Cultural Center; and Anna Schmidt, the Czechoslovakian girl friend of Harry Lime, an obscure actress with forged papers. Moving among them are three extraordinary principals, Holly Martins, a typical Greene creation, a hack American writer, a used-up second-rater; Colonel Calloway, a Scotland Yard type, chief of British Military Police; and Harry Lime (Welles), the corrupt two-bit racketeer, an utterly immoral, totally unreachable villain. These characters wander through rain-slick night streets, in and out of shabby cafés, over the rubble of bombed-out buildings, even into a *terrain vague* dominated by a huge Ferris wheel. The Vienna of THE THIRD MAN is a vast city that seems empty. Its streets are always damp, and water rushes through a system of sweet-smelling sewers underneath. It is a world of slinking cats and biting parrots, of people taking advantage of each other without pity. Its morality is summed up by Orson Welles in lines he wrote for himself. Speaking of his trafficking in stolen and diluted penicillin which has turned children into zombies, Welles excuses himself with the words: "After all, it's not that awful. You know what the fellow said: In Italy for thirty years under the Borgias they had warfare, terror, murder, bloodshed—they produced Michelangelo, Leonardo da Vinci, and the Renaissance. In Switzerland they had brotherly love, five hundred years of democracy and peace, and what did they produce? The cuckoo clock!" Colonel Calloway sums up the sense of entrapment when he speaks to Anna of Harry Lime's chances of escape: "Vienna is a closed city. A rat would have more chance in a closed room without a hole and a pack of terriers loose."

THE THIRD MAN meets the test of complexity. The characters interact, their stories conflict: A man who is supposed to be dead turns up alive, there is a question of whether two men or a "third man" carried off Lime's "body," there are conspiracies, deceits, and double crosses. Martins agrees to be the bait in a trap to catch Harry Lime if Calloway will get the Russians off Anna's back, but when Anna accuses him of being an informer he loses his nerve and decides to leave Vienna. He is only persuaded to be Calloway's "dumb decoy duck" when he is taken to the childrens' ward of a hospital and shown the damage that Lime has done. In the end he kills Lime,

Above: Director Carol Reed consults with star Orson Welles on location in the sewers of Vienna during shooting of THE THIRD MAN. Welles' characterization of Harry Lime, corrupt denizen of another atmospheric "night city," is unforgettable. Reed's precise direction, along with a brilliant script, a great score, and fine performances, makes this a nearly perfect film. Reed owes large directorial debts to Lang and Hitchcock, but his own contributions were immense.

his best friend, who in the last moments of his life becomes an almost sympathetic character, wounded, cornered, frightened, trying to crawl out of the sewers, his fingers twitching pathetically in a grille in the center of a moist, wind-blown, empty plaza.

Reed owes debts to Fritz Lang for some of his ideas: the geometrical shots, the montage of evidence, Welles' whistling, etc., but Reed has his own original visual style, particularly his use of a slightly tilted camera to produce so-called "Chinese angles," employed to project danger, foreboding, a twisted universe. He is also capable of providing suspense in the tradition of Hitchcock. One thinks particularly of Martins' mysterious "kidnapping," which turns out to be the result of a misunderstanding. He has been booked by mistake as a speaker to a literary society, and when his incompetence causes the audience to shuffle out, he gets into a verbal duel with Popescu, which only the two of them can understand. As in a Hitchcock film, we in the film audience also understand, but the other characters on the screen do not.

THE THIRD MAN is unique in the genre for its realism. Despite the complexities of plot, the characters are understandable, dimensional, emotionally genuine—a tribute to the fine ensemble playing and special, low-keyed acting style that is the cinematic equivalent of Graham Greene's writing.

Carol Reed was knighted for his excellence as a British filmmaker, and for a body of work that is notable for its good taste. It is this taste, of course, that works so well in THE THIRD MAN, but which has destroyed some of his other films, such as OUR MAN IN HAVANA, which require a certain amount of excess to make them work.

## Orson Welles' **Touch of Evil** 1958

One thing of which Orson Welles cannot be accused is too much good taste. He is flamboyant, excessive, doomed, it seems, to turn a number of films into magnificent failures. He is not known principally for his *policiers*, but his TOUCH OF EVIL must stand beside the very best in the genre. It is unmistakably Wellesian. Its dazzling sound track (a Welles signature since his early days in radio), its long, complicated tracking shots, its low angles, its expressionist lighting, the heightened theatricality of its performances, its dark, brooding photography, its extensive use of the wide-angle lens, its tortuous complexity, and self-contained fictional night-city world, all mark it as the vision of a startling genius of the cinema.

TOUCH OF EVIL may be the greatest B movie ever made. It is the genre film of genre films—in the sense that the French critics refer to the genres of Hollywood B production as places where talented directors work creatively within restrictive modes. On its face, TOUCH OF EVIL is a second-rate *policier,* with some absurd moments that give it the quality of a horror picture. But beneath that veneer it is a brilliant work of a great cinematic mind, exhibiting an encyclopedia of expressionist effects, and containing a tour de force of acting. (What besides tour de force can describe a situation in which the director of a film additionally plays its principal role?)

When Orson Welles is in a film his first appearance is always theatrical. One thinks, particularly, of THE THIRD MAN, when Harry Lime's face is suddenly illuminated in a doorway off a wet Viennese street. In TOUCH OF EVIL Welles' first appearance, as the crooked cop Hank Quinlan, is no less startling. A police car pulls up to the scene of a killing and suddenly there is Welles, sitting in the back seat, a huge mound of flesh, bigger than life, a cigar clenched between his teeth, his face unshaven, decadent, flabby, and also vulnerable, revealing that "touch of evil," that suggestion of corruption, that is the key to the fascinating and ambiguous character he plays. From that moment we are caught between admiration of his thousand brilliant directorial effects, and fascination with his characterization of Quinlan, a characterization which constantly energizes the screen.

Stanley Kubrick once said that the first shot of a picture should be the most interesting thing the audience sees after entering the theatre. Certainly, the first shot of TOUCH OF EVIL meets this test. It may be the most dazzling first shot to appear in any film, and Welles complains of having to explain to people how it was done.

In a single, constantly moving crane shot that lasts more than three minutes, we see, first, a close-up of a time bomb being set and a shadowy figure running to a parked car and placing the bomb in its trunk; second, an obviously wealthy businessman and his floozy girl friend appearing from the background, getting into the car, and driving toward the U. S.-Mexican frontier in the fictional border town of Los Robles (by this time the camera has tracked up and back and we have seen several extra-



Orson Welles as Hank Quinlan, the crooked cop, in his TOUCH OF EVIL. Grotesquely fat and bristling with unshaven stubble, swigging soda pop, growling at everyone, planting evidence and improvising the law, Quinlan is the essence of corruption in what is perhaps the greatest "B" movie ever made.

ordinary long views of the pseudo-Spanish, colonnaded environment which will contain the story); third, while the car stops at a traffic light the camera swoops back down and we see the Mexican detective, Vargas (Charlton Heston) and his blonde American wife (Janet Leigh) also walking toward the frontier; fourth, the camera tracks them for a while, then picks up again on the car as both Vargas and the car meet at the customs post; fifth, we overhear dialogue between Vargas and the border guard as the car pulls out of frame; sixth, we continue with Vargas and his wife as they walk into the United States until the explosion, which we have been awaiting all this time, overlaps on the sound track.

Unfortunately, Universal-International, which released the film, superimposed main titles over part of this shot, and as a result its fluidity is somewhat diluted. But if we ignore the titles and concentrate on the action we are prepared, by the time the car explodes, to say: "My God, Orson Welles is a genius. He has made the greatest crane shot of all time." In fact, this is precisely what he has done, charging the opening of his picture with unbearable suspense, and setting forth a brilliant visual style that will dominate and at times overwhelm the film. We have spoken of great opening expository shots by Hitchcock; his is the art that conceals itself, while Welles' is the art that cries out for attention.

Critics have written of TOUCH OF EVIL as if it were of ideological importance, finding great irony in the fact that the duel between the straight, incorruptible Vargas and the tainted, decadent Quinlan only ends when Vargas is forced to used Quinlan's dirty tricks to defeat him. Welles has said that "Hank Quinlan is the incarnation of everything I fight against politically and morally.... I firmly believe that in the modern world we have to choose between the morality of the law and the morality of basic justice."

If this is, in fact, the message of TOUCH OF EVIL, it is rather imperfectly expressed in the film. No, TOUCH OF EVIL is not great on account of its ideology, nor does its powerful impact have much to do with its convoluted plot. It is great on account of its succession of brilliantly staged and bizarrely played scenes; its images and its acting and its sound track are that things that make it memorable. Thus, it is a classic B movie. Its greatness lies wholly in how the story is told, and not at all in the message or material.

In addition to its fabulous opening, TOUCH OF EVIL contains other brilliant sequences:

The scene in which Quinlan throttles Grandi with one of Janet Leigh's stockings in a claustrophobic hotel



From TOUCH OF EVIL: Janet Leigh terrorized by motorcycle gang at the Mirador Hotel. Quinlan about to kill Grandi (Akim Tamiroff); he will not use the gun, but one of Janet Leigh's stockings. Right: Charlton Heston (with moustache) as the Mexican detective, Vargas.

room while a neon light flashes outside. Welles moves ponderously and inexorably toward Akim Tamiroff, who scurries about the room; we feel as though an elephant is stalking a mouse.

Two long (four- or five-minute) scenes in single takes in the murder suspect's apartment. Welles manipulates his cast with virtuosity. There is much overlapping dialogue as everyone talks at once, and half a dozen characters are brilliantly delineated.

The appalling terrorization of Janet Leigh at the Mirador Motel by a gang of leather-jacketed teen-agers.

The ambience of the parlor where Marlene Dietrich sits amidst the paraphernalia of her past, and while a pianola tinkles in the background, delivers some marvelous lines: "Darling, you're a mess," she says when she finally recognizes Quinlan beneath his layers of fat. And, when he asks her to tell his fortune: "Your future is all used up."

An extraordinary shot in which the camera dollies back as a group of characters cross a street, tracks them across a hotel lobby, leads them into a cramped elevator, and rides with them up five floors until Vargas, who has left them in the lobby, reappears at the very moment the elevator door reopens.

The final stalking scene in a nightmare world of pumping oil derricks and garbage heaps, with Quinlan's confession echoing off Vargas' receiver.

Perhaps the best thing about TOUCH OF EVIL is the strange, decaying atmosphere of its night city, a fictional space created by Welles out of bizarre locations in Venice, California. It is a weird world of flashing neon, tawdry hotels and night clubs, crumbling arches, peeling walls, twisting alleys, and everywhere, always, heaps of trash.

The history of the film is sad. Welles was hired originally just to play the part of Quinlan, but when the producer discovered that Charlton Heston had agreed to play Vargas only because he'd assumed that Welles would also direct, Welles was quickly signed as director, too. That accidental assignment was destined to change TOUCH OF EVIL from a B movie of average potential into a masterpiece of Gothic expressionism. But the final result confused executives at Universal-International, and when the film opened to poor business, they dumped it.

The box-office failure of TOUCH OF EVIL was harmful to Welles. For years afterward, despite his great critical reputation, no American studio would touch him. "Too eccentric, too grandiose," they'd say, shaking their heads over his "self-defeating genius."

# Howard Hawks' **The Big Sleep** 1946

The picture that usually springs to mind when considering that subgenre of intrigue and suspense, the private-eye film, is John Huston's THE MALTESE FALCON, an undeniably taut, tough, first-rate picture about greed and immorality and murder. Once Humphrey Bogart gets going as Sam Spade, emerging as sort of a tough-guy superman, the picture becomes powerfully magnetic. THE MALTESE FALCON (1941) is also the first of the great private-eye films and so is important for the way it stakes out a piece of territory in movie history. If it has faults, they are that it may take itself a bit too seriously and that it tries to be too logical. There are too many scenes in which characters sit around and explain things so we can follow the complex plot.

Howard Hawks' THE BIG SLEEP, on the other hand, moves so fast and with so little concern for whether or not its complexities are grasped that at times it becomes incomprehensible. For this incredible complexity, and for its speed, its wit, its sophistication, and the fact that for too long it has been ignored, we choose it as a summit in

From THE BIG SLEEP, Humphrey Bogart about to kiss Lauren Bacall. After appearing together in Hawks' TO HAVE AND HAVE NOT (1944), they became one of Hollywood's great acting couples. Below: Bogart as "shamus" Philip Marlowe, is menaced by Louis Heydt's gun, tied up, and stymied as Elisha Cook, Jr., inadvertently drinks poison, thereby adding himself to a mounting pile of bodies.

the subgenre, without meaning in any way to impugn the excellence of THE MALTESE FALCON. In the end, the question comes down to personal taste: Does one prefer Howard Hawks or the early John Huston, does one prefer a classic private-eye picture or a baroque one, does one prefer Bogart as Hammett's Sam Spade or as Chandler's Philip Marlowe? (The distinction between Dashiell Hammett and Raymond Chandler may not be apparent to the outsider, but to the aficionado of the detective novel it is crucial and basic.)

To speak of complexity in M, REAR WINDOW, THE THIRD MAN, and even TOUCH OF EVIL is to deal on a nursery school level with what is found in THE BIG SLEEP. The plot is so involuted, contains so many twists and turns, with bodies falling so fast, that summary is hopeless and comprehension is dicey. Even William Faulkner, who worked on the script, was confused about the plot. Someone once asked Hawks who had committed one of the murders, and Hawks, who wasn't sure, asked Faulkner. Faulkner wasn't sure either, so he and Hawks called Chandler, who told them, "The butler did it," to which Hawks is supposed to have replied: "You're crazy; the butler was at the beach house." This anecdote says something very important about THE BIG SLEEP: that though it meets every requirement of the superior thriller, being complex, entertaining, strongly visual, and depicting a demimonde, it is very much a put-on, not to be taken seriously at all.

Bogart was one of the few actors who didn't look ridiculous holding a gun. For ten years he played minor parts, until in 1941 he appeared as Sam Spade in John Huston's THE MALTESE FALCON. After that he was king of American *films noirs*, perhaps never so good as in THE BIG SLEEP.

THE THIRD MAN is a very serious picture. It is, ultimately, about the destruction of children. THE BIG SLEEP is not serious. It has to do with a bunch of whores, pimps, henchmen, killers, blackmailers, gamblers, a debutante who sucks her thumb and gets hopped-up on dope, and a decadent general who holds court in his greenhouse (where Bogart sweats like a pig). It has Mrs. Rutledge (Lauren Bacall), who gets involved with Bogart and with whom he has an incredible conversation, exceedingly daring for the time, in which they discuss sex in terms of horse racing, and it has Bogart as Philip Marlowe, a private eye who can go into a bookstore disguised as a homosexual (hilarious if a little vulgar in these days of Gay Liberation), and then go into a bookshop across the street and have a sexual matinée with a luscious, spectacled, bluestocking nymphomaniac, played by Dorothy Malone. The dialogue is racy, witty, tough, and full of erotic innuendos, so funny that before contemporary college audiences, more than a quarter of a century after its original release, THE BIG SLEEP brings down the house.

To make a critical analysis of THE BIG SLEEP is to take a skillful put-on entertainment too seriously. Suffice to say that it is richly satirical, that Bogart and Bacall together are marvelous, that there is good gunplay, fancy footwork, a Chinese statuette with a camera concealed inside, a pile of bodies, and that Bogart, as the "shamus," is at the top of his form. Perhaps some snatches of dialogue will convey something of the flavor:

Bacall's younger sister to Bogart: "You're a mess, aren't you?" Bogart's reply: "I'm not very tall either. Next time I'll come on stilts, wear a white tie, and carry a tennis racket."

Bogart re some bloodstains on the floor: "Maybe he had meat for dinner; maybe he likes to do his butchering in his parlor."

Bacall to Bogart: "You go too far, Marlowe." Bogart to Bacall: "Those are hard words to throw at a man, especially when he's walking out of your bedroom."

Two private-eye pictures were made in recent years in an attempt to revive the subgenre: Jack Smight's HARPER, starring Paul Newman, and Peter Yates' BULLITT, starring Steve McQueen. Among many other things they teach us that Humphrey Bogart is irreplaceable.

# Credits

## M

Germany; 1932; 99 minutes;
released in the U.S. by Janus.

**Directed by** Fritz Lang.
**Produced by** Nero Film A.G.
**Screenplay by** Thea von Harbou, after an article by Egon Jacobson, in collaboration with Paul Falkenberg, Adolf Jansen and Karl Vash.
**Photographed by** Fritz Arno Wagner.
**Art direction by** Emil Hasler and Karl Vollbrecht.
**Edited by** Paul Falkenberg.
**Music by** Edvard Grieg, abstract from "Peer Gynt."
**Cast:** Peter Lorre; Otto Wernicke; Gustaf Gründgens; Ellen Widmann; Inge Landgut; Ernst Stahl-Nachbaur; Franz Stein; Theodor Loos; Fritz Gnass; Fritz Odemar.

## Rear Window

U.S.A.; 1954; 112 minutes;
released by Paramount.

**Directed by** Alfred Hitchcock.
**Produced by** Alfred Hitchcock.
**Screenplay by** John Michael Hayes, from a story by Cornell Woolrich.
**Photographed by** Robert Burks.
**Art direction by** Hal Pereira, Joseph McMillan Johnson, Sam Comer and Ray Mayer.
**Edited by** George Tomasini.
**Music by** Franz Waxman.
**Cast:** James Stewart; Grace Kelly; Wendell Corey; Thelma Ritter; Raymond Burr; Judith Evelyn; Ross Bagdasarian; Georgine Darcy; Jesslyn Fax; Rand Harper; Irene Winston.

## The Third Man

Great Britain; 1949; 104 minutes;
released in the U.S. by Selznick Releasing Organization.

**Directed by** Carol Reed.
**Produced by** Alexander Korda.
**Screenplay by** Graham Greene.
**Photographed by** Robert Krasker.
**Art direction by** Vincent Korda.
**Edited by** Oswald Hafenrichter.
**Music by** Anton Karas.
**Cast:** Joseph Cotten; Alida Valli; Orson Welles; Trevor Howard; Bernard Lee; Paul Hoerbiger; Annie Rosar; Ernst Deutsch; Siegfried Breuer; Erich Ponto; Wilfrid Hyde-White.

## Touch of Evil

U.S.A.; 1958; 94 minutes;
released by Universal-International.

**Directed by** Orson Welles.
**Produced by** Albert Zugsmith.
**Screenplay by** Orson Welles, from the novel "Badge of Evil" by Walt Masterson.
**Photographed by** Russell Metty.
**Art direction by** Alexander Golitzen and Robert Clatworthy.
**Edited by** Virgil Vogel and Aaron Stell.
**Music by** Henry Mancini.
**Cast:** Orson Welles; Charlton Heston; Janet Leigh; Akim Tamiroff; Joseph Calleia; Joanna Moore; Ray Collins; Dennis Weaver; Marlene Dietrich; Joseph Cotten; Keenan Wynn; Zsa-Zsa Gabor; Mercedes McCambridge.

## The Big Sleep

U.S.A.; 1946; 113 minutes;
released by Warner Bros.

**Directed by** Howard Hawks.
**Produced by** Howard Hawks.
**Screenplay by** William Faulkner, Leigh Brackett and Jules Furthman, from the novel by Raymond Chandler.
**Photographed by** Sid Hickox.
**Art direction by** Carl Weyl.
**Edited by** Christian Nyby.
**Music by** Max Steiner.
**Cast:** Humphrey Bogart; Lauren Bacall; Martha Vickers; Dorothy Malone; John Ridgeley; Charles Waldron; Charles Brown; Regis Toomey; Louis Heydt; Elisha Cook, Jr.; Bob Steele.

# Comedies

# 3

The genre of comedy is bottom-heavy, which is to say that the "Golden Age of Comedy"—the silent era—has not been surpassed despite the advent of sound, color, and a hundred technical breakthroughs. In almost every other genre it is possible to argue that pictures got better as the art of the cinema developed, and that most old masterpieces look more like artifacts than movies in which a contemporary audience can become involved. But in comedy this is not true. The great silent comedy stars, Charles Chaplin, Buster Keaton, Harold Lloyd, Harry Langdon, and—by extension—Laurel and Hardy (for their style derived from the silents despite their success in the sound era) put Jerry Lewis, Woody Allen, Peter Sellers, and Danny Kaye to shame. One is left with the thesis that the silent screen was particularly amenable to comedy, especially in America; that the tradition of comic mime acting flourished in the early free-wheeling days of cinema; and that of all the different types of movies made during the silent period, comedy was perhaps the single one in which silence was an asset. (Chaplin certainly understood this. He continued to make mime comedies long after the advent of sound, and, of course, he was popular enough to get away with it.)

There is something about the sight gag that is universal. Show THE GENERAL to a morose college student today and watch him laugh. Show him IT HAPPENED ONE NIGHT and he'll tell you he can't "relate to it." Of course, he's right. The pictures of Chaplin and Keaton are universal, great, for all time. The situation comedies and screwball comedies of the thirties, forties, and fifties are, no matter how hilarious in their time, now mostly dated.

Mae West and W. C. Fields were very funny people, but their films were not all that great, and their comic attributes are amusing now mostly because of nostalgia. Of the talking comics only the Marx Brothers seem to have staying power. Their total and incorrigible outrageousness is universally accessible. There is something about their irreverent mockery of everything that is not too far from Abbie Hoffman appearing in a Minuteman costume to testify before the House Un-American Activities Committee.

There is a temptation, then, to say that the five

Preceding pages: Buster Keaton as Johnny Gray on cowcatcher of his beloved locomotive. THE GENERAL, in which both actor and train starred, was directed by Keaton and Clyde Bruckman. Above: Charlie Chaplin meets his opponent at start of famous boxing sequence in CITY LIGHTS.

greatest screen comedies are THE GOLD RUSH and CITY LIGHTS by Chaplin, THE NAVIGATOR and THE GENERAL by Keaton, and the Marx Brothers' DUCK SOUP. Such a statement treats the last forty years as a comic wasteland, which is, of course, an exaggeration. But if the Frank Capra social comedies, and the Howard Hawks screwball comedies, and the Wilder-Diamond situation comedies, and the British comedies of Guinness and Sellers, the fantasies of Kaye, and the dumbhead movies of Lewis all seem to have lost a lot of their comic savor, and often, if one is not in the precise mood, seem to fall completely flat, there do exist pictures from the last forty years which are funny.

Looking in vain for comic-actor geniuses, one turns to dependable directors. Hitchcock gives us THE TROUBLE WITH HARRY, which may be his worst picture. Welles, Renoir, Fellini, Ford, Buñuel, and Lang, though they may play at times in comic realms, are much too serious. Kubrick, on the other hand, provides an unexpected comic masterpiece—unexpected since he is generally accused of being cold and misanthropic, guilty of what Andrew Sarris calls "strained seriousness." It all adds up, though. Kubrick's cold formalism finds a voice in the comic mode called "black humor." DOCTOR STRANGELOVE, OR HOW I LEARNED TO STOP WORRYING AND LOVE THE BOMB is the black comedy of cinema. If it does not make us hold our sides, it forces us to smile at the absurdity of the world of men—another way of responding to the vision of Chaplin, Keaton, and the brothers Marx.

There also is Tony Richardson, a director who made his name as the most active filmmaker in the British Neo-Realist Movement, an interesting development in movie history which, unfortunately, produced no masterpieces. Richardson, however, did produce an enormously enjoyable comedy, TOM JONES, a riotous, broad, silly, bawdy costume satire, adapted by John Osborne from the lively eighteenth-century novel of Henry Fielding. It may be hard to argue that TOM JONES is in the same class as DUCK SOUP, or even DR. STRANGELOVE, but it meets the test of a great comedy, which far more subtle and sophisticated works by more proficient directors seem to fail. Years after its release it makes us laugh. And this, indeed, is what comedy is all about.

## Charles Chaplin's **City Lights** 1931

To speak of Chaplin's genius as comic and as filmmaker is to speak of that which everyone knows. The libraries are filled with books that explain him. Every critic has, at one time or another, written a Chaplin appreciation. In 1972, when Chaplin came back to America to receive his Academy Award, and the long overdue apologies of ignorant men who had tried to deprive him of honor, his films began to play again, and crowds flocked to them with pleasure. No comic is as loved as Chaplin. He may be the most famous movie actor in the world; certainly he is in the pantheon of every student of film.

It is almost impossible to locate the Chaplin masterpiece. One must choose from among THE KID, THE GOLD RUSH, THE CIRCUS, CITY LIGHTS, and MODERN TIMES. Which is most vintage? Impossible to say. The problem for the connoisseur of Chaplin is that the most recently seen of these five is always the favorite. The problem is complicated by the fact that the Tramp is always different, sometimes more jaunty and resilient, at other times more depressed, more crushed. And, too, there is the element of social comment. It is always there, but depending on one's taste in Chaplin one will prefer the film that contains the desired quotient. There is something touchingly, naïvely Marxist about MODERN TIMES. THE GOLD RUSH, on the other hand, though on one level concerned with problems of capital, cannot be considered ideological. Ultimately, just how funny does one want Chaplin to be? Purely funny, a comic acrobat, as in the early two-reelers, or with that famous pathos, which gives his characterizations an almost mystical dimension? Charlie the acrobat or Charlie the poet? The Tramp as extrovert or the Tramp who knows himself? Chaplin the fool or Chaplin the breaker of hearts?

The greatness of Chaplin resides in the wealth of possibilities he presents and from which his audience may choose. He did so many things so well, developed and changed so many times, showed so many facets while maintaining such originality, that the richness of his work may be mined by every taste.

Always, lurking behind every great Chaplin film, is Chaplin the director, the filmmaker-genius who understood the actor-genius and depicted him with perfection. With Chaplin we always have the feeling that he is entertaining himself; that he is behind the camera at the same time that he is in front of it, adoring his own antics so honestly that he can photograph himself with utter love.

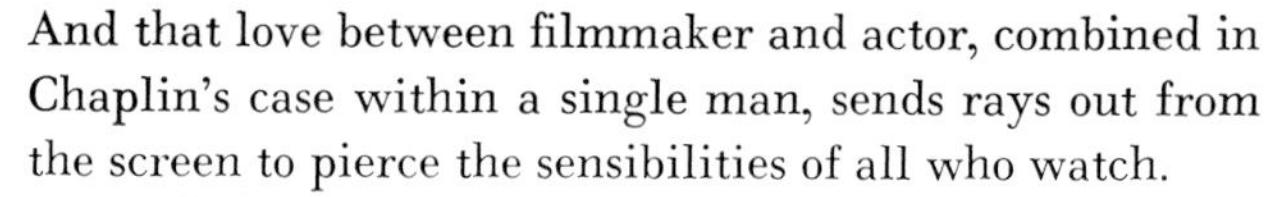

And that love between filmmaker and actor, combined in Chaplin's case within a single man, sends rays out from the screen to pierce the sensibilities of all who watch.

In many ways, CITY LIGHTS is the prototypal Chaplin film, containing most of the important elements of Chaplin's work at or near summits of perfection.

At War with An Object: Chaplin's famous scene along these lines is his extended battle with a Murphy bed, but when he swallows a whistle in CITY LIGHTS the result is the same, and the effect more humorous for being more subtle. He wants to conquer the whistle in his throat, but he cannot. Despite all his ingenuity, its trap is infernal. Variations are played out with perfect timing, hilarity mounts, and then, before there is repetition, Charlie is off to something else. There is a fascinating contradiction in Chaplin's numerous wars against things. While fighting with them, he makes them come alive. In the case of the whistle, he literally breathes life into it. At the same time, the humor derives from the fact that these objects are inanimate, that his wars against them are futile.

Trapped in A Situation: One sees this over and over again in Chaplin, though never so elaborately or comically refined as in the boxing match in CITY LIGHTS. For Charlie the boxing match appears at first to be a marvelous opportunity. He needs money for the blind girl, and there's a fifty-fifty split if he throws the bout. But in the dressing room, as the horror of what *might* happen is revealed, his partner suddenly withdraws and an ominous new combatant appears. The trap springs shut. Charlie is in an impossible dilemma, with no way out. He still needs the money; he must go on; a slaughter

Clockwise from left: Chaplin with blind flower girl (Virginia Cherrill) in one of their idealized love scenes. Boxing match is among finest acrobatic bits in the entire oeuvre of cinema. Chaplinesque surrealism has street-cleaning Tramp confronting herculean task posed by elephant.

is imminent. We know the ingenuity of the Tramp. Our wonder at how he will escape this situation fills us with suspense. What happens in the ring is the finest sort of acrobatics, timed perfectly, to the split second. The boxing match in CITY LIGHTS is as good as any stunt sequence in any early Chaplin short. But here, in a film of characters about whom we care, suspended in a story that must have an end, the boxing match is much more than a comic routine. It is a comic sequence wtih dramatic power.

The Girl, Idealized: She is always there, in Chaplin films, and in CITY LIGHTS Virginia Cherrill may be the ultimate example, though there are those who think her spirituality is overdone. Chaplin has a lot of heart, and his films are filled with sentiment, but the idealization of his women can never be considered sentimental, even in CITY LIGHTS where a blind heroine would seem to offer an irresistible opportunity to play for soap opera.

Social Comment: There is plenty of it in CITY LIGHTS: the millionaire, generous when drunk, hard-nosed when sober; his butler, who is a snob; the pomposity of the officials and patrons at the unveiling of the statue; the night-club sequence, which is brilliant social satire. Comparing the social comment in CITY LIGHTS and MODERN TIMES, one can say that in CITY LIGHTS the satire is less bitter and therefore more poignant.

Surrealism: Certainly a trademark of the Chaplin film is the controlled surreality of the world in which the action takes place. Chaplin's sets are always stylized, but not so much as to look artificial. In CITY LIGHTS he has created a city that is no city in particular, but which is every city in general, a city that is oppressive and also believable, a perfect place of torment for the Tramp.

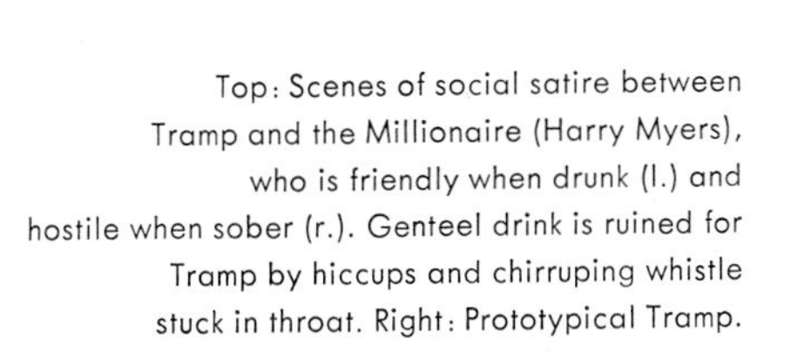

Top: Scenes of social satire between Tramp and the Millionaire (Harry Myers), who is friendly when drunk (l.) and hostile when sober (r.). Genteel drink is ruined for Tramp by hiccups and chirruping whistle stuck in throat. Right: Prototypical Tramp.

Pathos: There is no better example of the famous pathos of Chaplin than in the final minutes of CITY LIGHTS. The comedy, the slapstick, is somehow transscended. Suddenly one is in the realm of poetry. The expressions on Chaplin's face and on the face of the girl say so much on so many levels that they defy analysis. In fact, to try to analyze them is to risk the destruction of the poetry. Is this a sudden realization in which the Tramp grasps his own unworthiness? Has his gift of sight to the blind girl, for whom he has suffered and gone to prison, produced a gaze upon himself whose pity makes him wither? And are his teeth, bared through his grin, the remnants of a defense that has just been breached? Surely, there is here some moment of truth, some confrontation between a Tramp who is lovable and a Tramp who is pathetic. But to unravel it all is to know things which must forever be wrapped in mystery: Who is the Tramp? What are his origins? Why, above all, is he a tramp? For all the mystery, one thing in these final frames becomes clear to every Chaplin fan. The Tramp is much more than a lovable fool—much, much more.

What of Chaplin as filmmaker? In his autobiography, he writes that he spent more than a year shooting CITY LIGHTS because he had worked himself "into a neurotic state of wanting perfection." The Tramp's discovery that the flower girl is blind, a scene that lasts seventy seconds, took five days to shoot. The movies of Chaplin, which look so simple, are among the most carefully crafted of films. Mack Sennett had accidentally discovered —accidentally, because he really had no aesthetic—that the best way to shoot a comic sequence was to set up a camera, turn it on, and shoot the scene performed in front of it in long, single takes. Chaplin took this idea, totally opposed to the concept of montage, and carried it out with artistry. His shots are always perfectly framed. When he chooses an angle it is not merely to cover his antics, but to frame his scenes for eternity, to place a music-hall proscenium around them in the most perfect way he can devise.

The reason, perhaps, that people speak of Chaplin as a genius is that they cannot understand where he learned such things, how he was able to transform himself from a clown into an artist. Genius is the only word there is for talent that comes from sources deep within the self that can neither be traced nor understood. Chaplin's fall into the self-pity of LIMELIGHT, and the flatness of MONSIEUR VERDOUX, would not be noticeable in a man who had not reached dizzying heights in earlier years.

## Buster Keaton's **The General** 1926

Chaplin and Buster Keaton ruled the Golden Age of Comedy, while Harold Lloyd, Harry Langdon, and Laurel and Hardy worked within the territory they staked out. Chaplin and Keaton often have been compared, and the belief exists that they represent antipodes of expression. No one has stated their differences quite so eloquently as the film critic, Andrew Sarris, who wrote:

"The difference between Keaton and Chaplin is the difference between poise and poetry, between the aristocrat and the tramp, between adaptability and dislocation, between the function of things and the meaning of things, between eccentricity and mysticism, between man as machine and man as angel, between the girl as a convention and the girl as an ideal, between life as farce and life as fantasy."

James Agee came close to putting the essence of Buster Keaton's comic character into words when he wrote: "In a way his pictures are like a transcendent juggling act in which it seems that the whole universe is in exquisite flying motion, and the one point of repose is the juggler's effortless, uninterested face."

This repose, this sense of self-containment, this indifference to the madness of the world, this aloofness while pursuing some private goal, combined with the beauty of his face and his famous dead-pan look, endows his pictures with a unique quality perhaps nowhere better illustrated than in his masterpiece, THE GENERAL.

The first thing one notices about this film is its sense of cinema. While Chaplin's conceptions are often theatrical, Keaton seems to have had an instinctive grasp of the potential of the screen. Throughout THE GENERAL, in which Keaton plays a railroad engineer in Civil War times, there is a manipulation of trains running back and forth, while violent, comic, and extraordinary actions take place upon them, that gives the picture an enormous sense of movement. We see Keaton, poised against backgrounds that are constantly in motion, engaging in feats of acrobatics and in startling and ingenious comic stunts. Simultaneously, he is enmeshed in a dramatic story of strong suspense and epic grandeur. THE GENERAL, among



Buster Keaton performing with locomotive and cannon in a series of his famous battles with machines. At times they defy him, at other times they overwhelm him, and then there are sublime moments when he and they are in perfect harmony.

3
GENERAL

CSA

other things, is a comedy, an historical reconstruction, a chase movie, a war movie, and a film that exhibits the major theme of Buster Keaton's work: Man versus The Machine—a struggle between himself and a locomotive which resolves, at times, into a delicious harmonization.

The story is based on an actual incident of the Civil War, the so-called Anderson Raid, a daring exploit by a Northern spy who captured a Confederate train and tried to ride it back to Union lines, wreaking havoc along the way. Keaton was fascinated by the story and wanted to shoot it as authentically as possible, even going so far as to explore the possibility of shooting on the original Alabama-Tennessee railway line, where it had taken place. In the end, he shot in the lumber country of Oregon on a narrow-gauge track with Civil War-type wood-burning engines. (One of these started a forest fire which Keaton's extras, four thousand members of the Oregon National Guard, put out under his direction.) One of the extraordinary things about THE GENERAL is its sense of historical authenticity. It has the look, particularly in the Northern railway yard scene and in the great ambush scene, of photographs by Mathew Brady.

Throughout the film we are fascinated by the constant back-and-forth movement of the trains and the comic scenes played out upon them. After a series of increasingly ingenious pranks (including a phenomenal sequence in which Keaton barely avoids having his head blown off by a cannon) there suddenly appear alongside Keaton's train whole armies, literally thousands of men, a retreating Confederate force and a pursuing Union regiment, in one of the epic throwaway scenes in movie history. Keaton ignores this extravaganza with total composure and thus confirms Agee's description of his essence.

We are moved by Keaton and the films he designed, co-directed, and always edited himself, because of something ineffably human and poised in his being that tells us about ourselves and our weaknesses with good humor and infinite grace. There is a remarkable scene in THE GENERAL—a film filled with remarkable scenes and playful inventiveness—that illustrates this especially well. Keaton is furiously stoking his locomotive to escape two pursuing Union trains, and is desperate on account of his dwindling supply of wood fuel. He turns to find his girl, Annabelle Lee, nonchalantly sweeping wood chips out of the locomotive cabin and rejecting pieces of wood that do not please her eye. Keaton looks at her, mimics her gestures, grasps her by her neck, makes as if he is going to throttle her, and then embraces her with a loving kiss. No one can fail to be moved by so gracefully executed a sequence of gestures, illustrating that special combination of fury and love which men sometimes feel toward the women they adore.

Buster Keaton had the misfortune to fall from public favor. Billy Wilder dug him up as a "waxwork" for SUNSET BOULEVARD and Chaplin used him as an extra in LIMELIGHT. In the early days of television he was trotted out for variety shows, and nostalgia buffs were pleased to recognize his ruined face. In the last few years his genius has been recognized by many young critics, who have resurrected him to the pantheon. In a poll conducted by *Sight and Sound* magazine in 1972, THE GENERAL was voted the eighth greatest film of all time.

## The Marx Brothers' **Duck Soup** 1933

Like Chaplin and Keaton, the Marx Brothers came out of a background of poverty and a childhood on the vaudeville circuit, which may or may not say something about the origins necessary to become a great comedian. But while Chaplin and Keaton rose high above their vaudeville music-hall backgrounds, recasting themselves as great mime artists, the Marx Brothers, if anything, reduced vaudeville slapstick to its most debased level. In other words, they reveled in their vulgarity. Rather than try to rise above it and elevate themselves to artistry, they took lowbrowism and shamelessly pushed it to extremes.

They were neither poised nor poetic, not sublime or mystical, not skilled acrobats or breakers of hearts, or deeply tragic beneath their comic masks. They were cheap, sophomoric, scatological, reckless, excessive, lunatic, and asinine, all to such extremes that they turned everything impossibly bad into something extremely good. By being so thoroughly second-rate, without embarrassment or remorse, they made art out of the tawdry. And, of course, as much as they are loved by the hardhats, their greatest admirers are the intellectuals, whose best-kept secret is the acknowledgement that trash like DUCK SOUP is superior to phony art like DEATH IN VENICE because, when all is said and done, the Marx Brothers give pleasure by blasting at pretension, while Visconti is insufferable when he is sucking up to Art.



Keaton in cab; during rescue of his girl, Annabelle Lee (Marian Mack); and receiving hero's reward while taking salute. In final sight gag, the General starts to move, and couple – still seated on side rod and still in clinch – rise and fall, rhythmically and unheedingly.

Top: "If you think this country's bad off now, just wait 'til I get through with it," sings Groucho in opening reel of DUCK SOUP. Right: Four Marx Brothers (Zeppo at left) play at war. Far right: Groucho calls his troops collect. Below: Chico and Harpo ruin Louis Calhern (Ambassador Trentino). Comic genius of Marxes lies in special brand of contrived chaos and arrant lowbrowism.

The problem with the intellectuals' adoration of the Marx Brothers is that they feel they must justify their response by analysis and elevation—like the distinguished professor of English who enjoyed the music of the Beatles, and used methods of literary criticism to discuss them. By applying the self-conscious standards of official, certified art to material that is opposed to art, self-consciousness, and official standards, his analysis makes the Beatles sound unbearably pretentious. The situation is analogous to attempts to make sense out of the Marx Brothers, to explain their appeal in anything but the most obvious terms. The Marx Brothers give pleasure because, in addition to every other adjective heretofore applied to them, *they are outrageous.*

As for DUCK SOUP, it is undoubtedly the brothers' funniest film. This is not so much on account of its surrealism, well noted by intellectuals, or of the historical analysis which views it as striking a blow against fascism and war, but for the purity of its anarchy and absurdity, more valid than the self-conscious handling of these themes by Ionesco and Beckett.

Groucho plays Rufus T. Firefly, newly elected President of Fredonia, a self-contained universe of insanity. In other pictures Groucho played Captain Jeffrey T. Spaulding, Professor Quincey Adams Wagstaff, Otis B. Driftwood, Dr. Hugo Z. Hackenbush, J. Cheever Loophole, S. Quentin Quale, Wolf J. Flywheel, Ronald Kornblow, and Sam Grunion. Margaret Dumont, who in DUCK SOUP plays the wealthy Mrs. Teasdale, in other Marx Brothers' pictures played Mrs. Rittenhouse, Mrs. Potter, Mrs. Claypool, Mrs. Emily Upjohn, Mrs. Dukesbury, and Martha Phelps. The juxtapositions of these names explain all one needs to know about the famous Groucho-Dumont relationship. Their exchanges are legendary, sequences of put-downs and deflations seemingly without end. In DUCK SOUP, Firefly and Teasdale speak:

GROUCHO: What about your husband?

DUMONT: He's dead.

GROUCHO: He's just using that as an excuse.

DUMONT: I was with him to the end.

GROUCHO: No wonder he passed away.

DUMONT: I held him in my arms and kissed him.

GROUCHO: So—it was murder?

DUCK SOUP is filled with such delicious garbage, so stuffed with it, in fact, that the viewer barely has time to catch his breath. A random sampling should give a notion of the texture of the picture, and perhaps will convince the reader who has not seen it to rush out next time it comes around and laugh his head off.

The antics of Harpo and Chico: They are double agents in DUCK SOUP, spies of Ambassador Trentino of Sylvania, and cronies of President Firefly, as well. In their great scene with Trentino, Chico freaks him out with a spiderweb of verbal non sequiturs, while Harpo takes over the physical side, cutting off his tie, his coattails, and when asked to produce Firefly's "record," pulls out a phonograph record, throws it at the ceiling, fires at it with a pistol, and reduces it to crumbs. Harpo also uses a welder's torch as a cigar lighter, glues a newspaper to Trentino's derriere, and indulges in so many other acts of controlled violence that when the two depart Trentino's office they leave behind a man who has been wrecked.

In another scene, outside Firefly's presidential palace, which has nothing to do with anything in the picture but is more in the nature of an entr'acte skit in a vaudeville show, Harpo plays out his smiling hostility with a lemonade vender acted by slow-burning Edgar Kennedy. Again the physical and psychological destruction is total.

In a long sequence of interlocking slapstick scenes in Mrs. Teasdale's mansion, the three brothers have an opportunity to play together. One piece of mischief tops another until the three meet in what has become one of their two most famous scenes: the mirror sequence. (The other one is the jammed-stateroom sequence in A NIGHT AT THE OPERA.) In the mirror sequence, Groucho has just escaped from being locked in the bathroom, an inevitable consequence of the brothers' scatological tendencies. Chico and Harpo have taken turns impersonating him with the bewildered Mrs. Teasdale, and when Groucho confronts Harpo, dressed as himself, Harpo must evade detection by pretending to be Groucho's mirror-image. This routine is an old vaudeville stunt, done many times before and since DUCK SOUP, but for some reason, in this particular context, it is hilarious beyond belief, culminating when the two do a half circle and thus pierce through the "mirror," and breaking apart when Chico arrives, also dressed as Groucho. Suddenly there are three Grouchos staring at one another on the screen.

This kind of nonsense reaches depths of excess when Fredonia and Sylvania go to war. Harpo does a parody of a Paul Revere ride to awaken the threatened citizenry, Groucho sends orders to his troops "collect," and Chico deserts Trentino's headquarters after the following exchange:

TRENTINO: "There's a machine-gun nest on Hill 22. I want it cleaned out."

CHICO: "Good, I'll tell the janitor."

To put a film critic's problem vis-à-vis the Marx Brothers into perspective, consider the following possibility: Forced to attend a double feature consisting of Bergman's HOUR OF THE WOLF and the Marx Brothers' A NIGHT AT THE OPERA, and being deeply moved in the first instance by the anguish suffered by the creative mind, and in the second by a sore stomach caused by excessive belly-laughing, the critic can only reconcile his schizophrenia by concluding that the cinema is both a fine art and a debased, vulgarian entertainment form. No amount of pantheon-erecting, or theory, or inventing of *politiques* will ever explain this anomaly away. If there is anything beside pure pleasure to be derived from the films of the Marx Brothers, it is this essential lesson.

## Stanley Kubrick's **Dr. Strangelove**, or How I Learned to Stop Worrying and Love the Bomb 1963

In the late 1950s, we were confronted with books by technocrats instructing us to "think about the unthinkable."

In DR. STRANGELOVE, Stanley Kubrick does not ask us to "think about the unthinkable." He asks that we laugh about it. America's military and political leaders, hot-lines and fail-safe points, Strategic Air Command (whose motto, incredibly, is "Peace Is Our Profession"), computer technology, obsessions with Communist plots, former Nazi scientists, and the entire military-industrial complex are used by Kubrick as objects for merciless mockery. These things are funny all right, but we don't laugh too long. At the end of DR. STRANGELOVE, as we watch a lyrical sequence of mushroom clouds and listen to Vera Lynn sing "We'll Meet Again," we chuckle a little and then hold our guts.

DR. STRANGELOVE, then, employs the comic values of the 1960s. It mocks the most serious things, turns a death rattle into gales of laughter, makes us titter and then makes us bleed. It is what some intellectuals would have us find in DUCK SOUP, a surrealist comedy, an outrageous tract against war, power, and pretension. But the difference between these pictures could not be more consequential. Rather than being anarchic, open-ended and absurd, DR. STRANGELOVE is put together like a fine watch, charged with suspense, and, despite the claims of the U. S. Air Force, believable. In addition, because it was created intellectually, as opposed to being improvised from a series of slapstick sketches, it is, unlike DUCK SOUP, subject to analysis.

The action takes place at three locations: Burpelson Air Base, ruled by its insane commander, General Jack D. Ripper, a man obsessed with the idea that fluoridation is a plot hatched by Communists to taint the purity of "our precious bodily fluids"; the War Room at the Pentagon where President Merkin J. Muffley and Chairman of the Joint Chiefs, General "Buck" Turgidson, enact a duel of ideologies in exchanges that employ the equally fatuous language of Cold War liberals and conservatives; and the cockpit of a B-52 bomber, commanded by Major T. J. "King" Kong, flying toward military targets in the Soviet Union. These three locations, which are physically realistic, become the stages for outrageous if internally logical events.

The suspense of the picture is dependent upon the way Kubrick (and his editor, Anthony Harvey) cut back and forth between the locations. We become involved in a race against time: Will Group Captain Mandrake obtain the recall code from General Ripper? Will the President reach Major Kong in time? Will the B-52 be recalled, or will it drop the bomb and set off the "doomsday device"? Whenever a scene at Burpelson or the War Room comes to an end, Kubrick cuts to the B-52, flying ever closer to its target over snowy Arctic terrain. Computers click, the pace quickens, the cuts are faster, and suspense plays against comedy until, despite our better judgment, we find ourselves at the edge of our seat. The comic thrust of DR. STRANGELOVE is not open-ended. It fights against a clock.

Into this tight drama about the destiny of man, Kubrick installs a half-dozen fine comic performances. Peter Sellers, the most famous comic actor of the day, plays three parts. As Group Captain Lionel Mandrake he is the epitome of the British officer, calm in the face of disaster, a satirical composite of all the Group Captains we've seen in an endless succession of movies about the Battle of Britain. As President Muffley he is the platitudinous liberal ("Gentlemen, you can't fight in here; this is the War Room!"), and when he gets on the hot-line with the Soviet Premier he talks like a resident in pediatrics trying to reason with a sick child. As Dr. Strangelove, he is a crippled ex-Nazi whose black-gloved wooden arm constantly threatens to give President Muffley a Nazi salute, and even tries to strangle Strangelove himself. When the "doomsday device" is triggered, Strangelove's withered legs are miraculously cured. "Mein Führer," he says to Muffley, "I can walk!"—surely one of the great



George C. Scott as General "Buck" Turgidson and Peter Sellers as President Merkin J. Muffley in DR. STRANGELOVE, OR HOW I LEARNED TO STOP WORRYING AND LOVE THE BOMB. Although Sellers was the famous comedian and played three parts, Scott gave the comic performance of the year.

Director Kubrick worked with a brilliant cast (l. to r.): Peter Sellers as Dr. Strangelove ("Mein Führer, I can walk!"); Scott as General Turgidson ("You got to watch them Ruskies"); Sterling Hayden as General Jack D. Ripper ("We must protect our precious bodily fluids. . . ."); Sellers as Group Captain Mandrake; Keenan Wynn as Colonel "Bat" Guano ("If you want to know what I think, I think you're some kind of deviated prevert"). Below: The War Room. (Muffley: "You can't fight in here. This is the War Room!") Opposite: Slim Pickens as Major Kong in cockpit of unrecallable B-52 bomber which will set off "doomsday device."

moments in screen comedy.

As General "Buck" Turgidson, George C. Scott—not known up to that time as a comedian—gives the comic performance of the decade, screwing up his face, broadly satirizing the emotions of cunning and rowdiness, at times assuming ape-like stances, often ending his speeches with his gestures frozen.

Turgidson, however, is the lightweight "heavy" of the film. General Ripper (played by Sterling Hayden) is the brooding maniac. Hayden is very good, and would be even funnier if it weren't for the fact that shortly before the release of the film a U. S. Army general was retired from active duty for spouting similar paranoic sentiments. Keenan Wynn, as Colonel "Bat" Guano, gives a marvelous performance as the man who won't shoot the lock off a Coke machine to retrieve a dime to make a phone call that might save the human race, and Slim Pickens, as Major "King" Kong stunningly satirizes a plane commander, particularly in his pep talk to his crew.

The film is rich in sexual humor, making a constant equation between sexuality and war. Under the opening titles we see one jet plane refueling another in an aerial ballet devised to resemble copulation. General Turgidson is reluctant to go to the War Room, despite the possibility of nuclear war, because he wants to conclude a sex session with his secretary. "Bat" Guano speaks obsessively of "deviated preverts." General Ripper tells Mandrake that he first suspected the fluoridation plot when he found himself impotent during sexual intercourse. Major "King" Kong rides the phallic-shaped bomb orgasmically whooping his Stetson. And Dr. Strangelove's plan to save a sampling of the human race by installing high military and political leaders at the bottom of mine shafts with attractive women at a ratio of one to ten puts gleams of sexual avarice into the eyes of everyone.

Kubrick has said that he started out with the intention of making a serious film about the problems of accidental nuclear war, but that the longer he allowed his imagination to dwell on this theme the more apparent it became that "the only way to tell the story was as a black comedy, or, better, a nightmare comedy, where the things that make you laugh are really the heart of the paradoxical postures that make a nuclear war possible."

His film is not only daring in its subject matter, but is stylistically ingenious, too. The scenes inside the B-52, for example, are staged as they might have occurred, with source lighting and an overpowering sense of realism. The attack against Burpelson Air Base is shot in a *cinéma-vérité* style with hand-held cameras, mostly operated by Stanley Kubrick himself. The effect is like a newsreel, perhaps the first staged battle scene to look totally convincing.

This stylistic realism heightens the impact of DR. STRANGELOVE, making us laugh and think at the same time. Like the picture's suspense, it works against the comedy, making us choke on our laughter, and leaving a bitter taste—the inevitable effect of "black humor."



Stanley Kubrick with machine gun and camera. He himself shot much of the attack on Burpelson Air Force Base (r.) with hand-held camera in *cinéma-vérité* style. Although wildly comic, DR. STRANGELOVE is a disciplined film, brilliantly edited to heighten suspense.

# Tony Richardson's **Tom Jones** 1963

TOM JONES appeared the same year as DR. STRANGELOVE. Both pictures survive as great comic entertainments, and yet are totally different in terms of comic thrust. STRANGELOVE is intellectual; TOM JONES is silly. STRANGELOVE is futuristic; TOM JONES is historical. STRANGELOVE is controlled; TOM JONES is wild. The sexual humor of STRANGELOVE is witty; the sexual humor of TOM JONES is bawdy. STRANGELOVE is cold; TOM JONES is warm. The differences between them are the differences between irony and slapstick, the drawing room and the burlesque hall, the cool grin and the belly laugh, a comedy that matters and a comedy of manners. At one point, Kubrick decided to end his final war-room sequence with a custard-pie fight. He actually shot the scene and then dropped it from his final version because he realized it was out of place. In TOM JONES a custard-pie fight would have been consistent with the style, whether relevant or not.

TOM JONES was a popular success and as a result has been attacked by highbrow critics. The principal fault they find is that the picture is academic. Though appearing to be a helter-skelter comedy, it is academically contrived. The charge of academicism is valid, but irrelevant to the picture's success as a comedy. Certainly, TOM JONES self-consciously employs the full gamut of New Wave devices: speeded-up action, frozen frames, superimposed titles, an ironic narrator, spiral wipes, iris dissolves, etc. (which were not, of course, invented by New Wave directors, but were resuscitated by them from the Mack Sennett comedies). And, of course, these devices are not employed with abandon, but with the calculation of filmmakers trying hard to produce an entertainment.

Perhaps the most academic thing about the picture is the warm, rich, precise cinematography of Walter Lassally, which, combined with very careful costuming and a certain amount of Neo-Realist historicism, gives the picture its famous "Hogarthian" look.

But it seems a little silly to find fault with TOM JONES because it does not look shabby, or because it lacks the spontaneity of silent two-reelers, or to question, for example, the use of a helicopter shot in the stag-hunt sequence because such a shot does not simulate an eighteenth-century point of view. Whatever faults the picture may have, it is redeemed by the fact that it makes no attempt to take itself seriously, or even to remain very faithful to Henry Fielding. TOM JONES is a film that mocks itself, its own devices, its own origins. It even allows its characters to turn to the lens and address the audience, thus breaking down the barrier between audience and screen, and disrupting suspension of disbelief.

The most marvelous of these to-the-camera moments occurs when Mrs. Waters receives the news (which turns out later to be false) that the Tom Jones with whom she has made delightful love is really her son. She shrugs at us as if to say: "Oedipus, schmoedipus!"

There are great sequences in TOM JONES (the nocturnal machinations at Upton Inn, the stag hunt at Squire Western's estate, etc.), but the dining sequence between Tom and Mrs. Waters is the high point of the film, and must be counted among the all-time great comic scenes in movie history. Their devouring of food is so erotic that the scene outclasses, on a purely sexual level, any of the frank, nude lovemaking scenes which began to appear on the screen in the 1970s. Lobsters, chickens, oysters, and fruits are sucked, gobbled, licked, and bitten with riotous obscenity.

In TOM JONES, Tony Richardson has no cast of comic geniuses like Chaplin, Keaton, or Groucho Marx, or even Peter Sellers and George C. Scott. His actors—Albert Finney, Hugh Griffith, Susannah York, and Edith Evans—are all fine straight performers, but are not breathtakingly poised (like Keaton) or hopelessly sloppy (like Groucho). The pleasure of TOM JONES does not derive from watching the people so much as from becoming entranced by the absurd and complex situations and the parodies of eighteenth-century manners. By cutting the picture fast, and employing every trick he knows, Richardson keeps TOM JONES going at a feverish pitch, much like a juggler performing an absurdly complicated balancing act. If his social satire has sometimes too bitter a taste (as in the bloody spur-bitten flanks of the horses in the stag hunt, or the poor farmer incredulously holding up his trampled goose), Richardson manages to subdue his social conscience long enough to produce an extraordinarily entertaining comedy, funny enough to blot out thoughts of its trivial flaws.

It is interesting that Richardson manages to do this, because his best-known pictures—LOOK BACK IN ANGER, A TASTE OF HONEY, THE LONELINESS OF THE LONG-DISTANCE RUNNER—all were made in the Angry Young Man mood that cries out its commitment and importance. Richardson may be one of those filmmakers who are corrupted by Art. When he tries to make statements he fails to be moving; when he merely tries to entertain he can make people laugh.

Albert Finney as Tom Jones in Tony Richardson's period comedy. Below: Tom and Mrs. Waters (Joyce Redman) in hilarious eating sequence in which they swallow oysters, bite meat, suck at lobster, and gobble fruit in a magnificent parody of the sexual delights to come.

# Credits

## City Lights

U.S.A.; 1931; 87 minutes;
originally released by United Artists.

**Directed by** Charles Chaplin.
**Produced by** Charles Chaplin.
**Written by** Charles Chaplin.
**Photographed by** Rollie Totheroh, Gordon Pollack, and Mark Marklatt.
**Art direction by** Charles D. Hall.
**Music by** Charles Chaplin.
**Cast:** Charles Chaplin; Virginia Cherrill; Florence Lee; Harry Myers; Allan Garcia; Hank Mann; Albert Austin; Henry Bergman; John Rand; Jean Harlow.

## The General

U.S.A.; 1926; 80 minutes;
originally released by United Artists.

**Directed by** Buster Keaton and Clyde Bruckman.
**Produced by** Joseph M. Schenck.
**Screenplay by** Al Boasberg and Charles Smith.
**Photographed by** J. Devereux Jennings and Bert Haines.
**Cast:** Buster Keaton; Marion Mack; Glen Cavender; Jim Farley; Frederick Vroom; Charles Smith; Frank Barnes; Joe Keaton; Mike Denlin; Tom Nawm.

## Duck Soup

U.S.A.; 1933; 70 minutes;
released by Paramount.

**Directed by** Leo McCarey.
**Screenplay by** Bert Kalmar and Harry Ruby, with additional dialogue by Arthur Sheekman and Nat Perrin.
**Photographed by** Henry Sharp.
**Art direction by** Hans Dreier and Wilard Ihnen.
**Edited by** LeRoy Stone.
**Music and Lyrics by** Bert Kalmar and Harry Ruby.
**Cast:** Groucho Marx; Harpo Marx; Chico Marx; Zeppo Marx; Margaret Dumont; Louis Calhern; Raquel Torres; Edgar Kennedy; Edmund Breese; Leonid Kinsky.

## Dr. Strangelove, or How I Learned To Stop Worrying and Love the Bomb

Great Britain; 1963; 94 minutes;
released by Columbia Pictures.

**Directed by** Stanley Kubrick.
**Produced by** Stanley Kubrick.
**Screenplay by** Stanley Kubrick, Terry Southern, and Peter George, from the novel "Red Alert" by Peter George.
**Photographed by** Gilbert Taylor.
**Art direction by** Ken Adam.
**Edited by** Anthony Harvey.
**Music by** Laurie Johnson.
**Cast:** Peter Sellers; George C. Scott; Sterling Hayden; Keenan Wynn; Slim Pickens; Peter Bull; Tracy Reed; James Earl Jones.

## Tom Jones

Great Britain; 1963; 125 minutes;
released by United Artists.

**Directed by** Tony Richardson.
**Produced by** Tony Richardson.
**Screenplay by** John Osborne, based on the novel by Henry Fielding.
**Photographed by** Walter Lassally.
**Art direction by** Ralph Brinton.
**Edited by** Antony Gibbs.
**Music by** John Addison.
**Cast:** Albert Finney; Hugh Griffith; Susannah York; Edith Evans; Joyce Redman; Joan Greenwood; David Tomlinson; Jack MacGowran; Diane Cilento; Wilfrid Lawson; Peter Bull; David Warner; Julian Glover; Rosalind Knight; Lynn Redgrave; George Devine; George A. Cooper.

# Musicals

4

People seem either to adore musicals or to detest them, and logic will not sway their opinions on this not-too-crucial issue. People either go to the movies to be entertained and to escape reality, or else they go to be engaged by themes and to be moved by art. To the first group (a vast majority), musicals are the raison d'être of the cinema, and to the second they are evidence of its debasement. Of course, both groups are wrong.

It is important to give musicals their due and to honor them in proportion to their worth. Some bridge the gap by claiming that Europeans are best at making art films, and that Americans are preeminent in escapist genres. Hollywood was a dream factory, their argument goes, and its greatest products were escapist fantasies: thrillers, westerns, musicals.

Though this position is much too doctrinaire, and has a patronizing air about it, one must risk the wrath of the musical cultists and say that it comes fairly close to the truth. Musicals are the most escapist of genres, and Americans seem to be most excellent at making them. This may be accounted for by the size of the country and its traditions, the quality and diversity of American song-writing and of its singing and dancing entertainers, plus the reservoir of material and people provided by the musical stage. And though the Hollywood studio system had many defects, most of them deriving from the fact that movie-making was considered above all else a business, no one can deny Hollywood's technical expertise, the craftsmanship and inventiveness of its artisans, and the respective sizes of its budgets and sound stages. Combine American talents, American expertise, American budgets, and a desire to manufacture an escapist product, and you come up with a peculiarly American genre, perhaps not an art form, but an entertainment form that must be admired. It generated, perhaps more by accident than design, a certain number of delightful works a cultist would call "masterpieces," but which a civilized person must recognize as belonging with such charming and minor things as Fabergé Easter eggs. At their very best, this is what musicals are. At their worst (and there are plenty of examples), they can be impossibly vulgar, akin to such awful things as plastic suction-cupped Madonnas, or as totally lifeless as lead balloons.

It has been pointed out that the first sound film, THE JAZZ SINGER, was, essentially, a musical. Also that Busby Berkeley was the first original talent to grace the genre with a fantastic vision, his elaborate and grandiose choreographies. From that time to the present, the history of the musical has been a history of famous names, stars, composers, and even some directors: Fred Astaire and Ginger Rogers, Jeanette MacDonald and Nelson Eddy, Shirley Temple, Judy Garland, Barbra Streisand, Julie Andrews, Doris Day, Cyd Charisse, Mickey Rooney, Bing Crosby, Frank Sinatra, Gene Kelly, Cole Porter, Harold Arlen, Irving Berlin, Richard Rodgers, Jerome Kern, George Gershwin, Ernst Lubitsch, Rouben Mamoulian, Vincente Minnelli, Stanley Donen, George Cukor, and many more. These people are the American musical, as are certain art directors, costume and set designers, choreographers, cameramen, and sound technicians. All of this says something important about musicals. As much as one may try, it is difficult to prove that great musicals can be attributed to great filmmakers, or that musicals are even a filmmaker's medium. Sometimes it is the star (a Fred Astaire, a Judy Garland) that makes a musical work. Other times it is the composer (a Jerome Kern, a Cole Porter), or a producer (an Arthur Freed), or a director (a Vincente Minnelli). But the number of superior film-

Preceding pages & above: Fred Astaire and Ginger Rogers in TOP HAT. In their marvelous duets, the most magical dancing ever seen on the screen, they enacted the conflicts between men and women, romance and sex.

makers who have failed with good musical material (Carol Reed with OLIVER!, Joshua Logan with CAMELOT, William Wyler with FUNNY GIRL, George Cukor with MY FAIR LADY, etc.) suggests that a musical is a precarious balance of many ingredients, and that filmmaking ability is not always the most important.

What, then, are the qualities that make a great musical, keeping in mind, of course, that the best of musicals are minor works? It is easier to say what these qualities are not. It is not necessary, for example, as some have said, that a great musical be an organic whole with the songs growing naturally out of the story (the Astaire-Rogers musicals do not meet this test and they are great; Fred Zinnemann's OKLAHOMA does and it is not). A great musical doesn't have to be an original work as opposed to a Broadway adaptation (originals like THE WIZARD OF OZ and SINGIN' IN THE RAIN are great, but so are adaptations like CABARET and ON THE TOWN; the original AN AMERICAN IN PARIS is about as pretentious as a musical can be, and the adaptation of WEST SIDE STORY is a feeble reminder of its glory upon the stage). A great musical need not emphasize dancing at the expense of singing, or, for that matter, the other way around. (Is Streisand less marvelous than Ginger Rogers? Is Fred Astaire better than the Beatles?) These are the kinds of assertions that devotees use to justify their favorites.

No, the criteria for a great musical are among the most elusive of things, for though it is obvious that a musical must work, that its diverse elements must come together in some way, this "way" remains mysterious and seems to depend upon something called "chemistry," which is a word used to describe a phenomenon that people recognize but can't rationally explain. Still and all, a great musical gives pleasure because of its lightness and artistry and the ebullience of its fantasy, because, like the Fabergé egg, or a trompe l'oeil ceiling, it is "right." And that, admittedly, is as dubious and subjective a standard as one can employ.

## Astaire and Rogers in **Top Hat** 1935

There can be no better example of pictures being "right," of things "working," and of "chemistry" in musicals than the films of Fred Astaire and Ginger Rogers. Their partnership is legendary, and the ten films they made together are remembered not for their stories (which were mostly inane), nor for the brilliance of their filmmaking (they were workmanlike, but not extraordinary), nor even for their music (some of which was extremely fine as popular music goes), but for the way Fred Astaire and Ginger Rogers moved together. He was sophisticated, elegant, graceful, and supple. She was fresh, charming, speedy, and engagingly maddening. Together they were sublime.

She made him vulnerable and he gave her class; she made him sexy and he made her look like a lady—these are the usual explanations for their famous chemistry. Like Spencer Tracy and Katharine Hepburn, Humphrey Bogart and Lauren Bacall, Fred Astaire and Ginger Rogers together combusted into something greater than

the sum of their separate selves, and that is saying something, since Rogers alone could be magnificent and Astaire was and is the greatest dancing star in motion pictures. However, it is interesting that unlike Tracy-Hepburn and Bogart-Bacall, Astaire-Rogers had little use for each other off the screen, which may say something about the special nature of musicals: that at their best they are worlds of fantasy where things can happen that are impossible in real life. Astaire and Rogers were impossible—impossibly well-matched, impossibly enchanting, an exemplary pair that could only exist in the dream-world of luminescent screens in darkened halls.

They came together by accident as second leads in FLYING DOWN TO RIO in 1933, and they stole the show from Gene Raymond and Dolores del Rio with their "Carioca," the first of a series of spectacular and innovative dances they premiered usually at the end of their pictures. ("The Continental" in THE GAY DIVORCEE, 1934; "The Piccolino" in TOP HAT, 1935; the wild "Yam" in CAREFREE, 1938; etc.) For five years they flourished until in the last number of CAREFREE, "I Used to Be Color-Blind," they kissed for the first time. The dance and the kiss were shot in slow motion, a tantalizing reply to the demands of their fans that the time had come for Fred to kiss Ginger. After CAREFREE, THE STORY OF VERNON AND IRENE CASTLE in 1939 was something of a letdown, and a decade later, when they played in THE BARKLEYS OF BROADWAY, their duets were but a pale reprise of magic that was lost and could not be recaptured.

The kiss in CAREFREE was, quite possibly, the logical end to their collaboration. When Astaire and Rogers danced together they achieved a delicate tension between reality and abandonment, infatuation and realization. Astaire was always in pursuit of Rogers and she always pretended she wasn't interested. In their duets things usually proceeded to the point where it seemed as though Astaire could sweep her away, that after dealing with her many rebuffs he could carry her to the point of capitulation. And then, on the verge of oneness, there would occur one of their famous pauses, and Rogers would charmingly pull back. It is in these heightened moments of pause, when fantasy (his) and earthiness (hers) lie in the balance, that one may observe the essence of their chemistry. By his seductiveness and her feigned indifference and haughty withdrawals they enact wooing patterns, dance out the basic duel between men and women, and symbolize the conflict between romance and sex. Watching them swirl together, one feels them approaching a oneness of deep intensity. It is clear that they belong together, that they perfectly fit. But the source of their power to enchant is the tension between them, and once it was released in the kiss at the end of CAREFREE that power was gone. It had to happen. Their magic was too delicate a thing to last forever. It is remarkable that it lasted through eight films and five years.

To select the best of these films is a difficult task. One searches for the picture with the greatest number of great duets. TOP HAT is a likely choice, for here, as in FOLLOW THE FLEET and CAREFREE, one finds an additional empathy between Astaire and Irving Berlin to reinforce that of Astaire and Rogers. One also finds Astaire's trademark solo, his famous "Top Hat" number, that sums up better than anything else he ever did the elegance and élan of his screen character.

Astaire and Rogers were genuine stars, so it was appropriate that their films were viewed by producers as "star vehicles." It didn't much matter what the story was, as long as it provided opportunities for the pair to dance. The story of TOP HAT is as forgettable and irrelevant as the story of any Astaire-Rogers film: A dancer falls for a haughty model and chases her up and down Europe, tap-dancing most of the way. The journeyman direction of Mark Sandrich (who directed five of their ten pictures) is appropriate for this sort of material. No mastermind, no Busby Berkeley, he does not manipulate people like pawns. No heavyweight director, no Vincente Minnelli, he does not impose a fantasy concept or try to impart a strong directorial style. Rather, Sandrich does the only logical thing that a director can do with Astaire-Rogers—he lets them dance.

TOP HAT may be the best of the Astaire-Rogers films, because in addition to the songs of Irving Berlin and the excellence of the dances, it is the simplest and most pure. And it was made early enough in the collaboration that Astaire's and Roger's elation at the miracle of their chemistry shines through and adds to its prevailing charm.



"Isn't It A Lovely Day" number in London bandbox (above) and ebullient "Top Hat" solo (opposite) were among picture's many delights.
"Chemistry" between Astaire and Rogers has never been surpassed by another screen couple. Any of six films could be judged their best.

The
by L.Frank Ba

# The Wizard of Oz 1939

Nineteen thirty-nine was a key year in the history of motion pictures. In France, Jean Renoir was depicting the social confusion of Europe in his biting and satirical RULES OF THE GAME. At Columbia Studios, Howard Hawks was staking out the themes and motifs of the adventure film with ONLY ANGELS HAVE WINGS. In Monument Valley, John Ford was reinventing the western with STAGECOACH. And at MGM, Victor Fleming was directing a sheerly pleasureful bit of fluff called THE WIZARD OF OZ. One can only speculate on whether there is significance in any of this, and particularly in the fact that while Europe was threatened by war and the depression was not yet over in America, Hollywood was turning out escapist fantasies.

THE WIZARD OF OZ was the first of a series of musicals produced for MGM by Arthur Freed which would give that studio dominance in the genre for many years. Freed, who encouraged and gave free rein to such people as Vincente Minnelli, Gene Kelly, and Stanley Donen, and who produced such remarkably fine musicals as CABIN IN THE SKY, MEET ME IN ST. LOUIS, ON THE TOWN, SINGIN' IN THE RAIN, IT'S ALWAYS FAIR WEATHER, and a good thirty more of varying quality but consistent commerciality, harbored a definite conception of what a musical should be.

It should be an organic whole, an entertainment in which story, songs, and dances are integrated and unified by a strong dramatic line. Songs, according to Freed's concept, must flow out of the dramatic material and advance the story, rather than serve merely as intermezzos between action that stops when music begins and resumes when music is finished. An obvious corollary to his theory was that a song, no matter how tuneful or pleasure-giving, that did not advance the story should be scrapped, which is precisely what happened to "The Jitterbug" in THE WIZARD OF OZ, and which almost happened to the picture's most famous song "Over the Rainbow." In addition, Freed believed that the transition from dialogue to music should be as smooth as possible, triggered usually by the emotion of a character whose enlarged exuberance would make a burst into song natural and inevitable. Freed's influence lay not so much in the novelty of his ideas, but in the fact that he formulated them into a definite concept, and then applied that concept to all the musicals under his jurisdiction. The result of his success was a clamp upon the musical so binding that new approaches have emerged only in recent years.

THE WIZARD OF OZ was the first musical calculatedly fashioned according to this formula, and therefore it is important for historical reasons. But it is also special on several additional counts. It has a magnificent score: songs by Harold Arlen and lyrics by E. Y. Harburg. Arlen's elaborate and sophisticated music combusts "chemically" with the teasing *joie de vivre* of Harburg's rhymes, and the result is one of the few scores that appeals equally to children and adults. Also, the very idea of making a musical out of L. Frank Baum's classic was brilliantly inspired, akin to Disney's use of "Snow White" for his first feature-length cartoon. Baum's book contains the very fantasy elements that the musical film is best equipped to deliver: special architecture, magical effects, and the distortion of normal space-time. Finally, and especially notable about THE WIZARD OF OZ, is the performance of Judy Garland.

Garland: Her place in the history of the American musical is as important as that of Fred Astaire. THE WIZARD OF OZ, by no means her greatest work, is representative of the first phase of her remarkable career. She almost didn't get the part. Originally it was to go to Shirley Temple, who was to be borrowed from Twentieth Century-Fox in exchange for Jean Harlow and Clark Gable. When Harlow died the deal fell through, and MGM decided to risk everything on Garland. She was sixteen years old at the time, but was able to look eleven or twelve and to exude a wholesome, innocent, bouncy freshness that was charming because she achieved it without being cute. As Dorothy she was perfect, and one squirms now at the thought of Shirley Temple in the role. Garland's performance in THE WIZARD OF OZ endeared her to the public. People watched with fascination as her adolescent wholesomeness gave way to the all-heart sincerity and emotional directness of her performance in MEET ME IN ST. LOUIS in 1944, and then mutated again until, by the time of A STAR IS BORN in 1954, she had become urgent, electric, quivering, self-destructive, and altogether stunning for the way she made these qualities work for her in what may be the greatest piece of dramatic acting in the history of the musical genre. Garland was unique in movies. No other singer, with the possible exception of Edith Piaf, has ever matched her musical passion.

THE WIZARD OF OZ begins in black and white in a bitterly real America of stern faces and endless plains.



From left, Ray Bolger (Scarecrow), Jack Haley (Tin Woodman), Frank Morgan (The Wizard), Judy Garland (Dorothy), and Bert Lahr (Cowardly Lion) posed for studio publicity shot before a giant copy of L. Frank Baum's THE WIZARD OF OZ. Bit player Margaret Hamilton won enduring fame as Wicked Witch.

Dorothy, the innocent dreamer, is swirled from this place to a Technicolor dreamland "somewhere over the rainbow." Here she eludes peril, overcomes enemies, and finds loving friends. And when she returns her innocence is intact. THE WIZARD OF OZ is one of those films, like Disney's SNOW WHITE and Douglas Fairbanks' ROBIN HOOD, on which people are brought up and which they never forget. Children and parents who go to see THE WIZARD OF OZ year after year never seem to tire of it. How to account for this timeless appeal? There is no way except to repeat that like all great escapist fantasies it is, somehow, "right."

## Kelly and Donen's **Singin' in the Rain** 1952

SINGIN' IN THE RAIN is considered by those who are connoisseurs of the genre to be the summit of the Hollywood musical. Perhaps they are right, for SINGIN' IN THE RAIN is light, frothy, unpretentious, and funny, contains good songs, good dances, good performances, and is unified by an inspired idea.

It was produced for MGM by the ubiquitous Arthur Freed and meets his conception of the film musical more completely than any of his other calculated efforts. Freed also wrote the lyrics to the songs, and they are fine, especially the title number "Singin' In the Rain," which Stanley Kubrick reprised with such fascinating perversity in A CLOCKWORK ORANGE. But the magic and strength of SINGIN' IN THE RAIN lie in its story, written by Betty Comden and Adolph Green, whose chemistry was also responsible for ON THE TOWN, IT'S ALWAYS FAIR WEATHER, and BELLS ARE RINGING. SINGIN' IN THE RAIN is a satire on show business and Hollywood, an exposé of the ruthless ambition of idolized stars, and it is built around the comic possibilities implicit in the problems faced by actors and studios making the transition from silent films to talkies in the late 1920s. This situation, in which an industry that deals in fantasy and illusion must adapt itself to a new technology, was actually tragic for several film stars who, because of lack of diction and disparity between image and voice, were undone by the demands of the talking film. Whoever decided to use it as the unifying theme of a musical comedy (Freed, Comden and Green, or whoever) must receive credit for enormous inspiration. Hollywood is often at its best when feeding upon itself.

SINGIN' IN THE RAIN is the tale of a sex goddess, played by one of the great impersonators of the "dumb



Sequences of Dorothy's Kansas home are in black and white, Oz is in color. Movie has timeless quality of a fairy tale, a magnificent score by Harold Arlen and E. Y. Harburg, and a lovable performance by Judy Garland. Clara Blandick was Auntie Em, Charley Grapewin was Uncle Henry.

blonde," Jean Hagen, who cannot sing, cannot talk, cannot enunciate a single word without creating mounting hysteria in an audience. The Hollywood where she and her co-star, Gene Kelly, work, is depicted as a lovably phony place. Hagen, of course, is thoroughly despicable, and is in love with Kelly who cannot stand her and is himself in love with the lovely, modest, and talented Debbie Reynolds. Kelly is unscrupulous and superficial, though there are plenty of indications that he knows he is involved in a put-on business. Anyway, Hagen achieves stardom on Debbie Reynolds' voice, dubbed in for her execrable singing, grows vicious and arrogant, and is mercilessly debunked by the machinations of Kelly and Donald O'Connor. Debbie, in the end, is reconciled with Gene, who, it turns out, is not such a bad guy after all.

SINGIN' IN THE RAIN is rich in references to the old days of Hollywood, and the satire on moguls, stars, and show business is sharp and sometimes devastating. It is also rich in musical film styles. Each of its three great production numbers is presented differently, and their juxtaposition gives the picture its notable qualities of variety and lightness. "Singin' In the Rain" is a simple and emotionally direct Garlandesque solo by Gene Kelly. "You Were Meant for Me," in which Kelly and Reynolds sing and dance their love duet on an empty sound stage is more in the Astaire-Rogers tradition. And the big production number, "Broadway Ballet," is a surrealistic Busby Berkeley-type extravaganza filled with magic, unexpected transitions, a huge cast, and spectacular uses of light, color, costumes, and sets, plus marvelous balletic dancing by Kelly and Cyd Charisse. In addition, there is Donald O'Connor's acrobatic and amusing "Make 'Em Laugh," and a couple of other numbers which enrich the mixture, heighten the ebullience, and make the picture an anthology of musical styles and techniques.

The Comden-Green collaboration is reinforced in SINGIN' IN THE RAIN by the chemistry between Gene Kelly and Stanley Donen, who co-directed the film. Kelly as a performer is nearly as important in the history of the musical as Astaire-Rogers and Judy Garland, although he never achieved their popularity. People liked Kelly for his brashness and his very American brand of charm, his extraordinarily virile footwork, and their feeling that he was on the verge of winking at them from the screen. But for some reason he was difficult to love. Perhaps his famous grin seemed painted on. But if he was important as a performer, he became legendary as a choreographer and director. With Stanley Donen, in addition to SINGIN' IN THE RAIN, he made ON THE TOWN and IT'S ALWAYS FAIR WEATHER, all of which were produced by Arthur Freed and based on screenplays by Comden and Green. Taken together, they constitute an *oeuvre* of such lightness and dazzle that they must be considered the ultimate works of a certain kind of film, the apotheosis of the organic, unified, smooth-flowing musical developed and nurtured at MGM.

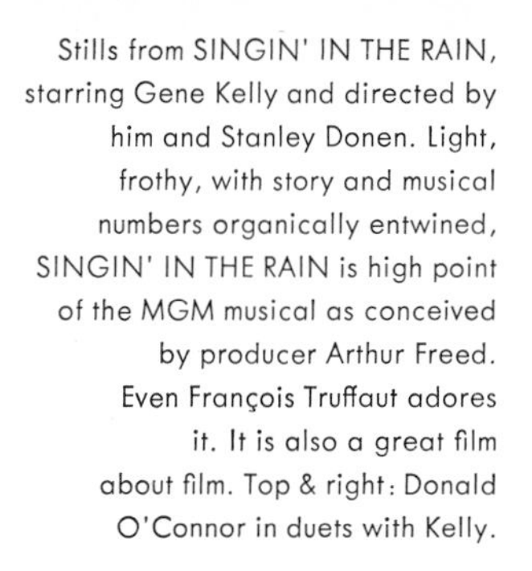

Stills from SINGIN' IN THE RAIN, starring Gene Kelly and directed by him and Stanley Donen. Light, frothy, with story and musical numbers organically entwined, SINGIN' IN THE RAIN is high point of the MGM musical as conceived by producer Arthur Freed. Even François Truffaut adores it. It is also a great film about film. Top & right: Donald O'Connor in duets with Kelly.

# Cabaret 1972

The musicals of the 1960s were characterized by bigness, expensiveness, and the degeneration of an outmoded principle. Some made fortunes, like Robert Wise's THE SOUND OF MUSIC, perhaps the most perfectly contrived piece of sticky, sentimental, tear-jerking kitsch ever manufactured by Hollywood. Others, like WEST SIDE STORY and MY FAIR LADY, typified Hollywood's knack for ruining great properties, in the first instance when an expressionist fantasy was staged in the streets of New York instead of on a sound stage (an example of the tyranny of the notion that a film will be good if it is made on location), and in the second by such rigid direction and lifeless staging that one can only think of it as an embalming. Still others, like STAR, SWEET CHARITY, and DR. DOOLITTLE, have so little to recommend them that they are significant only as casebook studies of failed "chemistry." No matter how elaborate the production numbers, how engaging the stars, how successful the Broadway productions (when they were adaptations), or how talented the choreographers imported from New York, something in the musicals of the 1960s was lacking and that something was life force.

Arthur Freed's conception of the integrated musical, by then imitated by producers at all the studios, was worn out. The time had arrived for a new formulation, and when it finally came it turned out to be in fact two separate concepts, sufficiently interesting to cause one to quit shaking one's head over the demise of the genre.

The first new approach came from the recognition that there were great filmic possibilities in the new music called rock. The second, and the one that concerns us here, involved a rejection of the Arthur Freed principle. Taking off from the premise that there is nothing wrong with an unintegrated musical, a musical in which songs and dances are separated from story, the thinking went that since the natural transition from dialogue to music had become a cliché, why not simply abandon it and start again from scratch? The breakthrough musical of this type was CABARET, and though it is still too early to know whether or not it is a freak, its quality and success may establish it in movie history as a pivotal work.

CABARET, in the first place, is tough, stinging, satirical, and acid. None of the sweetness of Rodgers and Hammerstein here; none of the wholesome goodness of THE SOUND OF MUSIC in which life is depicted with utter falsity as one big happy songfest. CABARET owes more to the Weill-Brecht spirit of THE THREEPENNY OPERA, an uncompromising, hard-nosed look at life consistent with the coming of age of America in the 1960s. CABARET is the first musical to exploit the notion, now generally recognized by the public and for too long ignored by the industry, that life is fascinating because it is ambiguous, and that the intensity of a character's experiences is more interesting than an imposed wholesome personality. This is not to say that CABARET is some kind of thinking man's musical, and that because it confronts the facts that (a) people use one another, (b) homosexuality exists, (c) Nazism had its seductions, (d) decadence can be fun, etc., it is any less escapist than THE WIZARD OF OZ. On the contrary, CABARET is an escapist fantasy of a new kind. If the wholesome fantasy of THE WIZARD OF OZ is the sort that audiences needed when the reference points of American culture were midwestern and small town, CABARET is the sort they need and crave now that urban and political turmoil are the hallmarks of the age.

CABARET uses music in an exciting new way. Characters do not burst into song to express their emotions. Rather, a sleazy night club called the Kit Kat becomes a place where satirical comment on the lives and problems of these characters is made in striking, entertaining, and often savage dances and songs. Unlike a street in Spanish Harlem or a meadow in the Austrian Alps, the Kit Kat Klub is a logical place for music, and yet the entwining of the music performed in the cabaret and the story of Sally Bowles and her friends is as unnatural as the drama-music mix in any musical. The difference is that the fantasy in CABARET is not disguised by the pseudonaturalism of the integrated musical. It is clearly artificial and no attempt is made to have it any other way.

Moreover, like all great musicals, CABARET is "right." Liza Minnelli (daughter of Judy Garland and Vincente Minnelli) is the catalyst. She enlivens the story by her gifts for dramatic acting, and becomes bigger than life when belting out songs on the Kit Kat Klub stage. She is the force that unifies the sly, cruel satire of Joel Grey (the cabaret's emcee and the personification of a decadence beyond good and evil), the superbly stylized art direction inspired by German expressionist painting, the handsome and intricate camerawork, and the choreography and dramatic direction of Bob Fosse. CABARET is not unforgettable, it is not profound, it is not great art, but it is great entertainment, a daring piece of diverting escapism that hopefully will revitalize a tired form.

# Richard Lester's **A Hard Day's Night** 1964

And then there came rock. . . .

For many years the split in pop music was between the tawdry trash beloved by teen-agers and the kind of classy pop known as "show music" (the songs of Porter, Berlin, Rodgers, etc.). But in the 1960s a reversal took place. Rock-'n-roll flourished with a brilliance that even exceeded the flourishing of the cinema in the same decade. People like Bob Dylan, the Beatles, The Rolling Stones, The Who, The Grateful Dead, Crosby, Stills, Nash and Young, and countless other artists and groups took over rock, refined it, and raised it from its more or less barbaric origins to the level of an art form.

Though many rock music cultists sincerely believe that this process sapped the greatest strength of rock—its primitive power—and that sophistication in this sort of music is more of a curse than a triumph, to the unbiased ear it is clear that the new rock music has transcended itself and has become the new "class" pop, and that conventional "show music" has gone into decline.

The cinema has not yet come firmly to grips with rock. Its potential as a new base for filmed musicals has been recognized, but the final form of these musicals has yet to be devised. Documentaries like WOODSTOCK, MONTEREY POP, DON'T LOOK BACK, and the very great GIMME SHELTER are, in a sense, a new kind of musical film, though not of the sort we are discussing here. Rock has been used, too, to embellish and heighten certain dramatic films. One thinks of the important contribution of Simon and Garfunkel to THE GRADUATE and the "score" of EASY RIDER made from preexisting rock songs written and recorded by a variety of vocalists and groups. One film, Richard Lester's A HARD DAY'S NIGHT, starring the Beatles, stakes out new ground. It synthesizes the new music with the new cinema in an exciting way, suggests a new format, and is, moreover, a great musical film.

Some would deny to A HARD DAY'S NIGHT the right to be called a musical. It was not made in Hollywood, after all, and contains no dream sequences, no dancing, no fantasy, and was not even shot in color. In fact, A HARD DAY'S NIGHT is a truer musical than the embalmings that have been passed off as musicals in recent years.

Like any Astaire-Rogers film, A HARD DAY'S NIGHT was contrived as a star vehicle. It was commissioned in frantic haste by United Artists as an exploitation film about the Beatles. Executives of UA were convinced that the group's popularity would crest in 1964 and were most anxious that the film be completed before the bubble burst. (How badly they misunderstood the temper of the times. There is no question that the Beatles' place in musical history is more secure than that, for example, of Julie Andrews, but then film-industry executives, whose business presumably is fantasy fulfillment, rarely have shown much understanding of what the public craves.)

A HARD DAY'S NIGHT, like any great musical, is totally informed by music. It is a musical about music, a pseudodocumentary about an immensely popular rock band whose members' lives center around music and who attempt both to escape from and build rapport with their many thousands of screaming fans. There are plenty of songs, some played voice-over, some rendered live from the concert stage; the final seventeen minutes, which were shot in a single day with six movie cameras and three TV cameras, is as much of a fantastic extravaganza as anything ever cooked up by Busby Berkeley.

Fantasy? The whole film is a fantasy, an entertaining vision of how the Beatles live and the absurd claustrophobic world they inhabit.

Comedy? The Beatles are natural-born comedians of the Mack Sennett school, and Lester has used many revitalized Mack Sennett devices to reinforce and heighten their comedic personalities.

Lightness? Exuberance? Froth? Escape? A HARD DAY'S NIGHT has all of these, and is surrealistic and satiric as well. The rising shot of the Beatles as they cavort around a field in a kind of mad ballet is a perfect example of lightness of touch in musical filmmaking. Their final concert is the picture's great escapist production number. Their relationships with each other, the "clean old man," their managers, and their public are enriched by put-down dialogue delivered with ingenuous charm. Only the most obtuse viewer believes that A HARD DAY'S NIGHT is a documentary. It is clearly contrived and a good deal of the froth and fun of the film lies in the way it calls attention to its many contrivances, and, in fact, flaunts them.

Magic? Chemistry? If seeing is believing, then the evidence is on the screen, both of the chemistry among the Beatles (which the bitterness of their breakup further confirms) and between them and their fans. A HARD DAY'S NIGHT is a filmmaker's film, a bold, inventive work by Richard Lester, whose flashy, jumpy style combusts with the exuberance of his stars into an explosion of joy at being young and alive.

From Kit Kat Klub sequences of CABARET. Liza Minnelli (l.) as Sally Bowles; Joel Grey is the bawdy emcee. CABARET represents a departure from "integrated musical" of Arthur Freed. Singing and dramatic elements are separated, and wholesomeness (as in THE SOUND OF MUSIC) is finally abandoned in favor of adult themes.

Scenes from A HARD DAY'S NIGHT, with Director Richard Lester (bald) posing with the Beatles during shooting (bottom l.). With decline of show music, it was inevitable that the filmed musical would turn to rock 'n roll. Lester's "documentary" approach was another breakthrough.

# Credits

## Top Hat

U.S.A.; 1935; 105 minutes;
released by RKO.

**Directed by** Mark Sandrich.
**Produced by** Pandro S. Berman.
**Screenplay by** Dwight Taylor and Allan Scott.
**Photographed by** David Abel and Vernon Walker.
**Art direction by** Van Nest Polglase.
**Choreography by** Hermes Pan and Fred Astaire.
**Songs by** Irving Berlin.
**Cast:** Fred Astaire; Ginger Rogers; Helen Broderick; Edward Everett Horton; Eric Blore; Erik Rhodes.

## Singin' in the Rain

U.S.A.; 1952; 103 minutes;
released by MGM.

**Directed by** Stanley Donen and Gene Kelly.
**Produced by** Arthur Freed.
**Screenplay by** Betty Comden and Adolph Green.
**Photographed by** Harold Rosson.
**Art direction by** Cedric Gibbons and Randall Duell.
**Choreography by** Stanley Donen and Gene Kelly.
**Songs by** Nacio Herb Brown and Arthur Freed.
**Cast:** Gene Kelly; Debbie Reynolds; Donald O'Connor; Cyd Charisse; Jean Hagen; Millard Mitchell; Douglas Fowley; Rita Moreno.

## The Wizard of Oz

U.S.A.; 1939; 101 minutes;
released by MGM.

**Directed by** Victor Fleming.
**Produced by** Mervyn Le Roy and Arthur Freed.
**Screenplay by** Florence Ryerson, Noel Langley and Edgar Alan Woolf, from Frank L. Baum's story.
**Photographed by** Harold Rosson.
**Art direction by** Cedric Gibbons and William Horning.
**Choreography by** Bobby Connolly.
**Songs by** Harold Arlen and E. Y. Harburg.
**Cast:** Judy Garland; Ray Bolger; Jack Haley; Bert Lahr; Billie Burke; The Singer Midgets; Frank Morgan; Margaret Hamilton.

## Cabaret

U.S.A.; 1972; 122 minutes;
released by Allied Artists.

**Directed by** Bob Fosse.
**Produced by** Cy Feuer.
**Screenplay by** Jay Allen, based on the musical drama "Cabaret!" written by Joe Masteroff and based on the play "I Am A Camera" by John Van Druten and stories by Christopher Isherwood.
**Photographed by** Geoffrey Unsworth.
**Art direction by** Rolf Zehetbauer.
**Choreography by** Bob Fosse.
**Songs by** John Kander and Fred Ebb.
**Cast:** Liza Minnelli; Joel Grey; Michael York; Helmut Griem; Marisa Berenson; Fritz Wepper.

## A Hard Day's Night

Great Britain; 1964; 87 minutes;
released by United Artists.

**Directed by** Richard Lester.
**Produced by** Walter Shenson.
**Screenplay by** Alan Owen.
**Photographed by** Gilbert Taylor.
**Songs by** The Beatles.
**Cast:** John Lennon; Paul McCartney; George Harrison; Ringo Starr; Wilfrid Branbell; Norman Rossington; Victor Spinetti; John Junkin; Anna Quayle; Kenneth Haigh; Richard Vernon; Eddie Malin.

# War

5

More movies have been made about war than about any other subject. War stories are so amenable to the cinema that in other chapters of this book there are at least fifteen pictures from which one could draw several perfectly acceptable lists of great examples of the genre: DR. STRANGELOVE, THE SEVEN SAMURAI, HIROSHIMA, MON AMOUR, THE GENERAL, and THE WILD BUNCH, or DUCK SOUP, GONE WITH THE WIND, LAWRENCE OF ARABIA, THE BATTLE OF ALGIERS, and HENRY V, etc.

There are so many good war films that it is difficult to make a valid selection. One may choose from such Second World War action classics as Howard Hawks' AIR FORCE, John Ford's THEY WERE EXPENDABLE, and William Wellman's STORY OF G. I. JOE, Sergei Eisenstein's great war pageant ALEXANDER NEVSKY, such antiwar warhorses as John Huston's THE RED BADGE OF COURAGE, Lewis Milestone's ALL QUIET ON THE WESTERN FRONT, and Bernard Wicki's THE BRIDGE, plus many films about people caught up in the drama of war: Edward Dmytryk's THE YOUNG LIONS, Vittorio De Sica's TWO WOMEN, Roberto Rossellini's GENERAL DELLA ROVERE, William Wyler's THE BEST YEARS OF OUR LIVES, Don Siegel's HELL IS FOR HEROES, and so on.

War is a subject that invites every sort of portrayal by every sort of filmmaker, usually with the common goal of condemning its pain, uselessness, and waste. The history of the war film is mostly a history of well-meaning attempts to save the world. Henry King shows us that he comprehends the anguish of war but can also justify its cost in TWELVE O'CLOCK HIGH. Mike Nichols is fascinating and pretentious in his black-comic CATCH-22. Carl Foreman's ironies are simple-minded but strong in THE VICTORS. Stanley Kramer's moralizing is graceless but convincing in ON THE BEACH. Darryl Zanuck and Co. are exploitive in THE LONGEST DAY, but many of its scenes are forceful. Even the Sanders brothers deserve some credit for their self-righteous short film, A TIME OUT OF WAR.

The purpose of these critical remarks is not to condemn these pictures (flawed, but still better than ninety-five percent of the genre), but to debunk the widely held belief that a great war film must, by its very nature, be antiwar. In fact, this is probably true, but not in the sense that most filmmakers think—namely, that if their war movies are antiwar they are half-way to greatness already. Since it is so easy these days to be antiwar, one is inclined to admire the now unfashionable, prowar propaganda films of Hawks, Ford, and Wellman, and to be suspicious of the exploitation of antiwar sentiment by filmmakers who justify depiction of the most violent and revolting details of combat on the grounds that since their message is noble their vulgarity can be excused.

It is not enough that a war film be antiwar, or that it be measured solely on the basis of the skill of its scenes of combat, its verisimilitude or its politics. (The five pictures discussed here contain, all together, fewer minutes of actual combat than a single reel of THE DIRTY DOZEN.) To be great, a war film must view the madness that is war in the context of characters in conflict; then it must probe that madness, take its measure, and render it convincingly on the screen. The five selected films do these things well, and each, too, is the work of a unique sensibility that has come to grips with the endemic phenomenon of war in an original way.

## Jean Renoir's **La Grande Illusion** 1937

The question surrounding the legendary LA GRANDE ILLUSION is what, precisely, is the "great illusion" of its title? Is it the belief, widely held after 1918, that the First World War was the war that would end all wars? Is it the idea that war is a noble enterprise? Is it the myth that nation-states are the things that separate men, when, in fact, it is social differentiation? Or is it the "illusion" that these disparities of class can be overcome? The beauty of this title is that it is open to so many lines of interpretation, and thus reflects the richness and complexity of a film that probes the nature of war in the compassionate and profound style so characteristic of Jean Renoir.

But since 1936, when LA GRANDE ILLUSION was conceived and shot, a new interpretation of the title has emerged, an interpretation which the makers of the film did not anticipate. This is the possibility that Jean Renoir and his co-writer Charles Spaak suffered from a "great illusion" in thinking that they could change the world by making a work of art which would also be one of the strongest and most luminous pleas ever made for peace and brotherhood between men. Jean Renoir put it most poignantly when he made a written reply to a question posed by Robert Hughes, who was assembling a book about films having to do with war and peace, and who asked, in effect, whether such films ever really altered the public consciousness. Renoir wrote: "In 1936 I made a



Preceding pages: Alec Guinness staggers from sweatbox in THE BRIDGE ON THE RIVER KWAI. Opposite: Stills from LA GRANDE ILLUSION. Bottom: Erich von Stroheim as von Rauffenstein and Pierre Fresnay (also at top, hand in pocket) as de Boeldieu. Portraits, from top: Jean Gabin, Marcel Dalio, Director Jean Renoir.

VERKAUF

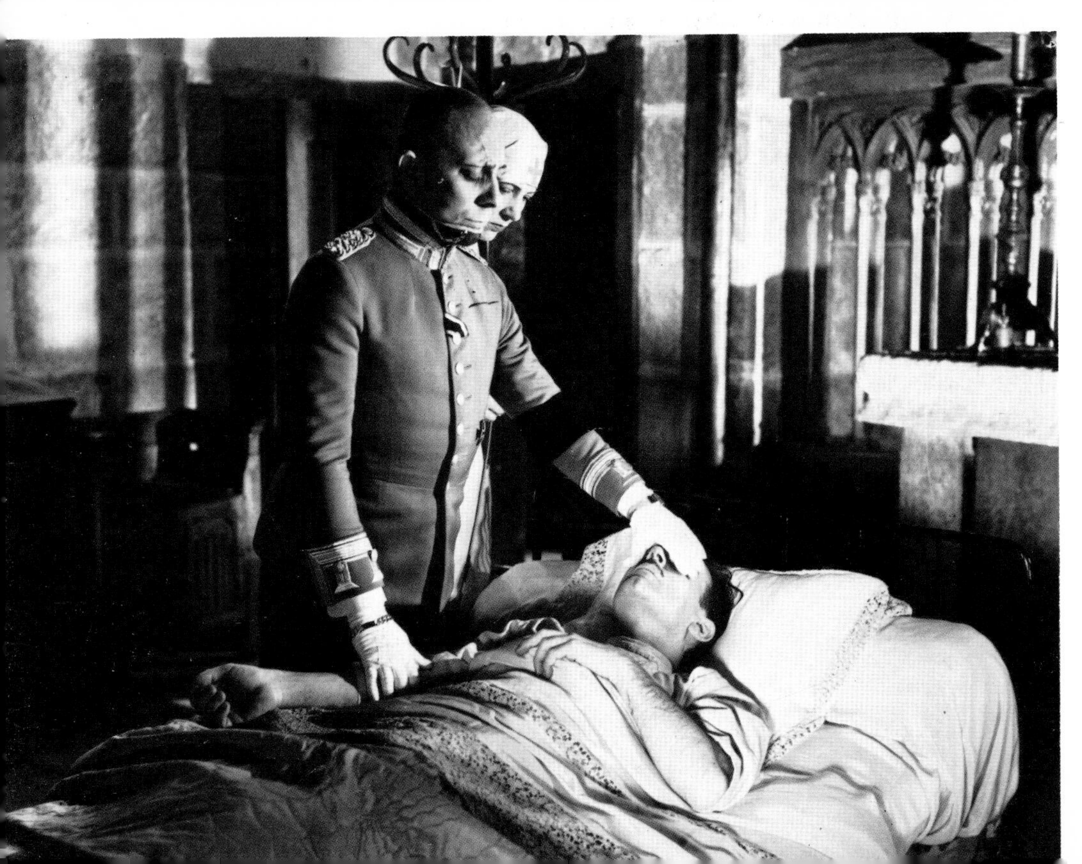

picture named LA GRANDE ILLUSION in which I tried to express all my deep feelings for the cause of peace. Three years later the war broke out. That is the only answer I can find to your very interesting enquiry." Could, then, in this ironic and retrospective way, the film itself have been a "great illusion"?

LA GRANDE ILLUSION is of that subgenre of war films which does not deal with combat or the horrors of war, but with the effects of war upon men removed from the fighting fronts, in this case men who are prisoners.

Though the settings of LA GRANDE ILLUSION are German prisoner-of-war camps in World War I, and the plot contains many of the motifs of prison-camp films, the real story of this picture is not escape, brutality, etc., but the interlocking and ambiguous relationships of four men, and the way these relationships illuminate the nature of human conflict. The men are the German aristocrat, von Rauffenstein (Erich von Stroheim), the French aristocrat, de Boeldieu (Pierre Fresnay), the former French mechanic and now officer, Maréchal (Jean Gabin), and the rich Jewish French officer, Rosenthal (Marcel Dalio). Their relationships are complex on account of social differences (important, but overcome), and differences in nationality (meaningless, but not overcome). In this sense LA GRANDE ILLUSION is about the stupidities of war rather than its horrors. In Jean Renoir's own words, it is "a sort of reconstructed documentary, a documentary on the condition of society at a given moment."

Jean Renoir, goes the cliché, is humanistic. But the cliché is true. The story, acting, and theme of LA GRANDE ILLUSION are permeated by compassion, warmth, and humanity, as is the very particular, steady, unblinking gaze of Jean Renoir's camera upon the faces of his actors while they perform with a genuineness of emotions and a generosity of spirit that is so luminous it nearly blinds us to their faults. The scene between Rosenthal and Maréchal in the snow is one of the perfect examples of this. Their split-up after their escape, Maréchal's anti-Semitic outburst and then the two men's reconciliation are a deeply moving dramatization of Renoir's belief that the nobility of a man is best demonstrated in moments when his most human failings are exposed.

Renoir is concerned with what he calls "the interior truth which is the one vital thing." In effect, he says, "it has to do with knowing what someone is really like, what stuff he has in him. Then, once one has got at him, one has to make the audience see it too...." This is the principle upon which all great Jean Renoir films have been built, and when brought to bear in LA GRANDE ILLUSION upon the subject of men in war, it results in something that is unique, tranquil, and altogether extraordinary.

The key to finding the interior truth of a character was, for Jean Renoir, resolved by the way he dealt with his actors. When Renoir cast Jean Gabin, he was the biggest star in France. Pierre Fresnay was extremely popular, and Erich von Stroheim was to Renoir something like a god. Stroheim and Renoir did not meet until after Stroheim accepted the role of Rauffenstein. They got along beautifully, Stroheim freely making suggestions, Renoir agreeing to build up his part. (The idea that Rauffenstein should wear an iron corset and a chin brace was Stroheim's.) Stroheim has written of Renoir's patience with his actors, the delicacy of his manners, his fervor, and his patience, too, in the face of enormous production difficulties. Every actor who has worked with Renoir has commented upon these qualities, and the intense and warm gaze with which he inspired their confidence and which is paralleled in his shooting style.

LA GRANDE ILLUSION was released in 1937, at a time when war in Europe seemed inevitable. It was applauded by the public as a plea for peace, and was later banned by Goebbels. All existing prints were confiscated during the German occupation. Of course, the Nazis hated this film. Its message that national boundaries are meaningless was taken as a direct attack upon the expansionist policies of the Third Reich. Renoir refers to the Nazis as men "who almost succeeded in making people forget that Germans are also human beings." His use of the word "almost" is characteristic. Despite the fact that his life's work was nearly destroyed by them, and they ridiculed his fondest dream of human brotherhood, his conviction that war and conflict are but the ignoble acts of an otherwise noble creature, remained unshaken.

In the early 1950s, Renoir bought back the rights to LA GRANDE ILLUSION, which was being shown in various mutilated versions. He discovered an untouched print in Munich, and from that reconstructed the picture in time for the 1958 Brussels World's Fair, at which it was judged one of the dozen greatest movies ever made.

Alec Guinness leads his ragged troops into Japanese prison camp in BRIDGE. Bridge blows up in dramatic finale (l.) which camp physician calls "madness, madness . . ." William Holden (above) is American commando killed along with Guinness in bloody Japanese counterattack. Opposite: Gabin and Dalio in LA GRANDE ILLUSION.

# David Lean's **The Bridge on the River Kwai** 1957

Like LA GRANDE ILLUSION, THE BRIDGE ON THE RIVER KWAI is an antiwar war film set in a prisoner-of-war camp milieu. But there the similarities cease. THE BRIDGE ON THE RIVER KWAI is an action movie in which the nature of war is explored in a contrived story executed by a director who is more concerned with spinning a climactic yarn than in making a social statement in an open-ended form. And if in LA GRANDE ILLUSION the characters are depicted by a great artist who cherishes their common humanity, in THE BRIDGE ON THE RIVER KWAI they are pushed to fulfill their destinies by a superb craftsman who values above all else suspension of disbelief.

The Japanese prison camp located near the Kwai River in Burma is an enclosed universe in which many familiar prison-camp motifs are played out. Escape is impossible but there is the inevitable talk of an escape committee; the prisoners are organized by their native commanders and are abused by brutal guards; the camp commandant is a psychopathic sadist; conditions are terrible—disease, poor food, a bad climate; morale fluctuates; the prisoners put on a musical in which they dress up as women; there are no significant female characters.

Into this essentially familiar situation comes Colonel Nicholson, a brave and admirable British officer, deeply concerned for the welfare of his men. Nicholson wants to prove to the Japanese that the British soldier is superior; he is convinced that if he can prove this his men will achieve a victory in their defeat. After an initial and fairly conventional struggle between Nicholson and the Japanese commandant over an obscure point of honor, the major situation of the story is introduced. Nicholson agrees to help the Japanese construct a bridge, and in his passion to find victory in defeat, loses sight of the fact that this bridge, which he insists must be a "proper bridge," will be used to further the war aims of the Japanese against other British troops.

In addition to the usual contending forces of a prison-camp picture, captors versus captives, and an interesting moral dilemma posed by the issue of the bridge, a third element is introduced: a commando force, led by a British major and an American escapee from the camp, whose mission is to blow up the bridge.

The film works to a climax. A Japanese train and the commando force converge on the bridge being completed by the British captives. The film cuts back and forth between the camp and the commandos, and the motives of Nicholson, the Japanese commandant, and the British major are fully explored. Each character has a perfectly valid reason for what he is doing, and each develops a relationship to the bridge that increases to proportions that are slowly and subtly revealed to be insane. Eventually, the suspense is relieved by a sensational climax in which the bridge is blown up, the Japanese train hurtles into a canyon, two of the commandos are killed, the commandant who was planning to commit hara-kiri is killed, and Colonel Nicholson dies, too, but not before he falls upon the plunger that sets off the explosives that destroy the bridge he has tried to save. In the words of a British medical officer who observes this finale from a hilltop, it is "madness, madness...."

Thus, THE BRIDGE ON THE RIVER KWAI deals with war in the form of a single incident in which well-developed and rational characters march reasonably and logically into an orgy of self-destruction. This, the film tells us, is what war is all about.

There are certain standard complaints leveled against THE BRIDGE ON THE RIVER KWAI, all of which seem to revolve around questions concerning the ending. Does Colonel Nicholson fall upon the exploder mechanism by accident or design? If by accident, is not the story ruined by a coincidence that is too farfetched, and if on purpose, is not his character inconsistent and absurd? If David Lean were really so precise a craftsman, his critics say, he would not have bungled an ending that must be clear in order to justify his film.

Let those who question the craft of David Lean's choreography look at the picture again. Many things happen very quickly at the end of THE BRIDGE ON THE RIVER KWAI, but a close inspection makes it clear that Nicholson finally realizes the insanity of what he has done, and is groping, in panic and shock, toward the plunger when he is shot. Perhaps it is a coincidence that he happens to fall upon it, but films of this kind are built around coincidences, possible in fictional terrains where internal logic creates a suspension of disbelief. The only valid question about a scene like this is not whether it is realistic, but whether it works as entertainment. Since the climax of THE BRIDGE ON THE RIVER KWAI is one of the most gripping finales in cinema, one must say that it works extremely well.

PHOTOGRAPHS BY BOB WILLOUGHBY



Frank Sinatra's singing career was in shambles when he entreated Harry Cohn of Columbia Pictures to cast him as Maggio in FROM HERE TO ETERNITY, then set for Eli Wallach. Wallach withdrew, Sinatra got part, won an Oscar, and made a phenomenal comeback.

# Fred Zinnemann's **From Here to Eternity** 1953

Unfortunately, FROM HERE TO ETERNITY is principally remembered for its role in the now legendary career of Frank Sinatra. "FROM HERE TO ETERNITY?" people say. "Oh, yes, wasn't that Sinatra's comeback film?" And recently the whole story has been sensationalized and distorted in THE GODFATHER. The real significance of FROM HERE TO ETERNITY is that it was one of the best pictures produced in America in the 1950s, a superb entertainment that has in common with THE BRIDGE ON THE RIVER KWAI a well-wrought war story about people with whom audiences can become intensely involved.

It may seem odd to refer to FROM HERE TO ETERNITY as a war film, since so much of it deals with the peacetime army. But war is very important to this film. The December 7 attack on Pearl Harbor is its end point, the culmination of a merciless attack on the military mind.

FROM HERE TO ETERNITY views war as the monstrous cloud that hangs over its characters' lives. Throughout the film one feels a terrifying sense of déjà vu. One knows that the Japanese attack on Pearl Harbor will be the climax of the story, but since the characters do not know this and cannot anticipate the momentous event that will so deeply affect their destinies, one's inclination is to shout a warning to them.

When the attack comes it is brilliantly staged, one of the superb action sequences in war films. The Japanese planes are first only heard. Then there are explosions. Confused men rise from Sunday breakfast; the planes dive and strafe the quadrangle of the barracks while men run back and forth. When a noncom refuses to issue arms the men break down the door, take machine guns to the roof and blaze away. When they finally shoot down a plane they are exhilarated by their first taste of combat.

With this one powerful scene all the interlocking relationships which have been the substance of the story (between the bugler, Prewitt, who lives by his own very special code of honor—Montgomery Clift; Prewitt's buddy, the tough little guy, Maggio—Frank Sinatra; the sadistic Sergeant of the Guard at the stockade—Ernest Borgnine; Sergeant Warden, the man who cannot imagine himself as an officer—Burt Lancaster; Warden's lover, the estranged wife of his company commander—Deborah Kerr; her husband, a Captain whose principal concern is winning a divisional boxing tournament; and Donna Reed, Prewitt's girl friend, a paid companion at the New Congress Club) are permanently altered. A huge event diminishes these characters' sufferings and passions. World War II is a force that changes everything. Clift, Sinatra, and Borgnine die, the company commander resigns from the Army, Donna Reed and Deborah Kerr return to the mainland without their lovers, and Burt Lancaster has ahead of him an heroic career. War, in this picture, is bigger than people, and its sinister nature is explored by way of the relationships of the characters in the remote, confined, peacetime world of Schofield Barracks.

James Jones' novel, which sold millions of copies, was considered so offensive by the military that it took considerable pressure before the Department of Defense agreed to help with the filming of the attack. Daniel Taradash, who wrote the screenplay, has written that Harry Cohn of Columbia Pictures felt (undoubtedly by that infamous sense of instinct ridiculed by Herman Mankiewicz in his marvelous quip: "Imagine—the whole world wired to Harry Cohn's ass!") that Prewitt should blow his bugle before the sequence when he plays taps for Maggio. This led to one of the picture's more interesting scenes, when Montgomery Clift, perhaps the most brooding and introspective of American movie stars, plays a flamboyant and mournful blues in an enlisted man's club to express his rage at the way his beloved army is mistreating him. Other fine scenes include the great romantic-erotic encounter between Lancaster and Kerr at twilight on a beach (perhaps the most remembered sequence in the film, and quite daring in its day); Maggio's various encounters with Borgnine; and many short scenes of army life, in the barracks, on the drill field, and at the enlisted man's haven, the New Congress Club.

Fred Zinnemann's film closely follows James Jones' novel in style and technique. The omniscient and realistic direction of FROM HERE TO ETERNITY is Zinnemann's trademark. At the peak of his form (not apparent in HIGH NOON), he is capable of merging naturalistic acting and theatrical staging with a discipline that controls the first and prevents the second from looking phony. FROM HERE TO ETERNITY, his best picture, is one of those rare films in which the characters seem to have lives beyond the confines of the scenes in which they appear. The intersection of the attack on Pearl Harbor and the lives of Prewitt, Maggio, Warden, and the two women is a moving and eloquent statement of how war (a disinterested force) collides with the destinies of people and hurls them into a maelstrom.



Montgomery Clift as the bugler-boxer Prewitt in FROM HERE TO ETERNITY. Fred Zinnemann refused to direct the picture unless Clift played the lead, in which Cohn wanted to cast Aldo Ray. Cohn conceded, and Clift gave an extraordinary performance, perhaps the best of his career.

Burt Lancaster (l.) as Sergeant Warden, Deborah Kerr (above) as Karen Holmes. FROM HERE TO ETERNITY was one of greatest hits of the 1950s. Costing little more than $2 million, it earned a fortune and won eight Academy awards.

# Stanley Kubrick's **Paths of Glory** 1957

In PATHS OF GLORY war is viewed in terms of power. This urgent, pulsating film about an episode in World War I combines Jean Renoir's idea that class differences are more important than national differences with the cannon-fodder theory of war, the theory that soldiers are merely pawns in the hands of generals who play at war as if it were a game of chess.

PATHS OF GLORY is a great film despite certain serious defects. The dialogue has an overwritten, literary quality that is not enhanced by the flat American accents of actors who sometimes seem out of place in French uniforms and kepis. Because of the strong ideological content of the story, many of the characters seem to represent ideas rather than personalities. One does not find here the kind of naturalistic acting that leads to audience identification as, for example, in FROM HERE TO ETERNITY. But perhaps the major failing of this film is that its story—basically about three men ceremoniously court-martialed and executed to justify the incompetence of their corrupt commanders—is a thoroughly stacked deck. A picture about the consequences of military tyranny, power plays by generals, corruption in high places, blind obedience, men using one another ruthlessly for professional advancement, and class struggle between officers and men (officers dance while poor men wait to die, etc.), it often has the stink of a heavy-handed antiwar message picture. And its ending, when Colonel Dax (Kirk Douglas) watches while a German girl (Susanne Christian, later to become Kubrick's wife) is forced to sing for drunken French troops, and then stirs recognition in them of her and their shared humanity—a scene that is either moving or sentimental depending upon one's taste—is a forced and too-symmetrical windup to an already overly symmetrical structure.

Despite these faults, which all are arguable, PATHS OF GLORY is redeemed by the brilliant filmmaking of Stanley Kubrick. Even if one objects to the ideological formality of PATHS OF GLORY—the fact that the generals are too inhumane and corrupt, the enlisted troops too innocent and used, Colonel Dax, the man in the middle, too torn on account of his peculiar blend of obedience and moral outrage, and a forced, pseudohumanistic ending—one can still admire the formality of its execution. Imagine, for an instant, the result if Stanley Kramer had made this film; consider how bland, soft and dull such a version would be. In the hands, however, of another Stanley the visual excitement of PATHS OF GLORY is so great that it overwhelms the viewer and covers up the defects of the material. PATHS OF GLORY is a director's film. One feels in every scene that one is in a director's hands. The

From PATHS OF GLORY: General Mireau (George Macready) inspects trenches (l.). Kirk Douglas as Colonel Dax (above). Opposite: Futile attack on "the anthill"; General Broulard (Adolphe Menjou) arrives at château; the trial sequence.

power of the picture lies in what the French call the *mise en scène*, the way it is all put together.

This power is the result of the way Kubrick uses his camera to express visually the content of his scenes. No one who has seen PATHS OF GLORY will ever forget the long travelling shots through the trenches, first when General Mireau inspects the troops, and then when Colonel Dax walks the trenches before the attack on the Ant Hill. While these wide-angle moving shots convey the claustrophobia of the trenches and the oppressed conditions of the soldiers, the elegant compositions inside the huge rooms of the chateau convey the coldness of the commanders and also their luxurious condition. The Ant Hill attack is a marvel of realistic filmmaking; one feels the confusion and desperation of an impossible assault. And the execution sequence, in which the camera moves relentlessly closer and closer to the stakes through lines of formally arranged troops, is one of the most suspenseful, geometric formulations in cinema. Alexander Walker has pointed out that the various shots of the Ant Hill assault made through binoculars express the way the commanders view the battle as a spectator sport. Similarly, the black-and-white squares of the château floors and the hierarchic arrangements of people in the court-martial scene express the way this occasion is a power play, a game of chess in which enlisted men are pawns being sacrificed to further the advancement of more powerful pieces.

This amazing film, which Winston Churchill is said to have admired for the verisimilitude of its combat sequence, cost a mere $900,000, of which more than one-third went to Kirk Douglas. It was shot in Germany, with German policemen cast as extras. Six cameras were used to shoot the attack on the Ant Hill; there were five "dying zones" and each extra had a slip of paper which told him in which one he should "die." For a while after it opened, PATHS OF GLORY was banned on American military bases, and it is still banned in France, where the military establishment considers it a vicious slander against its honor.

In Kubrick's career, PATHS OF GLORY is a formative work that shows traces of the influence of Max Ophuls, so famous for his endless dolly shots, and also of the Soviet cinema, with its formal framings, rhythmic cutting, and dialectically balanced stories. It led to Kubrick being hired by Kirk Douglas to direct SPARTACUS, which in turn led to his being taken seriously as a director, presumably on the theory that a man who directs a $10 million picture has got to be serious. The result has been the emergence of one of the great talents in contemporary cinema, the master who created 2001: A SPACE ODYSSEY, and whose greatest work is yet to come.



Priest comforts "cowards" before rifle squad receives order to fire. Entire execution sequence is elaborately choreographed and cut for maximum "build." Kubrick staged scene in formal geometric compositions in keeping with hierarchical themes of film.

# Robert Altman's M*A*S*H 1970

When Stanley Kubrick dealt with war again, in DR. STRANGELOVE, OR HOW I LEARNED TO STOP WORRYING AND LOVE THE BOMB, he pushed the absurdity he had described with such seriousness in PATHS OF GLORY into the realm of black comedy. M*A*S*H has also been described as a black comedy about war, but is actually part of the "service comedy" tradition, of which NO TIME FOR SERGEANTS and MISTER ROBERTS are probably the most famous examples. The "service comedy," a cross between the war film and the comedy, usually emphasizes the amusing aspects of being thrust into unfamiliar military situations, while minimizing the sinister realities of combat. But M*A*S*H is different. It combines broad, farcical routines with a significant and unblinking look at the nature of war, and is thus a film unto itself, perhaps the first picture in a new sub-subgenre that one might label the "blood comedy" on account of the large amount of scarlet fluid that dominates this movie's "look."

The Mobile Army Surgical Hospital, where most of the action in M*A*S*H takes place, is three miles from the front of the Korean War. Although we never see actual combat, we do see, over and over again until we are nauseated, the bloody results of fighting. War, in M*A*S*H, is a slaughterhouse, a huge, vicious machine that literally chews men up into so much bloody meat. It is against this situation, so gruesome and so horrendous, that the comedy is played. To stay sane the surgeons and nurses must indulge themselves with raucous and elaborately erotic games.

M*A*S*H is a very special film for reasons that elude those who shrug it off as trash. It is the first important film of Robert Altman, a highly original talent who develops here techniques he will use again in his superb western, MCCABE AND MRS. MILLER. These techniques, which result in a unique texture, may constitute one of the few original approaches to filmmaking in the last decade. The special look of M*A*S*H is the result not only of the lavish use of blood, but of its huge set constructed on mud flats at the Twentieth Century-Fox ranch in Malibu, California. The confused, asymmetrical arrangements of tents, supply dumps, field surgeries, and motor pool, crisscrossed by telephone wires, heaped with junk, and dominated by a public-address system that becomes, in effect, a major character, has the authentic feel of a mobile army surgical hospital, just as the town in MCCABE AND MRS. MILLER, in the very process of being built during the filming, conveys the sensual texture of the frontier. These sets do not look like sets. They are real spaces in which people live and work. And Altman, in both pictures, uses them this way. His casts actually inhabit these constructed environments, build up relationships with one another in them, improvise scenes and conversations, and literally live out their roles.

The extras in M*A*S*H were drawn from ensemble companies in San Francisco. Their realistic playing works in counterpoint to the foreground slapstick. In both of Altman's films one hears inconclusive pieces of conversation (often mumbled or cross-faded), and one glimpses relationships often left unresolved. Characters are revealed in bits and pieces rather than in conventional "character scenes." One has the sensation of exploring a particular world in a manner that is akin to one's experience in real life. In M*A*S*H one wanders through an environment, grasping its structure and meaning through the senses.

M*A*S*H was a big commercial hit. Despite the fact that it required more work from audiences than a more conventional film, it earned back its cost many times over. Like PATHS OF GLORY, it was considered an affront to the U. S. Army and was initially banned on American military bases. There is no solemnity in M*A*S*H, none of the heavy-handed pretentiousness that one finds in the brooding black comedy, CATCH-22, released in the same year. M*A*S*H has the vitality, the exaltation of life, that is typical of the American cinema at its best, and though its "Last Supper" sequence, derived from Leonardo da Vinci's famous painting, is not used with the same power as in Luis Buñuel's VIRIDIANA, it has in common with that great iconoclastic work the intention of mocking religion. M*A*S*H may have been the first commercial American film to do this openly. Religion—in the form of the "Last Supper," an incompetent surgeon who ludicrously prays, and a sanctimonious chaplain who wanders about giving spiritual comfort to men and women hourly confronted by blood and gore—is ridiculed without mercy. Religion, says Altman and his screenwriter, Ring Lardner, Jr., is of no comfort in the face of the insane carnage that is war. The only comforts, according to them, are the belly laugh, the sexual leer, and the marijuana cigarette.

From M*A*S*H: Elliott Gould and Donald Sutherland interrupt golt practice (l.) to examine X-rays. Bottom left: "Last Supper" sequence (compare with Buñuel's in VIRIDIANA, page 185). Bottom center: Director Robert Altman (with beard). M*A*S*H is notable for its ensemble playing, constructed environment, and bizarre blend of free-flowing blood and slapstick comedy.

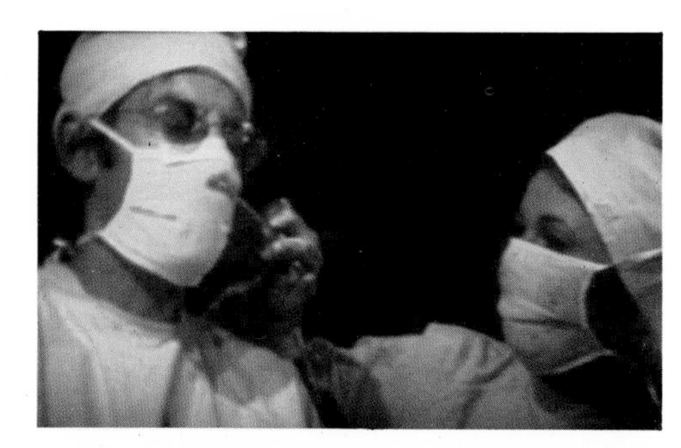

# Credits

## La Grande Illusion (The Great Illusion)

France; 1937; 117 minutes; originally released in the U.S. by World Films.

**Directed by** Jean Renoir.
**Produced by** Frank Rollmer and Albert Pinkovitch.
**Photographed by** Charles Matras and Claude Renoir.
**Screenplay by** Charles Spaak and Jean Renoir.
**Edited by** Marguerite Renoir (Marguerite Marthe-Huguet).
**Art direction by** Eugène Lourié.
**Music by** Joseph Kosma.
**Cast:** Jean Gabin; Pierre Fresnay; Erich von Stroheim; Marcel Dalio; Julien Carette; Gaston Modot; Jean Dasté; Georges Péclet; Jacques Becker; Sylvain Itkine; Dita Parlo; W. Florian.

## The Bridge on the River Kwai

U.S.A.; 1957; 161 minutes; released by Columbia.

**Directed by** David Lean.
**Produced by** Sam Spiegel.
**Screenplay by** Carl Foreman and Michael Wilson, based on the novel by Pierre Boulle.
**Photographed by** Jack Hildyard.
**Edited by** Peter Taylor.
**Art direction by** Donald Ashton.
**Music by** Malcolm Arnold.
**Cast:** Alec Guinness; William Holden; Jack Hawkins; Sessue Hayakawa; James Donald; Geoffrey Horne; Andre Movell; Peter Williams; John Boxer; Percy Herbert.

## From Here to Eternity

U.S.A.; 1953; 115 minutes; released by Columbia.

**Directed by** Fred Zinnemann.
**Produced by** Buddy Adler.
**Screenplay by** Daniel Taradash, from the novel by James Jones.
**Photographed by** Burnett Guffey.
**Edited by** William Lyon.
**Art direction by** Cary Odell.
**Music by** Morris Stoloff.
**Cast:** Montgomery Clift; Frank Sinatra; Burt Lancaster; Deborah Kerr; Ernest Borgnine; Donna Reed; Philip Ober; Mickey Shaughnessy; Harry Bellaver.

## Paths of Glory

U.S.A.; 1957; 86 minutes; released by United Artists.

**Directed by** Stanley Kubrick.
**Produced by** James B. Harris.
**Screenplay by** Stanley Kubrick, Calder Willingham, and Jim Thompson, based on the novel by Humphrey Cobb.
**Photographed by** George Krause.
**Art direction by** Ludwig Reiber.
**Edited by** Eva Kroll.
**Music by** Gerald Fried.
**Cast:** Kirk Douglas; Ralph Meeker; Adolphe Menjou; George Macready; Wayne Morris; Richard Anderson; Joseph Turkel; Timothy Carey; Peter Capell; Susanne Christian.

## M*A*S*H

U.S.A.; 1969; 116 minutes; released by 20th Century-Fox.

**Directed by** Robert Altman.
**Produced by** Ingo Preminger.
**Screenplay by** Ring Lardner, Jr., from the novel by Richard Hooker.
**Photographed by** Harold E. Stine.
**Art direction by** Jack Martin Smith.
**Edited by** Danford Greene.
**Music by** Johnny Mandel.
**Cast:** Donald Sutherland; Elliott Gould; Tom Skerritt; Sally Kellerman; Robert Duvall; Jo Ann Pflug; Rene Auberjonois; Roger Bowen.

# Adventure

# 6

The adventure film, like the western and the suspense picture, is a degraded genre, a genre of B pictures. Its purpose is to entertain an audience and make money, not to illuminate human experience and be honored as art. But like the western and the suspense picture, the adventure film can be a work of art. A great director, working within the conventions of the genre, can rise to heights of expressiveness.

The adventure film stands for everything that is anathema to Women's Liberation, a closed male world whose values the women's movement finds false and ugly. The pictures are always about men, alone or in groups, engaged in difficult action enterprises that reveal the male attributes of the characters. The enterprises are such things as the accomplishment of a difficult or impossible mission (a heist, a rescue, a search for treasure, a military campaign, or an act of revenge), involving encounters with harsh terrains (jungles, mountains, deserts), extremes of danger (natives, bandits, wild beasts, terrifying storms), and various forms of human baseness (killing, torture, betrayal, war). The revealed attributes are such things as bravery, ruthlessness, physical superiority, the assertion of power, and other aspects of machismo currently in disrepute.

If the story is about a solitary adventurer, it will concern his attempt to meet his own standards of honor. If it is about a group, it will concern camaraderie, the need for each man to measure up to the group code. The men of adventure films are hard, tough, determined, and physically skilled. The women, if they exist at all, are usually minor characters, sex objects, sometimes degraded, other times impossibly romanticized, or outsiders who must prove themselves before they can be admitted to the male world. A final convention is a subterranean stream of male love—love of man for man, expressed in an acceptable way, never tinged with effeminacy—which some observers cannot resist labeling latent homosexuality.

It is possible that the adventure story derives from some archetypal myth residing in the collective unconscious of man. From the time of Homer, stories of male exploits have been enormously popular. From the earliest days of the human race, men have sat around fires listening to other men tell stories of adventure. Someone once said that the cinema is the most perfect means ever devised to tell a story. Adventure films have been one of the economic pillars of the industry. Perhaps because they fulfill some need for vicarious experience they rarely fail to find an audience.

Ask someone to name his favorite films, and chances are he will give you a list of works which have been officially certified as art. Narrow the question and ask him to name the films he has most enjoyed, and chances are he will name one or more of the following five pictures, all of which are masterpieces of entertainment.

## Howard Hawks' **Only Angels Have Wings** 1939

ONLY ANGELS HAVE WINGS is, perhaps, the basic adventure film of the American cinema, demonstrating all but one of the conventions of the genre in full development. The convention that is not fulfilled is the convention of great action sequences. In terms of production values, ONLY ANGELS HAVE WINGS is a modest film in which the subject is the meaning and consequences of adventure, rather than the adventures themselves.

It is a film with a very special mood. Most of the action takes place at the Dutchman's saloon, but this one-set arena is surrounded by a dark world of dangerous mountains, treacherous storms, and sudden, lonely death. The characters, civil aviators working for a small mail-run outfit in the port town of Barranca, presumably near the high Andes region of Peru, form an enclosed, all-male world in which the performance of work—getting the mail through and thus measuring up to standards set by the group—is the substance of life. In this world a man's self-respect determines the poise of his behavior. Here personal honor is a function of his professionalism and the esteem of his peers.

In this isolated masculine world a cast of adventurers is assembled: Cary Grant, the stoical commander of the unit who must conceal his deep feeling for his men lest he lose the poise necessary to inspire their respect; Grant's best friend, a character called Kid (Thomas Mitchell), older than Grant and subordinate to him, a man who will not admit that his vision is failing because flying and the camaraderie of the group are his life; another flier named Bat McPherson (Richard Barthelmess), who must prove to himself his right to be part of this elite because of a shameful incident in his past; and the pilots, Joe, Les, Tex, Sparks, and others.

Bat's wife (Rita Hayworth) knows the subordinate



Preceding pages: Tim Holt, Humphrey Bogart, and Walter Huston in John Huston's THE TREASURE OF THE SIERRA MADRE. Opposite: Cary Grant and Jean Arthur in Howard Hawks' archetypal adventure melodrama ONLY ANGELS HAVE WINGS. At rear: Victor Kilian, Thomas Mitchell, Allyn Joslyn.

role that a woman must play in this sort of world. Jean Arthur, who becomes involved with the young flier, Joe (and later with Grant), does not understand and threatens its cohesion. When Joe dies because he takes an unacceptable risk in order to get back in time to meet her for a dinner date, Jean Arthur's outburst disrupts the cool, hard way the pilots know they must respond to the death of one of their own. In a world where death lingers everywhere, where the threat of death hangs over every one of them at every moment he is in the air, an outward callousness toward disaster is the only way to cope. At first Jean Arthur is appalled by this. When she comes to understand it, when she is initiated into the special world of Barranca, she becomes one of the guys.

The male attribute of not showing pain, of not weeping over the death of a friend, of maintaining the unspoken code that says that the way Joe died proved he wasn't "good enough," didn't have the character to give proper precedence to the job and the people who were counting on him to fulfill it—this code, finally, becomes her own, and when she understands it, we do, too.

ONLY ANGELS HAVE WINGS exemplifies the masculine ethos which is at the core of all great adventure films. This ethos is delineated by scenes which have become part of the vocabulary of films of this sort: camaraderie exhibited in the group sing; the initiation of a woman into a male world; the stoical hero who finally breaks down because even he, and therefore no one, can really take such pressure; the scenes which show why the job is more important than the individual; the austere life style of the adventurer who leaves no possessions behind, nothing except the status of his honor at the time he falls; and, finally, the scenes where a single man tests himself against danger, tempts death, and then defies it.

There are people who find ONLY ANGELS HAVE WINGS a corny film, filled with clichés, stock characters, and embarrassing moments whose excess makes them cringe. In a sense they are right. The film has blemishes, amplified perhaps by the fact that its ethos has become unfashionable. But its flaws are not important enough to obscure its brilliance as a film of conflicting relationships, played out in a strange and special world, in which the nature of adventure and the consequences of being an adventurer are laid bare.

If there is a literary equivalent of ONLY ANGELS HAVE WINGS it is in the works of Antoine de Saint-Exupéry, particularly *Night Flight,* in which the same philosophy of life is spelled out. It is also the philosophy of Howard Hawks, himself a physical adventurer, hunting companion of Hemingway, single-seat aviator, racing-car driver, and supreme technician of cinema, who made so many fine films over a period of many years, always denying that he was trying to do anything except tell a good story. In his career he created the parameters of the adventure film, not only with ONLY ANGELS HAVE WINGS, but with his two great westerns, RIO BRAVO and RED RIVER (which see), his Hemingway adaptation, TO HAVE AND TO HAVE NOT, his action war film, AIR FORCE, and many others. Hawks' pictures place him in the elite of Hollywood directors. Like the heroes of his adventure films he is a professional among professionals, the highest compliment that can be paid in the Hawksian universe.

# Akira Kurosawa's **The Seven Samurai** 1954

A totally different kind of adventure film is Akira Kurosawa's THE SEVEN SAMURAI. It is a classic action movie following the exploits of a group of men accomplishing an impossible mission at great expense—i.e., the death of most of the adventurers. We have seen this story many times, in Peckinpah's THE WILD BUNCH, Brooks' THE PROFESSIONALS, Aldrich's THE DIRTY DOZEN, etc., but never in the history of the cinema have we seen it told so well, with such intensity and passion.

ONLY ANGELS HAVE WINGS is a confined entertainment. THE SEVEN SAMURAI is a vast work of art. While Hawks is concerned with the psychology of adventurers, Kurosawa is concerned with their physical exploits. Both pictures deal with camaraderie and the code of men under stress, but while Hawks demonstrates the meaning of the code, Kurosawa shows it in full practice, played out, literally, on the battlefield. Intelligence, bravery, physical superiority, self-sacrifice—the "male" values are all here, imbedded in a great outdoor action picture. THE SEVEN SAMURAI is about the vanity of human endeavor: how the brave and the mighty, who dare risk all to perform exemplary deeds and who fling themselves into life without caution, must always lose in the end, before the timeless circles of existence as played out by lesser men.

It is ironic that this best-loved of all Japanese films has rarely been seen at its original three-hour, twenty-minute length, and doubly ironic that the worst of three butchered versions was distributed in the United States under the title, THE MAGNIFICENT SEVEN, only to be withdrawn in 1960, when John Sturges made a picture with the same title, transposing Kurosawa's story to the American West. (The only resemblance between Takashi Shimura and Yul Brynner is that they both have shaven heads.) Such are the vicissitudes of filmmaking. For a long time the original of THE SEVEN SAMURAI was thought to have been lost, but now that it has finally been uncovered, we can only marvel at the fact that it stands up for every one of its two hundred minutes, a feat most rare in the history of the very long film, and certainly not true of the most famous of "lost" originals, the full-length GREED.

Kurosawa has said of THE SEVEN SAMURAI: "I wanted to make a film which would be entertaining enough to eat." After a year of difficult shooting ("we didn't have enough horses;...it rained all the time"), clashes of temperament, threats by Toho Studios to close down the production, and the expenditure of over half a million dollars (which, till then, was the greatest sum ever spent on a Japanese movie), Kurosawa had in his hands an extraordinary vision, which he proceeded to edit himself.

Kurosawa had created what amounted to a film repertory company. His actors and technicians had worked with him over and over again, and the essence of this sort of collaboration (unique in the world, with the exception of Bergman's group in Sweden) was that he was able to put his vision onto film as close as possible to the way he harbored it in his mind.

With this sort of atmosphere, and the addition of many innovative techniques (a consistent and audacious use of the long lens to telescope action, give the impression that men moving toward the camera are running in place, and thus bring action into the viewer's lap; constantly tracking and panning his camera; and a surprising use of slow motion in the early reels during moments of great stress), Kurosawa was able to create a universe, people it with characters from his imagination, set them against one another in a story of conflict, and stage all action so that his film forecloses any extraneous thoughts that might cross a viewer's mind. With THE SEVEN SAMURAI he literally possesses us, grabs hold of our attention, and does not let it go until the last frame has faded from the screen. As Pauline Kael has written: "Kurosawa achieves... the excitement of the senses."

One of the impressive things about this picture is that we always know precisely what is going on, even in the last rapid and chaotic moments of combat, when much of the action is obscured by a driving rainstorm, the cutting is swift, and the camera is constantly in motion. This is partly the result of Kurosawa's skill as an action director, his use of multiple cameras for each scene, and also his use of a clever map of the village and its defenses. The device enables Shimura to explain his tactics simply and to record the progress of the fight by brushing out a symbol each time an enemy bandit is killed.

(If anyone should question the importance of this point, he need only look at Richardson's THE CHARGE OF THE LIGHT BRIGADE, in which the culminating battle scenes are so badly staged that it is impossible to know what is happening, and, for that matter, who is fighting whom.)

Among the superlative moments of action in this film: the duel when we first see Kyuzo, the master swordsman; the awe of the villagers when they go to town and see the samurai marching back and forth on the streets, swords over their shoulders; Toshiro Mifune's antics when he goes out to steal a rifle from the bandits (his sloppy and comic adventure is beautifully contrasted with Kyuzo's austere approach to the same mission); and, of course, always the battles—great swirling contests of charging horses, rushing enemies, thrusting spears, fired arrows, and slashing swords, including an incredible final sequence in wind and rain.

Woven into all this action are subtle intimations of character. We know and understand each of the seven samurai, and are particularly fascinated by Mifune, the half-comic, half-serious madman whom we finally come to understand the best. His finest character scene is so moving that it bears description in detail.

Mifune has discovered that the villagers have

Six of THE SEVEN SAMURAI in Akira Kurosawa's remarkable film. Takashi Shimura is at left. Toshiro Mifune, whose performance is one of the greatest in Japanese film history, is second from right. Bottom: Bandits attack the village defenses.

Furious action and fantastic battle sequences form the backbone of THE SEVEN SAMURAI. But the film is rich, too, in characterization and in philosophical dialogue on the doomed role of the superior samurai and the survival of the downtrodden farmers. Below: Shino and Katsushiro in love scene. Opposite: At burial of Heihachi, Mifune plunges sword into grave mound. Above & right: Typical scenes. Kurosawa revels in the use of telephoto shots of men running toward his camera; illusion of running in place may suggest his attitude toward violence and war.

3

secreted away many samurai weapons and suits of armor. He brings these things to the other six, who are instantly appalled, since they know that these objects were stripped off dead samurai, whom the villagers, their employers, may even have killed. Mifune answers them in a stunning speech, most of it addressed to the lens of the camera, so that we feel he is speaking to us, too.

"Well, what do you think farmers are? Saints? They are the most cunning and untrustworthy animals on earth. If you ask them for rice, they'll say they have none. But they have! They have everything! Look in the rafters. Dig in the ground. You'll find rice, salt, beans, sake. Look in the mountains—there are farms hidden everywhere. And yet they pretend to be oppressed. They are full of lies. When they smell a battle they make bamboo spears and then they hunt. They hunt down the wounded and defeated. Farmers are miserly, craven, mean, stupid, murderous. You make me laugh so hard I'm crying. But then who made animals out of them? You! You samurai! All of you damned samurai! And each time you fight you burn villages and destroy fields, steal food, rape women, enslave men. You kill them when they resist—you damned samurai!"

Mifune has delivered this speech while shouting, crying, laughing, full of hate and spite and irony and compassion. It is a fantastic scene, because after it we know that he is a farmer's son who, sickened by the craven cowardice of farmers, and wishing to be proud and noble, has proclaimed himself a samurai warrior. Yet at the same time he hates being a samurai, because he knows that the cowardice of farmers is caused by them. Thus his character is boxed. All his snorting bravado, his enormous rage, huge stamina, and boundless humor come out of the pressure of this paradox. Here, in the midst of a film of action and high adventure, we find a revelation of character as profound as any in any film made anywhere. This is Kurosawa's art: a rare combination of fully developed characters participating in violent action.

## John Huston's **The Treasure of the Sierra Madre** 1948

THE SEVEN SAMURAI deals with the impossible mission. Another great theme is the search for treasure. Here, again, a group of men face an ordeal where courage, stamina, and sacrifice must carry them through. THE TREASURE OF THE SIERRA MADRE is a story about a search for treasure, but the adventurers do not measure up to their ordeal. THE TREASURE OF THE SIERRA MADRE is a picture about the breakdown of the adventurer's code. Under pressure the principal character becomes cowardly and selfish, the adventure fails, the treasure is lost, the camaraderie dissolves. As an action film THE TREASURE OF THE SIERRA MADRE works extremely well; it holds the audience by providing vicarious exhilaration. But there is more to it than that. Besides being an action picture it is a psychological thriller with a moral bias, always human and never allegorical.

Indisputably, the success of the picture is due to the talents of its writer/director, John Huston, and its star, Humphrey Bogart, who collaborated on no less than six films over a period of fifteen years. Bogart's performance in THE TREASURE OF THE SIERRA MADRE is unique in his career. In the course of two hours we see him change from a likable and fair-minded guy on the bum, into a nervous paranoic, and finally into a madman capable of killing his best friend in cold blood. And the cause of his deterioration is gold, the cursed metal whose quest is the plot and whose ability to corrupt is the story of the film.

In an early scene, Bogart is sitting in a flophouse in Tampico, Mexico, with his friend Curt, listening as a wiry old prospector named Howard (Walter Huston, the director's father) says that once a man has had a taste of gold, he is never satisfied until he has more. "No," says Bogart, "that wouldn't happen to me—not to Fred C. Dobbs." Thus the theme of the movie is laid bare. Despite fair warning of what is to come, Dobbs is corrupted and then devoured by greed. His gold destroys him, and at the end, insane with fear and thirst, he is cornered and slaughtered by ruthless bandits, and his treasure is scattered to the winds.

The production of TREASURE was an adventure in itself. Huston had wanted to make the film for years, and chose it as his first production after returning from World War II, where he had honed his craft making documentaries for the Army. He wrote a screenplay based on the novel by the elusive author B. Traven. Huston mailed his screenplay to Traven, and when he received back a long letter, he asked to meet with the author to further discuss the filming of his book. He was instructed to appear at the Hotel Reforma in Mexico City for an interview. Huston waited there several days, but Traven



Hand-to-hand combat in a driving rainstorm: Spears are thrust, arrows fired, horses slip, and swords slash in the phenomenal climactic battle as samurai lead embattled peasants to victory over the bandits — perhaps the greatest action sequence ever filmed.

Bottom, far right: John Huston, director of THE TREASURE OF THE SIERRA MADRE, sits between Humphrey Bogart and father Walter Huston. Both Hustons won Academy awards, John for screenplay and direction, Walter as best supporting actor. Above (on burro): Alfonso Bedoya scored in small, juicy role of Gold Hat, the sinister Mexican bandit.

didn't show up. As he was about to return to Hollywood a man handed him a card which read "H. Croves, translator, Acapulco," and a note from Traven saying, "This man knows my work better than I do." Huston hired "Croves" as a technical advisor on the film, but throughout the production "Croves" refused to be photographed. When the filming was over Huston somehow got hold of a rare photograph of Traven and showed it to Bogart. "That's Croves," said Bogart, but the "mysterious" author had disappeared and Huston never saw him again.

The film was one of the first major postwar Hollywood productions to be shot entirely on location, for which Huston had to have the special permission of Jack L. Warner, president of Warner Bros. The shooting was difficult and the conditions primitive. While Huston was casting extras his Mexican production manager told him that the men would normally receive ten pesos a day, but if Huston was willing to pay them fifty, he could shoot them in an arm or a leg. He was warned, however, that they were not to be killed!

There were many battles with the studio as costs mounted to nearly $3 million and Jack Warner insisted that the Bogart character not die. (Huston's early films always seemed to climax in difficult and bitter fights with his backers. Then, for a long period, he seemed to lose his will to fight and became involved in mediocre projects.)

B. Traven's novel rambles along through a thicket of Marxism, while Huston's film is a direct and hard-hitting attack on the accumulation of wealth, without once mentioning the word "capital." This may constitute its superiority over Erich von Stroheim's GREED. Stroheim hits his audience over the head with a long, ambitious attempt to make a Great Statement. Huston conceals his statement in a comparatively modest and austere story of believable characters, whose obsession grips the audience and becomes their own. In THE TREASURE OF THE SIERRA MADRE we seldom feel that we are watching a "message film." The picture is pure entertainment, and its ironic ending, in which the gold dug out with such difficulty blows back into the hills where it was mined, is barely tarnished by the final echoing laughter of Walter Huston on the sound track. This laughter may represent less the irony of John Huston than the triumph of a wise old man whose predictions have come true.

The film is striking for its purity of technique—its clean cuts and avoidance of tricky angles and attention-calling shots. Its sense of movement is as great a credit to Huston the screenwriter as it is to Huston the director. His construction is economical, spare, always correct. We feel that each shot and each scene is exactly as it should be.

Many of the moments in THE TREASURE OF THE SIERRA MADRE have become classic: the glint in Bogart's eyes as Walter Huston weighs out the gold; the night the three adventurers decide that each man will take care of his own "goods"; Walter Huston's trusting look back when he is taken off by peaceful Indians; the shadow of the desperado, Gold Hat, when he appears behind Bogart at the water hole; the way the bandits seem to pick over Bogart, even before they kill him.

There is one sequence that is rarely mentioned, and that seems to sum up the artistry of this film especially well. This occurs when Gold Hat and the remnants of his band go into town to sell Bogart's burros. Someone spots a brand on one of the burros, a boy runs to the police, people in the marketplace stall the thieves, surround them, and then turn them over to the Federales for immediate execution. The scenes goes on for nearly a reel, the entire dialogue is in Spanish, not one word of English is spoken, and yet every moment is comprehensible, and we are never really aware that we are listening to a foreign language. In a scene like this, Huston is telling his story visually, at the highest level of film art.

## Michael Curtiz' **Casablanca** 1943

The Casablanca of CASABLANCA is a unique piece of fictional turf. The picture opens on maps while a narrator explains that Casablanca is the second-last resting place on the long, tortuous refugee route from war-torn Europe. (The last resting place is Lisbon; the mecca is New York.) As one character puts it: "The scum of Europe has gravitated to Casablanca." Another says: "Human beings... they're Casablanca's leading commodity." "In Casablanca," says the Nazi Major Strasser, summing it all up, "human life is cheap." It is a place, in short, where anything is possible and everything is negotiable, a place of drama, adventure, and intrigue, a place where a man may be shot on the street in front of a portrait of Marshal Pétain, or where an attractive young lady may secure an exit visa by spending the night with the Préfet de Police.

The center of the action in this world is Rick's

Humphrey Bogart in his quintessential adventurer's role, posing before Rick's Café Américain in a publicity still for CASABLANCA. Rick's café is an arena of incredible adventures, harboring arrogant Nazis, Free French, black marketeers, idealists, murderers, refugees, and S. Z. Sakall.

As Time Goes By: Bogart presides over his domain
while Dooley Wilson plays piano. Center: Bogart with Paul Henreid,
Ingrid Bergman, and Claude Rains. Bottom: Bogart about
to kill Major Strasser (Conrad Veidt). Opposite: Bogart
and Bergman in one of their "with-the-whole-world-crumbling-
we-pick-this-time-to-fall-in-love" moods.

Café Américain, conveniently located across the street from the airport, which is where most of the people in Casablanca want to go. Rick's café is an incredible place, owned and operated by Humphrey Bogart, a combination bar, night club, and gambling casino, where the pastry chef formerly was the leading banker of Amsterdam, and where the rooms seethe with conspiracies, black-market activities, and plots and counterplots of all sorts. A member of the Free French underground circulates with a ring that conceals a Cross of Lorraine; a marvelous black singer-pianist named Sam plays nostalgic tunes; and the roulette wheel is fixed to stop at number 22 on command.

CASABLANCA is one of the few adventure films where the adventures take place indoors. There are no fights, no outdoor adventures here. There are, instead, adventures of verbal jousting, of dialogue and innuendo, and they are dominated, in fact ruled, by a supreme adventurer, Rick.

Rick is the quintessential Bogart character, who has absolutely nothing in common with the psychopathic Fred C. Dobbs of THE TREASURE OF THE SIERRA MADRE. He is more urbane than Sam Spade in THE MALTESE FALCON or Philip Marlowe in THE BIG SLEEP. The Bogart of CASABLANCA is the Bogart who has been posthumously idealized by the young, resurrected by them from a temporary oblivion.

In the 1940s, audiences who attended Bogart films thought of him as a good actor who appeared in interesting movies. Since the mid-1950s, however, when informally arranged Bogart festivals were booked into college movie theatres, he has been rediscovered and his cult born. Youngsters had never seen his like before. They adored him, the way he smoked and talked out of the corner of his mouth and held a gun as if he knew how it worked and meant to use it. Girls found him sexy and young men wished to emulate him. He was idolized for his toughness, his vulnerability, and his implicit freedom. He had the aura of a man who did what he liked doing; he didn't work for wages and he was nobody's patsy. Of all the Bogart characters (and most of them were facets of the same man), none stirred these young audiences so much as the Bogart of CASABLANCA. Who is this Rick/Bogart? What is his magic? What is the secret of his appeal? Portions of dialogue from CASABLANCA give hints. When added together they make something of a portrait of a supreme adventurer.

His Irony:

Asked to explain why he came to Casablanca, Rick says: "I came to Casablanca for the waters."

"What waters? We're in the desert."

"I was misinformed," he says.

His Politics:

We learn that in 1935 he ran guns to Ethiopia, and in 1936 fought on the Loyalist side in Spain. "I was well paid on both occasions," he says, but the Préfet de Police points out that "the winning side would have paid you twice as much." Rick, we come to understand, is on the Nazi blacklist—their "role of honor."

His Erudition:

Rick is a man who can tell by the sound that a piece of distant artillery is "the new German 77." Listening a little more closely he can estimate its distance from Paris at thirty-five miles "and moving closer every minute."

His Sex Life in Casablanca:

A brief exchange with a girl explains a lot:

"Where were you last night?" she asks.

"That's so long ago I don't remember."

"Will I see you tonight?" she insists.

"I never make plans so far in advance."

His Cynicism:

Twice he says: "I stick out my neck for nobody." When asked who he thinks will win the war, he replies: "I haven't the slightest idea....The problems of the world are not my department—I'm a saloon keeper," he says. And on another occasion, when pressed for a commitment, he replies: "Your business is politics—mine is running a saloon."

His Fastidiousness:

He never drinks with his customers.

His Sentimentality:

To Ingrid Bergman in Paris: "With the whole world crumbling we pick this time to fall in love...."

To Bergman and her husband at the Casablanca airport: "The problems of three little people don't amount to a hill of beans in this crazy world."

His Pain:

The look on his face when he throws away Ingrid Bergman's letter as his train pulls out of Paris. (The rain has washed away the ink of her hurtful words.)

The look on his face when Ingrid Bergman appears in his café. "Of all the gin joints in all the towns in all the world," he says, "she walks into mine."

His Bitterness:

When he accuses Ingrid Bergman of having had other lovers: "Were there others in between? Or aren't you the kind that tells?"

His Urbanity:

"What is your nationality?" asks Major Strasser.

"I'm a drunkard," says Rick.

His Mystique:

Claude Rains explains it to Ingrid Bergman: "Rick is the kind of man that if I were a woman I would be in love with Rick."

Bogart dominates CASABLANCA, but there are other characters too, fascinating ones, revealed at breathtaking speed in the first few reels, delineated clearly by snatches of their own dialogue, by comments others make about them, or by their own peculiar and very striking presences:

Claude Rains, the police prefect, infinitely charming, infinitely corrupt: "I blow with the wind; the prevailing wind blows from Vichy."

Conrad Veidt, the Nazi major who has come to Casablanca to impose the influence of the Gestapo: "You speak of the Third Reich as if you expect there to be a fourth."

Paul Henreid, the goody-goody character, underground resistance leader, Bergman's husband, stiff and pompous. As Claude Rains says of him: "He succeeded in impressing half the world; it's my job to see that he doesn't impress the other half." At the same time that Henreid refuses to tell the names of the underground leaders in the capitals of Europe, he assures Veidt that if the men are caught "from every corner of Europe hundreds, thousands will rise up to take their places."

Sidney Greenstreet, owner of the Blue Parrot and chief of the black market: "As the leader of all illegal activities in Casablanca, I am an influential and respected man."

Peter Lorre, a psychotic, two-bit black marketeer and murderer: "You despise me," he says to Rick. "I trust you because you despise me."

A girl who has apparently slept with every man in the story: "In her own way she may constitute an extra second front."

A refugee couple: "We hear very little and we understand even less."

Ingrid Bergman, Bogart's lover: She is simply there—beautiful, soft, remote, warm, mysterious, the impossible object of an impossible romance, the dream lover of every man.

Of course, the interaction of these adventurers results in some moments of pure corn: the Paris flashbacks; the Marseillaise versus the Horst Wessel Song sequence; the "Here's looking at you, kid," toasts; the "Play it, Sam" pleas of Ingrid Bergman; the discarded bottle of Vichy water at the end; the line of Paul Henreid: "Welcome back to the fight. This time I know our side will win"; and the lyrics of "As Time Goes By." But all this corn is delivered with enormous style, and is satisfying in an uncanny way. It is conventional now to admire CASABLANCA for its camp qualities. "It's so good it's bad," is what a lot of people like to say. Actually, CASABLANCA is good on its own merits. It is extremely well written and very well directed by Michael Curtiz. The two long sequences at Rick's Café, in which a dozen characters and nine or ten subplots are developed with wit and clarity, are unbeatable examples of shorthand storytelling. Obviously, it is not a work of art, but just as obviously it is a masterpiece of entertainment.

CASABLANCA was big when it opened thirty years ago, a week before the wartime Casablanca Conference, and it has been big ever since, particularly on campuses. In fact, it is possible that CASABLANCA has ruined the summer vacations of many college students who have gone to the city expecting to find the glamor and excitement of the movie, and have found instead a huge, impersonal metropolis, the Chicago of Morocco.

# David Lean's **Lawrence of Arabia** 1962

*I consider myself an entertainer. . . .*
*I like a good strong story. I like a beginning,*
*a middle, and an end. . . . I like to be*
*excited when I go to the movies.*

*—David Lean, in an interview on the CBC, March, 1965.*

No amount of critical analysis will sum up the aesthetic of David Lean better than that quotation. Lean does not merely pay lip service to well-constructed, exciting stories. He makes them. His greatest achievement, in a career that has included the poignant romance, BRIEF ENCOUNTER (1946), the splendid period film, GREAT EXPECTATIONS (1947), and the great war picture, THE BRIDGE ON THE RIVER KWAI (1957), is undoubtedly LAWRENCE OF ARABIA, the adventure film of adventure films, one of the best-constructed and most exciting adventure stories ever to fill a screen.

LAWRENCE OF ARABIA has in common with THE SEVEN SAMURAI a rare combination of deep character penetration and enormous epic sweep. It is a masterpiece of

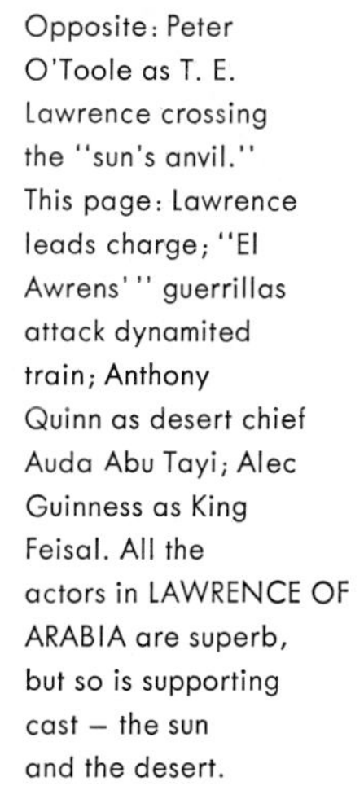

Opposite: Peter O'Toole as T. E. Lawrence crossing the "sun's anvil." This page: Lawrence leads charge; "El Awrens'" guerrillas attack dynamited train; Anthony Quinn as desert chief Auda Abu Tayi; Alec Guinness as King Feisal. All the actors in LAWRENCE OF ARABIA are superb, but so is supporting cast — the sun and the desert.

intimate moment and spectacular largesse. But while THE SEVEN SAMURAI is about a group of men, LAWRENCE OF ARABIA is the story of a solitary adventurer who lived, was romanticized, and has lately been debunked. Throughout the picture one has a sense of a man discovering his own unique dimensions. Lawrence always knew he was different, but in Arabia he discovered that his proportions were heroic. Perhaps this is the secret of LAWRENCE OF ARABIA—that at the bottom of all the violent action is a protagonist about whom one cares, an intriguing, enigmatic personality whom one glimpses but never fully understands.

All the conventional elements of the genre are at peaks of excellence here: a difficult terrain (the desert—when Lawrence leads men across the sun's anvil we pant with thirst); danger (it is everywhere, for LAWRENCE OF ARABIA is a film about guerrilla warfare); prowess (Lawrence crosses Sinai on foot!); torture (Lawrence in the hands of the Turkish bey); an impossible mission (to take Aqaba from behind); a rescue (Lawrence returns to the sun's anvil to pick up a man who has fallen from his camel); ruthlessness (Lawrence must kill the man he saved to give justice to his Arab allies; he shouts "take no prisoners" when his men decimate a Turkish column); austerity (Lawrence is an adventurer uninterested in possessions; for him glory is enough and he even renounces that when he returns to England and seeks anonymity); the subordinate role of women (there are none in the film, unless one counts the nurse who appears at the end and speaks one line). Every component is here, everything one needs for a great adventure film, and in addition there is a fascinating pivotal character whose mystery is grasped though never solved.

The usual complaint against David Lean is what some critics call his "impersonal style." What they really are objecting to is his superlative technique, craftsmanship that never calls attention to itself, but always serves the telling of his stories. LAWRENCE OF ARABIA represents an enormous achievement, a film, like THE SEVEN SAMURAI, that literally excites the senses.

There are many spectacular sequences in LAWRENCE OF ARABIA, each of them flawless: Lawrence's trek to rescue the fallen man (Lean cuts to the sun again and again, turning it into a character); the scene in Feisal's tent when Lawrence first talks with the King (as the characters pace and move into different pools of light the camera tracks back and forth with at least a dozen changes of focus, but the conversation flows with an effortless grace that obscures the technical accomplishment); Lawrence striding on top of a captured train, parading before rows of cheering Arabs; Lawrence in his encounters with Allenby and Bentley (to Allenby he confesses discovering a perverse pleasure in killing; when Bentley asks him what attracts him personally to the desert, he looks the man up and down and says, "It's clean"); the scene when Ali Ibn el Kharish (Omar Sharif) appears on his camel, an excruciatingly long take in which an ominous figure is first resolved out of waves of heat and then, as he draws closer, becomes a deadly threat to Lawrence's escort; the great slaughter scene when Lawrence discovers himself caked with blood and becomes horrified at the barbarism lurking beneath his civilized veneer; and the scene between Lawrence and Jose Ferrer illuminating Lawrence's strange perversity, a mixture of masochism and repressed homosexuality. (Some critics have complained that this scene is a copout because Lean doesn't show what happened. It is difficult to know what they want to see, why a literal act of sodomy is necessary when Lawrence's look and gestures, before and after, make absolutely clear what took place.)

There is not much more one can say about LAWRENCE OF ARABIA other than that it meets every test of the great adventure film and passes it with honors. The photography by Freddy Young, the script by Robert Bolt, and the acting by Peter O'Toole, Alec Guinness, Anthony Quinn, Jack Hawkins, Jose Ferrer, Anthony Quayle, Claude Rains, Arthur Kennedy, and Omar Sharif are so superb that LAWRENCE becomes one of the very rare breed, the superexpensive picture that is also good, the lavish spectacle that is deep, the big film that didn't get away from the director whose control one can feel in every frame.

Director David Lean (in white hat) on location in Jordan during filming of LAWRENCE. Raid on Aqaba and blasting of railroad were shot in Spain, slaughter of Turks in Morocco. Scenes of Cairo, Damascus, and Jerusalem, which had become too modern for period of film, were recreated in Seville.

# Credits

## Only Angels Have Wings

U.S.A.; 1939; 121 minutes;
released by Columbia.

**Directed by** Howard Hawks.
**Produced by** Howard Hawks.
**Screenplay by** Jules Furthman, from a story by Howard Hawks.
**Photographed by** Elmer Dyer and Joseph Walker.
**Art direction by** Lionel Banks.
**Edited by** Viola Lawrence.
**Music by** Dimitri Tiomkin and Morris W. Stoloff.
**Cast:** Cary Grant; Jean Arthur; Richard Barthelmess; Rita Hayworth; Thomas Mitchell; Sig Rumann; Victor Kilian; John Carrol; Allyn Joslyn; Donald Barry; Noah Beery, Jr.

## The Seven Samurai (Shichinin No Samurai)

Japan; 1954; 200 minutes;
released by Toho.

**Directed by** Akira Kurosawa.
**Produced by** Shojiro Motoki.
**Screenplay by** Shinobu Hashimoto, Hideo Oguni, and Akira Kurosawa.
**Photographed by** Asakazu Nakai.
**Art direction by** So Matsuyama.
**Edited by** Akira Kurosawa.
**Music by** Fumio Hayasaka.
**Cast:** Toshiro Mifune; Takashi Shimura; Yoshio Inaba; Seiji Miyaguchi; Minoru Chiaki; Daisuke Kato; Ko Kimura; Kunmnori Kodo; Kamatari Fujiwara; Yoshio Tsuchiya; Keiko Tsushima; Yukiko Shimazaki.

## The Treasure of the Sierra Madre

U.S.A.; 1948; 126 minutes;
released by Warner Bros.

**Directed by** John Huston.
**Produced by** Henry Blanke.
**Screenplay by** John Huston, from a novel by B. Traven.
**Photographed by** Ted McCord.
**Art direction by** John Hughes.
**Edited by** Owen Marks.
**Music by** Max Steiner.
**Cast:** Humphrey Bogart; Walter Huston; Tim Holt; Bruce Bennett; Alfonso Bedoya; Barton MacLane.

## Casablanca

U.S.A.; 1943; 102 minutes;
released by Warner Bros.

**Directed by** Michael Curtiz.
**Produced by** Hal B. Wallis.
**Screenplay by** Julius J. and Philip G. Epstein and Howard Koch.
**Photographed by** Arthur Edeson.
**Art direction by** Carl Jules Weyl.
**Edited by** Don Siegel and James Leicester.
**Music by** Max Steiner.
**Cast:** Humphrey Bogart; Ingrid Bergman; Claude Rains; Paul Henreid; Conrad Veidt; Sidney Greenstreet; Peter Lorre; Marcel Dalio; Helmut Dantine; Dooley Wilson; S. Z. Sakall; Joy Page; Leonid Kinsky; Madelaine LeBeau; John Qualen.

## Lawrence of Arabia

Great Britain; 1962; 221 minutes;
released by Columbia.

**Directed by** David Lean.
**Produced by** Sam Spiegel.
**Screenplay by** Robert Bolt.
**Photographed by** F. A. Young.
**Art direction by** John Box.
**Edited by** Anne Coates.
**Music by** Maurice Jarre.
**Cast:** Peter O'Toole; Alec Guinness; Anthony Quinn; Jack Hawkins; Jose Ferrer; Anthony Quayle; Claude Rains; Arthur Kennedy; Donald Wolfit; Omar Sharif.

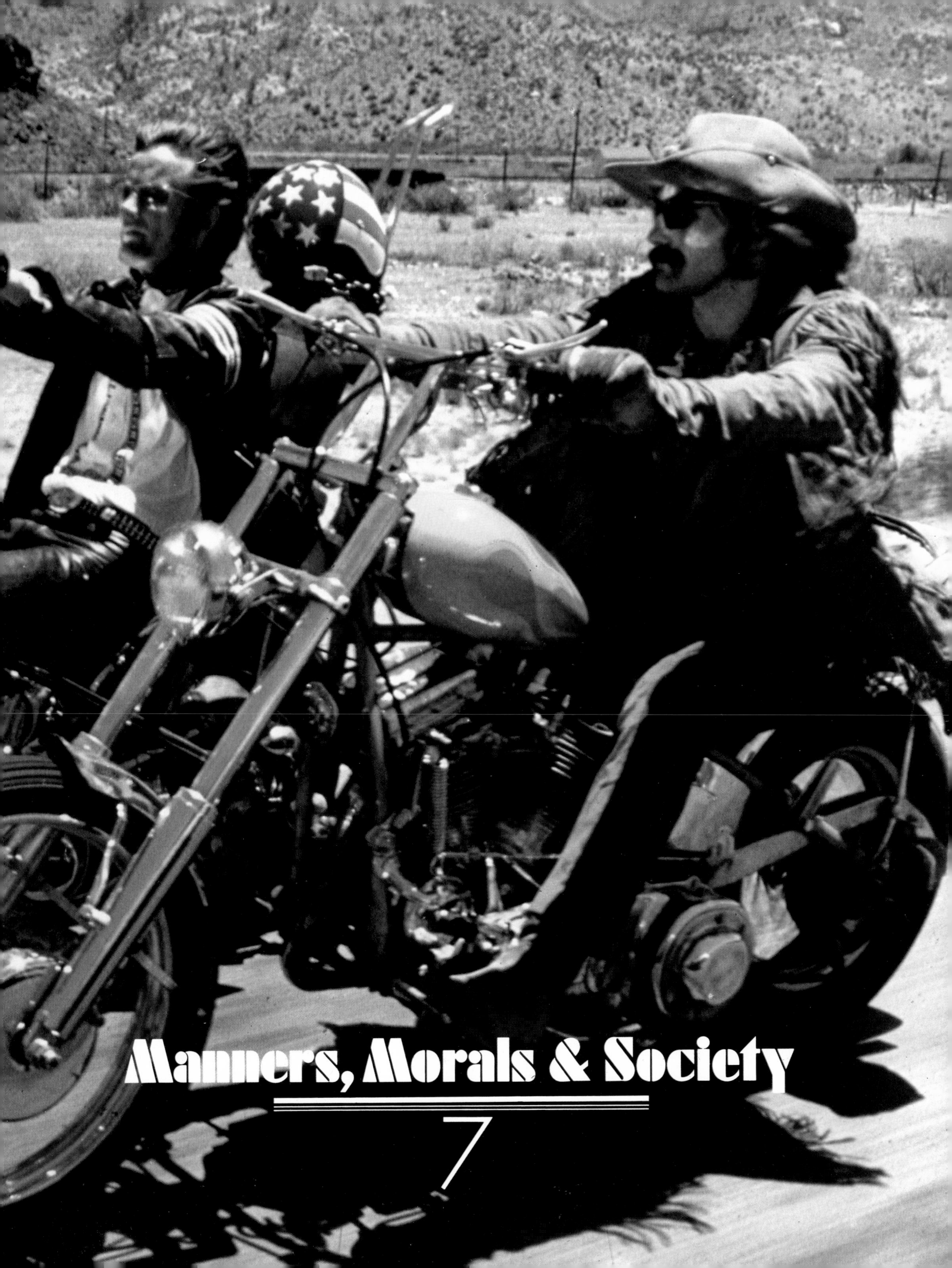

# Manners, Morals & Society

7

"Manners, Morals and Society" is not, of course, a classic motion-picture genre. It is a phrase that serves as a catchall, a means of linking pictures whose makers enjoyed a common desire to describe a social milieu. These are not the "message films" that take positions on specific issues or speak for those who have no voice. They are dealt with later on, in a chapter on "The Cinema of Concern." Here the focus is on movies which express filmmakers' visions of society, in widely varying styles and at different levels of artistic achievement.

This matter of artistry may present a problem. It is a fair question to ask why a sublime work like RULES OF THE GAME should be linked in any way with so crude a work as EASY RIDER. The question begs an answer. Otherwise, it might seem as though some fragile link between fine and popular art is being forged in order that the author might secure himself a base in each of the two great opposing critical camps, the camp of the highbrows, oriented toward the art cinema of Europe, and the camp of the slobs, who exult in the pop cinema of Hollywood.

Let that charge now be firmly met. The fact that the vision of Jean Renoir is refined and complex, and the vision of Dennis Hopper is crude and simplistic, has no bearing when it comes to judging the emotional strength of their respective works. It is the contention here that these distinctions are not relevant to "greatness." Who would now say that a "great" painting by Raphael is either better or worse than a "great" primitive sculpture by an unknown African Bushman? However wide the gulf between RULES OF THE GAME and EASY RIDER in matters of quality, style, and commercial success, they share an intensity that is rarely found in film.

Intensity—that, ultimately, was the basis for choosing the pictures in this chapter. Each of them is an enormously powerful vision of society, a picture which once seen cannot be shaken from the mind.

## Jean Renoir's **Rules of the Game** 1939

RULES OF THE GAME is a social comedy in the tradition of certain classics of the French theatre, the comedies of manners of Beaumarchais and Marivaux. An opening title protests that "This entertainment... does not aspire to be a study of morals"—a protestation one must rapidly dispute. Morals, or rather the absence of them, is what the picture is all about.

Renoir has spoken of his mood at the time he conceived the film: "It was between Munich and the beginning of the Second World War, and I was deeply disturbed by the state of mind of French society and the world in general." Clearly, he is referring to the well-known aimlessness and social corruption of that period, the macabre dance of a society headed for cataclysm. (His use of Saint-Saëns' "Danse Macabre" during the fête sequence is a stroke of genius.)

Rather than express his distress directly in the form of a serious protest film, Renoir decided to use the more subtle form of the comedy of manners. A large number of characters, representing many types, are confined in the Château la Colinière. In this miniature universe they become a ship of fools, and play out the manners and morals of society at large in a diverting, farcical, and tragic-grotesque style. In RULES OF THE GAME, Renoir does not allow us to identify too closely with any single individual. Rather, he paints on a broad canvas which we observe from an amused distance. And, as in French plays of this sort, when we laugh at the posturings of the characters we are really laughing at ourselves.

Like LA GRANDE ILLUSION, RULES OF THE GAME is an enigmatic title, a device of which Renoir, in the thirties, was especially fond. Just as the first question about LA GRANDE ILLUSION is what, exactly, is the "great illusion," so the first problem of RULES OF THE GAME is to identify the "game" and to understand what is meant by the word "rules."

The game is life. Life becomes a game in a society when human behavior has no meaning beyond pleasure and diversion. The rules are the manners and morals, the social code, by which such a society expects its members to live. In the world of La Colinière these rules are closely allied with the metaphor of poaching. There is no morality, everyone cheats, everyone trespasses, everyone lies. Politeness is more important than sincerity. Being amusing is more important than being honorable. Discretion and charm are highly valued, commitment and honesty are in disrepute. The Marquis de la Chesnaye rescues the rabbit-poacher Marceau from the clutches of his gamekeeper Schumacher, and hires him to serve inside the house where he poaches on Schumacher's wife. The aviator, Jurieu, who has himself been poaching on la Chesnaye's wife, Christine, no longer can abide a hypocritical



Preceding pages: Peter Fonda as Wyatt and Dennis Hopper as Billy discover America on choppers in Hopper's EASY RIDER. Despite dubious values, such as dope-selling heroes, film was an enormous hit, created the myth of "youth-oriented films." Opposite: Actor-director Jean Renoir in RULES OF THE GAME.

relationship; he wants to marry Christine after settling the matter honorably with la Chesnaye. The great irony of the film is that the two characters, Schumacher and Jurieu, who live by the rules of an earlier time, when personal honor was paramount and poaching in all its forms was a crime, become the protagonists in the final tragedy. Schumacher shoots Jurieu after a series of absurd misunderstandings. When Jurieu is killed, la Chesnaye informs the other guests that there has been a "deplorable accident"—a startling euphemism for a grotesque tragedy that is the logical ending to a preposterous tale. The game is finished because two of the players, Schumacher and Jurieu, played by different rules.

RULES OF THE GAME is an admirably complex picture in which a number of characters are closely observed and an exceedingly large number of subplots are intricately entwined. The parallel lines of the story, scenes between nobles and scenes between servants, games played at the top of society and at the bottom, are reconciled at the end when the social boundaries merge and Schumacher kills Jurieu. It is not just the upper class that is on display in RULES OF THE GAME. It is the entire world whose blurred stratification was mourned by Boeldieu and Rauffenstein in LA GRANDE ILLUSION.

Much has been written about Jean Renoir's improvisatory methods, carried further in RULES OF THE GAME than in any of his other films. He and his writers share credit for the script with the members of the cast. Evidently, much of the dialogue and many of the characterizations were worked out during shooting. The spirit of collaboration, inspired by Renoir, may account for the picture's extraordinarily fine ensemble playing.

Special mention must be made of Marcel Dalio's performance as the Marquis de la Chesnaye. He is the central character, master of the château, arbiter of the world of La Colinière. Strange, at times absurd, almost desperately polite, he loves and collects automatons, and yet is able to make tenuous contact with human beings. Because his lies are softened by the style with which he lives them, he ultimately becomes a sympathetic character, perhaps the most rounded in the story.

In an interview with Dalio and Renoir made by French television in 1961 at locations where the picture was shot, actor and director reminisce and then agree that in the brief instant when la Chesnaye stands before his huge mechanical organ, his entire character is revealed, a "mixture of humility and pride, of success and doubt." Renoir goes as far as to say that those few seconds amount to "the best shot I've done in my life." This tells us much about Jean Renoir. To him the human being is the essential element in a film; the quality of an actor's performance is always more important than some use of the camera that will dazzle the audience, call attention to the director, and distract from the revelation of character.

The hunting scene and the fête are the two remarkable sequences in the film. At the hunt we are again confronted with a game played by certain rules. While servants beat the forest trees with sticks, driving birds and rabbits from their nests and holes, the nobles wait at their stations with ready guns. Renoir dwells upon the death throes of these little animals, the way their bodies crumple and twitch, until he evokes enormous anguish and pain. To those involved in this hunt, an extraordinary combination of pictorial beauty and merciless slaughter, the massacre is another game.

The fête is a grand farce, or rather a combination of so many farces that when le Chesnaye tells his majordomo to "Get this comedy stopped!", the confused Corneille must ask his master, "Which one, Monsieur le Marquis?" While Schumacher chases Marceau through the chateau and fires his revolver, the guests think it is just another of the amusing little skits that have been organized for their pleasure. At the fête, La Colinière becomes a merry-go-round: happenings, relationships, misunderstandings, and fights flare up and explode at breathtaking speed.

One marvels at the intensity of Renoir's vision, and his ability to filter his dismay through irony and present it in a classical theatrical form. Only a Frenchman could have made RULES OF THE GAME, and only Frenchmen could hate it. When the picture opened in Paris in 1939 it was poorly received. Audiences booed and hissed, and a perplexed Renoir, watching from the projection booth, could not still the furor no matter how many cuts and changes he made. Something about his vision cut too deep. During the Occupation the film was confiscated and banned, and in 1942 the original negative was destroyed when the GM film laboratories were hit by Allied bombs. After the war the picture could only be seen in mutilated prints until two Frenchmen, Jean Gaborit and Jacques Durand, reassembled it in 1958 from bits and pieces into its original form. The world owes these gentlemen an extraordinary debt.

Aristocrats and servants play various "games" by various "rules" in Jean Renoir's brilliant film about manners, morals, and society. Renoir acted role of the pompous failure Octave (this page, top). Film was booed at its premiere, was only recognized as a masterpiece when reconstituted twenty years later.

# Orson Welles' **Citizen Kane** 1941

It has been said many times, but let it be said again: Orson Welles' CITIZEN KANE is the greatest film ever made.

Let it also be said that CITIZEN KANE is not perfect. RULES OF THE GAME comes closer to perfection; the minor gem, THE THIRD MAN, is perfection itself. CITIZEN KANE is a work of great excess. It is an extravaganza, and like all extravaganzas it is riddled with imperfections. But it is interesting that when one uncovers and lists its flaws one's admiration remains undiminished. Who really cares that some of the characters recount incidents they could not possibly have observed? What difference does it make to a person sophisticated in film technique that many of the special effects, particularly the miniatures, are technically weak? Who is much bothered by the occasional patches of hokey dialogue, and the few overdrawn characterizations? Give Welles a B for precision, but give him A's for force, bravado, originality, effort, richness of texture, ability to entertain, power to compel, intensity of vision and personal expression. CITIZEN KANE is the greatest film ever made, and that is a fact there is no way around.

CITIZEN KANE is probably the most discussed film of all time. Books have been written about it, and those who are interested in balanced critiques and labored analyses should turn to them. Since almost everything there is to say about CITIZEN KANE has already been said, it seems appropriate to note down some random thoughts.

What is CITIZEN KANE about? It is about William Randolph Hearst, not literally, of course, but in the form of a fictionalized fantasy produced with the intention of exploiting public interest in a controversial man, and becoming, like Welles' "The War of the Worlds," a *succès de scandale*. One of the most delightful things about CITIZEN KANE is the way it uses Hearst against himself. CITIZEN KANE exploits him the way his papers exploited everyone else. CITIZEN KANE is yellow journalism. It sacrifices the truth about Hearst for the sensational aspects of his story.

CITIZEN KANE is also about money and power, aging and time, love and marriage, business and politics, and the futility of human aspirations.

CITIZEN KANE is a mystery story, a search, a quest. One of its themes is that the more one finds out about someone, the less one understands his character.

CITIZEN KANE is a mighty exposition of American society and a devastating critique of the American Dream.

CITIZEN KANE is a version of Faust, the story of a man who gains the world and loses his soul.

CITIZEN KANE is a circus. Many acts take place at once. One is diverted. One is amused. There is a leitmotif of comedy, and an exhilarating razzle-dazzle style. Welles is like a huckster pitching a fantastic notion. We know he is overselling but we are charmed by his spiel.

Orson Welles has said that CITIZEN KANE is "a portrait of a public man's private life," and that may be the best summary of all.

The jigsaw puzzle is the great metaphor of the story. The picture is about a journalist named Thompson trying to work out the puzzle of Charles Foster Kane. He collects various pieces from various persons, but at the end he cannot fit them together. With an actual puzzle in his hand he says: "I guess Rosebud is just a piece in a jigsaw puzzle—a missing piece." Crates of the things that Kane has accumulated in his life lie about like disconnected pieces. The puzzle of Kane, like the giant puzzles that Susan Alexander could never finish, cannot be solved. CITIZEN KANE does not pretend to explain the character of Charles Foster Kane. It offers glimpses but leaves the center murky. Just as it begins with the camera penetrating mists, then passing through the barriers around the mysterious world of Xanadu, so it ends with the camera withdrawing until mists cover the lens. Like the photographer in BLOW-UP, the closer we look the less we see.

Rosebud: It is too glib to call it parlor Freudianism. Rosebud is a powerful idea. The irony of Rosebud, of course, is that it doesn't make any difference that Thompson never finds out what it means. He finds out more on the route of his quest than Rosebud could ever tell him. But having set up Rosebud as the object of a search, Welles cannot leave us dangling. He explains Rosebud in a way that makes it clear that it is not the key piece, but at best a minor fragment of the puzzle. Yet the shot when the camera moves over the crates and toward the furnace where flames lick at the lettering on the sled is one of the most powerful in all of cinema. Those crates are the ruins of a life and say better than any words how greatly Charles Foster Kane had failed.

Some things that CITIZEN KANE is not: It is not the first film to use deep focus; it is not the first to use overlapping dialogue; it did not cost millions of dollars; it was not poorly received by critics when it opened.



Orson Welles, aged twenty-five, made the most impressive debut in cinema history as producer, director, star, and co-author of CITIZEN KANE. Opposite: Kane speaks at rally as candidate for governor before scandal wrecks his political career. This is perhaps the most famous movie still of all time.

KANE

SILENCE

Opposite: Welles at head, Everett Sloane (Bernstein) and Joseph Cotten (Leland) at foot of table. Note depth of field created by cameraman Gregg Toland. This page: Kane becomes newspaper publisher; scene from montage of Kane's failing marriage; Kane's wife (Ruth Warrick) confronts his mistress (Dorothy Comingore); Boss Jim Geddys (Ray Collins) in background.

Some facts about CITIZEN KANE:

Louis B. Mayer offered to reimburse RKO for the cost of the picture, if RKO would destroy its negative and all existing prints. The difference between him and General Hans Speidel is that the general didn't want to go down in history as the man who blew up Paris, but Mayer would have been content to be remembered as the man who destroyed CITIZEN KANE.

The production cost of CITIZEN KANE was either $686,033 or $842,000, depending upon one's source.

The apparently continuous shot when the camera passes through a neon sign, then penetrates a skylight and descends into the "El Rancho" cabaret, was achieved by a combination of miniatures and a life-size set, joined by an invisible cut camouflaged by a flash of lightning and a lap dissolve matched to the misting of the skylight by rain. Of all the virtuoso effects in the film this shot is the most phenomenal. One is tempted to stand up in the theatre and shout to everyone: "My God, Welles' camera has just passed through glass!"

All rumors to the contrary, Orson Welles, not Herman J. Mankiewicz, was responsible for CITIZEN KANE. Film is a collaborative art and many artists contributed to CITIZEN KANE. Without the brilliant camera work of Gregg Toland, the superb music of Bernard Herrmann, the astute editing of Robert Wise and Mark Robson, and the superior performances of the Mercury Theatre Company, CITIZEN KANE would not be the same film. The same thing applies to the work of the sound men and scenic artists at RKO, and the very important contribution of Herman Mankiewicz' screenplay. But CITIZEN KANE is Welles' film. He produced it, he directed it, he stars in it, and he worked on the script. Attempts to prove otherwise are as futile as attempts to prove that Shakespeare did not write Shakespeare's plays. CITIZEN KANE and Orson Welles are inseparable. As annoying as it is that Welles was only twenty-five years old at the time, and as annoying as it is that we cannot all be prodigies and create works of genius, facts are facts and credit must be given where it is due.

CITIZEN KANE is an encyclopedia of the cinema. Its flashbacks, its montages, its deep focus, its sound track, its sets, its structure, its camera moves, its cuts make it a treasury of superb examples of almost everything one can do in a film. One can look at CITIZEN KANE a dozen times and still not mine its riches. One can look at it fifty times —as many people have—and still enjoy its story. Familiarity does not make it tiresome. CITIZEN KANE remains unpredictable at each separate viewing. It is impossible to think of another film that gives so much pleasure so many times.

CITIZEN KANE is not a difficult picture; it is accessible to nearly everyone. Let those who think that a great picture must contain exotic symbols, be produced in a foreign language, and deal with abstract themes, think again. Let those who think that CITIZEN KANE is shallow name a picture that has a scene more profound than that in which Welles smashes up Susan's room.



Top, left: Another example of great depth of field in CITIZEN KANE. Top, right: Camera set up in pit for low-angle shot; KANE is notable for its visible ceilings. Opposite: At Xanadu, Susan Alexander (Dorothy Comingore) works huge jigsaw puzzle which is central metaphor of the film.

One of the great charms of CITIZEN KANE is its flamboyance. Its excesses, its bravado, its look-Ma-no-hands effects are forgivable and actually warm the heart because Welles delivers them with a wink. CITIZEN KANE is not as subtle as LA GRANDE ILLUSION, or as difficult as PERSONA, or as self-effacing as THE SEARCHERS. It proclaims its genius from every frame with the stylishness of a brilliant show-off magician whom we admire for taking enormous risks.

The newsreel sequence: Charles Higham reports that the aging of the early shots was achieved by rubbing the negative with sand. The newsreel, an amusing satire on "The March Of Time," is a brilliant device for the way it provides the structure of Kane's life in linear terms, making the nonlinear puzzle quality of the main body of the film scrutable.

A speculation: CITIZEN KANE is the watershed work of the cinema, approximately halfway between Griffith and now.

A question: Try to think of a personage in contemporary life who would be a suitable model for an updated Kane? Howard Hughes? The late Joseph Kennedy? Lyndon Johnson? Or don't they make them like Hearst anymore?

Another question: If you were the head of a Hollywood studio—not a patron of the arts, but a man concerned with profit and loss—would you give Welles the kind of total freedom he had at RKO, and which he claims he needs to make another masterpiece?

Some thoughts upon watching Orson Welles on a television talk-show: The great filmmaker has become the great pontificator. The twenty-five-year-old could play the old man, but the old man cannot play the twenty-five-year-old. The charm is still there, but something is missing—perhaps recklessness. If Welles made CITIZEN KANE today it might be ponderous.

A thought upon visiting San Simeon: It was more insane than Xanadu.

The first films of most great filmmakers are usually faltering and talented. One looks at them to discover the themes and motifs that are worked out with greatness in later pictures. Welles' first film is different. It is the monument of his career. CITIZEN KANE is an ultimate first film for the way it shouts out to the world that a new presence is at large in the cinema, that a giant has arrived and that the dwarfs had better scatter. Unfortunately, this announcement was not heeded, and the giant suffered when the dwarfs ganged up. Welles, of course, made other masterpieces: THE MAGNIFICENT AMBERSONS, LADY FROM SHANGHAI, TOUCH OF EVIL, CHIMES AT MIDNIGHT. But his career faltered after CITIZEN KANE until he became a symbol of the artist ruined by philistines.

There is a quotient of Charles Foster Kane in Orson Welles; there are rages and there are ruins left behind, grandiose schemes and a fall from glorious heights. One does not want to stress this point and say that CITIZEN KANE prophesied Welles' own life, but the parallels that exist are poignant.

# Federico Fellini's **La Dolce Vita** 1959

Looking at LA DOLCE VITA today, more than ten years after its original release, it is possible to find it quaint. Recalling the lines outside the theatres where it played, recalling the conversation piece it became, recalling its power as an exposé of the decline and decadence of European intellectual and aristocratic circles, recalling what a heavy indictment it then seemed of the boredom, uselessness, and self-hatred of people at the top, one is tempted to ask what all the hoopla was about. LA DOLCE VITA today seems positively tame. It is amazing how fast the world has changed, how what seemed so daring and depraved in 1959 appears now to be almost innocent and restrained. But who in 1959 would have predicted that by 1969 sexual intercourse could be legally shown upon the commercial screen?

Remember the scandal of LA DOLCE VITA? How it was attacked by the Vatican as an outrageous sacrilege, and championed by the Left as a profound exposure of ruling-class decadence? Remember the articles which described how the film was convulsing Europe, how anticipation built as the American opening neared, and the backlash when the highbrow critics discovered it was going to be a popular success? Remember the adjectives that were flung about: journalistic, superficial, hallucinatory, disturbing, putrid, Ziegfeldian, cinematic, breathtaking? While the educated bourgeoisie feverishly studied the dialogue in the Steiner sequence which, it was rumored, revealed important clues to the picture's meaning, intellectuals scoffed that the Steiner character was absurd, because none of them had ever been to a gathering where "intellectuals" spoke that way. Fellini was either a philosopher or a fraud, an artist or a huckster, and LA DOLCE VITA was either the greatest film ever made or a hulk of laborious trash.

Fellini, himself, must have been amused. In one stroke he had created a scandal and at the same time become the most famous and talked-about director in the world. And all of this for merely, as he put it himself, taking "the temperature of an ailing society, a society that has every appearance of running a fever."

Like Jean Renoir in RULES OF THE GAME, Fellini took on the task of describing the manners and morals of a society in a certain time and place. But unlike Renoir he was successful in making a picture of enormous influence. What LA DOLCE VITA may have lacked in aesthetic power, it more than made up for in popular accessibility. Despite its apparent tameness a decade after the fact, LA DOLCE VITA should not be underestimated. As a film of social comment it is extremely important, an opening wedge, the first in a phalanx of pictures that dissected the milieu of the rich and the successful, and helped to smash public confidence in the social order. It is possible to argue that the disorientation that characterized the social tensions of the 1960s, and the subsequent rejection by a good many people of what it is now fashionable to call "the establishment," may be attributed to the influence of certain films of which LA DOLCE VITA was the first.

Federico Fellini, like most filmmakers who have created popular hits, was ahead of his audience with LA DOLCE VITA—not so far ahead that they were left behind, but just enough ahead that he could carry them along as he showed them things which they had always suspected, but had not yet come around to articulating for themselves. Fellini in LA DOLCE VITA says that the "sweet life" that can be purchased with money and fame is dreary and ugly, that people who are beautiful and successful are



Pack of *paparazzi* signifies falseness and emptiness of life in modern Rome in Federico Fellini's influential LA DOLCE VITA. Photographers callously crowd around characters in moments of stress, invading privacy and turning life into an outrageous gossip column.

boring and neurotic, that sin is rampant in society, that sophistication is a curse and innocence a treasure, and that vulgarity and greed—symbolized by the refuse of the media, the *paparazzi* of Rome with their pitiless flashbulbs and cameras—have tainted everything and ruined even the most intimate moments of human feeling. So negative a message was enormously gratifying to people who wanted to discover that the people they envied were worse off than themselves, and who could enjoy the delicious taste of a gossip column at the same time. As a piece of fantasy fulfillment LA DOLCE VITA was more than satisfactory. It confirmed the secret desire of the filmgoing public for a put-down spectacle about a world they could never know.

LA DOLCE VITA is filled with what one calls Fellini-isms: empty piazzas at midnight, satiric anticlericalism, scenes set near the sea, clarity in the light of dawn after long night voyages of the soul, a young girl symbolizing innocence, elaborate scenes involving unexpected actions by groups of people, and the inevitable Fellini signature, the constant use of the "interesting" face.

It contains sequences which, though beautifully staged, are sometimes a little too self-conscious and overburdened with meaning: the opening, for example, in which one helicopter carries a huge statue of Christ over Rome, while Marcello in a second helicopter cannot communicate with the sunbathers on the apartment roof. The lack-of-communication motif recurs throughout the film. Marcello cannot hear the words of the innocent girl who calls to him at the end. Marcello ends up confessing his love from the echo-chamber at the aristocrats' villa to an uninterested woman kissing another man, etc. But this fashionable strain of alienation should not distract from the social satire, brilliantly displayed in such amazing and memorable sequences as the one in which Anita Ekberg runs up the staircase of St. Peter's in a dress that is a modified version of priestly attire, or the anguish implicit in the sequence when Steiner's wife learns of her husband's and childrens' deaths in front of a pack of camera-clicking *paparazzi*.

The false miracle is one of the supreme sequences in all the films of Fellini. The exploitation by television and the press of two little children who claim to have seen the Madonna, the milking of a neurotic aberration for publicity and profit, may say more about the manners, morals, and society that Fellini was depicting than any of the famous orgies, or the sequence where Anouk Aimée insists upon making love in a whore's bed.

Fellini based many of the incidents in LA DOLCE VITA on incidents he read about in newspapers. He said in an interview: "I just thought of it as a vast fresco... and then gradually characters and incidents merged to fill it in...." This may account for the film's fragmentary quality, a series of blackout sketches bound together by the recurrent figure of Marcello Mastroianni, the journalist mired in the "sweet life," who wanders through the inferno of modern Rome. But there is also in LA DOLCE VITA a strong personal dimension, a renunciation by Fellini of the world in which he became involved by virtue of being a well-known film director in an ultra-film-conscious town.

LA DOLCE VITA is a big film filled with bravura, but it is dwarfed by CITIZEN KANE. It is an omniscient view of a collapsing social milieu, but not so fine a one as RULES OF THE GAME. What it does have in common with these pictures is a swirling intensity, a life force. Despite the way time has blunted the impact of its "scandal," LA DOLCE VITA is still alive.

Scenes from LA DOLCE VITA (top to bottom): False "miracle"; striptease and orgy; Marcello Mastroianni (r.) as journalist Marcello Rubini; encounter with sea monster. Opposite: Anita Ekberg as Sylvia. LA DOLCE VITA was a scandal when it opened in 1959, principally because of its sexual candor and open anticlericalism, but it looks tame today.

# François Truffaut's **Jules and Jim** 1961

"My films are gambles," says Truffaut. "For me shooting a film is like laying a bet. People took a strong dislike to the script for JULES AND JIM. Distributors said: 'The woman is a tart; the husband will be grotesque, etc.' The gamble for me was to make the woman moving (without being melodramatic) and not a tart, and to prevent her husband from seeming ridiculous."

Truffaut gambled and won, for JULES AND JIM is one of the best of all postwar French films, a miracle of storytelling, acting, filmmaking, and audience involvement.

JULES AND JIM is, admittedly, a period film. It recreates the spirit and moods of the times before and after World War I with a remarkable economy of means. The past is recaptured not so much by costumes and sets but by newsreel segments, an ironic, omniscient narrator, brilliant performances, and a calculated, ebullient, and mannered style of filmmaking. Within the first few minutes we feel the Paris of pre-1914. Throughout the picture, silent-film devices (iris dissolves, masking off of portions of the frame, etc.) and a restless, probing camera (including the use of swish-pans with a wide-screen process—a hitherto "forbidden" technique on account of its tendency to induce nausea) become in Truffaut's hands a bag of cinematic tricks by which he conveys a period flavor.

But to think of JULES AND JIM primarily as a period film may be to miss its real point. On one level, of course, it is a romance. Two close friends meet a *femme fatale,* and an impossible triangular relationship begins as an idyll and ends in tragedy. But on a deeper level it is a film about three social outlaws and the price they must pay for living free of social restraint and by improvised and mostly self-serving standards. As far as manners and morals are concerned, Jules, Jim, and Catherine invent their own and suffer the consequences.

They are bohemians. They live spontaneously in permanent isolation from the social mainstream. It is interesting that we see neither of the men perform a particle of "useful" work, nor do we ever observe Catherine make a single compromise toward the standards of society at large. Even when Jules and Jim must fight (on separate sides) in the war, they maintain a distance from the grit of the trenches, and an alienation from the issues (if, indeed, there were any) over which the war was fought. To the degree that JULES AND JIM is a film about society, it is about a tiny privileged sector, the bohemian subculture that flaunted the manners and morals of the bourgeoisie.

Jules, Jim, and Catherine play life as if it were a game. Even in a movie theatre, watching footage of the Nazis burning books, they are more interested by the amusing coincidence of being in the same place at the same time than in the political reality descending upon their world. By the end it is clear that they have played too long. The fake world of joy and tenderness, freedom and spontaneity, which they have created is impossible to maintain. The rules they have improvised do not serve, jealousy and neurosis intervene, their dream existence decays and the cost is frightful: sorrow and isolation for Jules, death for Catherine and Jim.

But despite the fact that their *ménage à trois* becomes grotesque, Catherine's charming dominance turns perverse, Jules' passivity descends into self-pity, and Jim's *joie de vivre* crumbles into anarchy, they are sympathetic characters. They live with such passion that it is impossible not to be fond of them. Their attempt to create their own life style is brave, and they must be admired for



Opposite: Jim (Henri Serre) and Catherine (Jeanne Moreau) in François Truffaut's JULES AND JIM. Jim, Catherine, and Jules (Oskar Werner) appear at separate bedroom windows suggesting their *ménage à trois.*
Above: Three principals with Truffaut.

having made it. Though in manuscript form they may have seemed repulsive to distributors, in Truffaut's hands they come alive and exude a warmth that makes their tragedy chilling. At one time or another everyone has wanted to live in total freedom; these three who tried and failed evoke nostalgia for our long-lost dreams.

JULES AND JIM begins as an ode to bohemianism and gradually turns dark. We are charmed when the two friends, whose relationship is so tender and sincere, rush off to Greece just to see the smile on a statue. When they meet up with Catherine, whom they instantly adore for having the same smile, we are enchanted by their romps, their outings on bicycles and to the beach, their runs across bridges and meadows. They are living at the highest of degrees, and despite the fact that the world is crumbling around them, their attempt to turn life into a "fiesta," to use Hemingway's word, is irresistible.

Of course, their idyll cannot go on forever. Social isolation leads to madness. Destructive traits within the human psyche cannot be willed away. When Catherine drives herself and Jim off the end of a broken bridge, following through on the self-destructive urge hinted at in earlier and jollier scenes, she smiles the enigmatic smile of the Greek statue, which is revealed to have been a smile of selfish triumph. All the innocence turns out to have been a fantasy. JULES AND JIM is like a seductive dream that suddenly turns into a nightmare and jars the sleeper awake.

There are brilliant and memorable scenes in this picture: the one (said to be improvised) when Jim tells of the soldier who fell in love with a girl he had known for half an hour on a train; Thérèse listing her lovers for Jim when he meets up with her again in a café; Jeanne Moreau listing all the great wines of France in response to Jim's delight in German beer; Catherine jumping into the Seine; the burial sequence in which black comedy reinforces the shock of the finale; and the amazing scene when Catherine's dress catches fire from the flames of her burning love letters, and she remarks to Jim that she carries around a bottle of vitriol for "lying eyes."

## Dennis Hopper's **Easy Rider** 1969

A not-so-imaginary conversation:

"You're not serious about EASY RIDER being a great film?"

"I'm absolutely serious."

"But it's nothing but a chain of poorly executed sequences patched together with shots of a couple of guys riding motorcycles. When a director needs that many musical transitions you know he's in trouble."

"It doesn't matter what a director needs, or even if his work is uneven. The only important thing in a film of this kind is the final result. EASY RIDER is a powerful experience. If Dennis Hopper has only one-tenth the film craftsmanship of François Truffaut that does not in itself disqualify him from making a great film. Besides, the lunchroom sequence, the George Hanson scenes, and the finale are not 'poorly executed.' "

"What do you mean when you say 'a film of this kind'? Are you sure you're not creating special standards to make your case?"

"Not at all. By 'a film of this kind' I mean a film of such consequence that imperfections (which might be crucial in a picture that was self-consciously 'finely wrought') become trivial in relation to impact."

"Aren't you confusing the phenomenon of EASY RIDER with its stature?"

"No. The phenomenon of EASY RIDER is well known: The picture cost a few hundred thousand dollars and earned many millions; it destroyed the idea once held sacred in Hollywood that a few isolated executives could determine the fantasies the public was willing to buy; it caused innumerable firings of personnel who, in the light of the success of EASY RIDER, were rightfully considered useless; it inspired a series of imitations, pictures calculatingly manufactured for the 'youth audience,' which failed and are now rightfully referred to as 'youth culture rip-off pictures.' These things are facts, the side effects or the 'phenomenon' of the film. But today, several years after its release, when the phenomenal aspect has cooled down and the political and social environment is considerably different, EASY RIDER is still powerful and still unnerving. This is what I mean by 'impact' and this certainly has to do with the film's stature."

"But the premise is faulty. This idea that if you're free in America you're going to get killed, that if you have long hair some redneck will shoot you down—it's paranoic. And the idea that two cocaine dealers can be heroic is immoral and absurd."

"We can argue endlessly about the morality of

motion pictures. People hate Peckinpah's THE WILD BUNCH because they say it's immoral, too violent, etc. What would they have him do? Make a picture like MARY POPPINS? Would Dennis Hopper be any more moral if he had made DR. DOOLITTLE? The whole point of being a filmmaker is to express oneself, and God knows, EASY RIDER expresses the convictions and vision of Hopper and Peter Fonda. Call the premise paranoic, but in the context of various assassinations and violent urban outbreaks it seems pretty realistic to me. Anyway, it's pointless to argue about the premise of a film. Some people can't stand the worlds of Hitchcock or Fritz Lang, but very few people deny the richness of these worlds or the power with which they are expressed. Give Hopper credit for having articulated a world that had never before been articulated on film. His is the first and only authentic picture about the youth culture. His perceptions—that America is violent, that the spirit of the counterculture descends from the spirit of the pioneers, that the one thing that enrages people trapped by their lives is the flaunted freedom of outsiders—may seem clichés now, but before EASY RIDER they had not been expressed on the screen."

"Aren't they expressed better by all that pop music he uses, than by anything he did himself?"

"He chose the music. What's the difference between using someone else's music and basing a picture on someone else's novel? The job of a filmmaker is to mold the work of collaborators toward a specific personal goal. This Hopper does admirably well. All those pop tunes certainly enrich the vision, and as a matter of fact one could say that Hopper's use of music is almost classic in the sense that the music becomes a chorus that comments on the action and defines its meaning."

"Aren't you confusing a film of fantasy fulfillment with a work of art when you put EASY RIDER in the same chapter as RULES OF THE GAME and CITIZEN KANE?"

"What is a movie? Some miles of celluloid and some chemicals arranged so that light projected through them will render images and sound. Film is fantasy, and a successful film is a form of fantasy fulfillment. As for CITIZEN KANE and RULES OF THE GAME, they too are based on arguable interpretations of society.

"To say that a picture is great is not the same thing as to say that it is a great work of art. It can be a great work of entertainment, a great articulation of an idea, a great example of a new technique, or a great work of personal expression. Let's simply think of the word 'great' as a superlative to be applied to pictures that distinguish themselves in an important way. EASY RIDER is one of the most distinguished pictures of fantasy fulfillment of the 1960s, for it certified an apprehension about America that was harbored in a vague form in many people's minds, and when they saw it rendered so intensely in this particular story they instantly recognized that it was true."

"You keep using words like 'powerful' and 'intense.' Do you think these are really the most important qualities in films?"

"In films that are interpretations of society—yes. A delicate and sensible EASY RIDER, or a thinking man's EASY RIDER would not be very interesting. By its very nature EASY RIDER must be polemical; the only way it can enforce its vision is to describe it on the most emotional and visceral level. To create two protagonists, a gentle 'Captain America' and a discontented 'Billy' (who, by the way, are not meant to be 'heroic'), to mount them on two incredible, gleaming motorcycles, to send them down the roads of America, first past some of the most spectacularly beautiful scenery in the world, and later down roads that border ecological and neon wastelands, to arrange for them to intersect with various social alternatives en route, and then, after several adventures, to have them gunned down gratuitously, is to engage in highly imaginative mythmaking on a powerful emotional level. It only seems easy and obvious after the fact. I think the thing that really bothers people about EASY RIDER is that it was cooked up by a couple of long-haired acid-trippers, instead of by a self-appointed artist like Losey or Visconti. And that lines like, 'We blew it,' and the recurring use of the word 'man' don't go down with people who think civilized movies must contain elegantly written dialogue. I'll tell you one thing, though. The image of the motorcycle exploding into flames contains as many cultural cross references as Renoir's use of French theatrical farce in RULES OF THE GAME: self-immolations and napalmings in Vietnam, for example, and the American Dream going up in smoke. Besides, it is an unforgettable image, as strong in its own primitive way as the final sled-burning in CITIZEN KANE. EASY RIDER is a primitive work, but then 'primitive' has perhaps ceased to be a pejorative word."

"If I read you correctly, you are saying that it is the primitive power of EASY RIDER that makes it great."

"You are reading me correctly. You can rip EASY RIDER apart for poor technique and dubious morality, but you cannot fault the intensity of its vision, even if you think it is sophomoric. It is authentic, a film that is true to itself. The people who made it were sincerely concerned about what they were saying, and the emotion they put into it rushes out each time it is projected. As Penelope Gilliatt put it (and no one can accuse her of lacking 'civilized values'): 'EASY RIDER is the real thing.' "

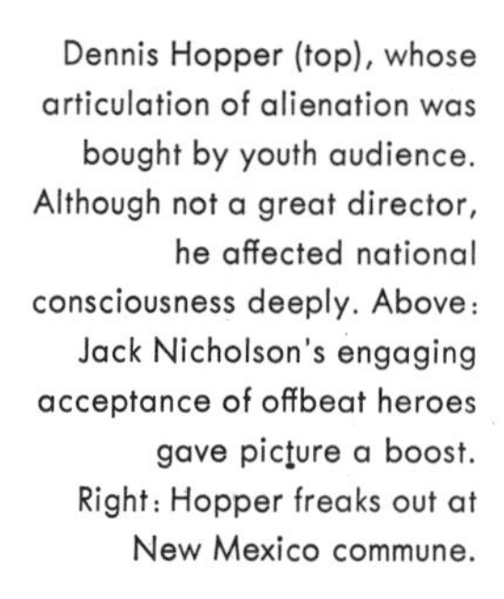

Dennis Hopper (top), whose articulation of alienation was bought by youth audience. Although not a great director, he affected national consciousness deeply. Above: Jack Nicholson's engaging acceptance of offbeat heroes gave picture a boost. Right: Hopper freaks out at New Mexico commune.

# Credits

## Rules of the Game (La Règle du Jeu)

France; 1939; 113 minutes;
released in the U.S. by Janus.

**Directed by** Jean Renoir.
**Produced by** Jean Renoir.
**Screenplay by** Jean Renoir, Karl Koch, Camille François and the cast, derived from "les Caprices de Marianne" by Alfred de Musset.
**Photographed by** Jean Bachelet.
**Art direction by** Eugène Lorié.
**Edited by** Marguerite Houlet-Renoir.
**Music by** Monsigny, Chopin, Saint-Saëns, Rosi, Salabert, and J. Strauss, arranged by Roger Désormières.
**Cast:** Marcel Dalio; Nora Grégor; Roland Toutain; Jean Renoir; Mila Parély; Paulette Dubost; Gaston Modot; Julien Carette.

## Citizen Kane

U.S.A.; 1941; 119 minutes;
released by RKO.

**Directed by** Orson Welles.
**Produced by** Orson Welles.
**Screenplay by** Herman J. Mankiewicz and Orson Welles.
**Photographed by** Gregg Toland.
**Art direction by** Van Nest Polglase and Perry Ferguson.
**Edited by** Robert Wise and Mark Robson.
**Music by** Bernard Herrmann.
**Cast:** Orson Welles; Joseph Cotten; Dorothy Comingore; Agnes Moorehead; Ruth Warrick; Ray Collins; Erskine Sanford; Everett Sloane; William Alland; Paul Stewart; George Coulouris; Fortunio Bonanova; Gus Schilling; Philip Van Zandt; Georgia Backus; Harry Shannon; Sonny Bupp; Buddy Swan; Richard Baer; Joan Blair.

## La Dolce Vita (The Sweet Life)

Italy; 1960; 175 minutes;
released in the U.S. by Astor.

**Directed by** Federico Fellini.
**Produced by** Giuseppe Amato and Angelo Rizzoli.
**Screenplay by** Federico Fellini, Tullio Pinelli, Ennio Flaiano and Brunello Rondi.
**Photographed by** Otello Martelli.
**Art direction by** Piero Gherardi.
**Edited by** Leo Cattozzo.
**Music by** Nino Rota.
**Cast:** Marcello Mastroianni; Walter Santesso; Anouk Aimée; Anita Ekberg; Yvonne Furneaux; Lex Barker; Alan Dijon; Alain Cluny; Valeria Ciangottini; Renée Lonarini; Annibale Ninchi; Polidor; Magali Noël; Giulio Questi; Nadia Gray.

## Jules and Jim (Jules et Jim)

France; 1961; 105 minutes;
released in the U.S. by Janus.

**Directed by** François Truffaut.
**Produced by** Les Films du Carrosse/SEDIF.
**Screenplay by** François Truffaut and Jean Gruault, based on the novel by Henri-Pierre Roché.
**Photographed by** Raoul Coutard.
**Edited by** Claudine Bouche.
**Music by** Georges Delerue.
**Cast:** Jeanne Moreau; Oskar Werner; Henri Serre; Marie Dubois; Vanna Urbino; Sabine Haudepin; Boris Bassiak; Jean-Louis Richard; Michel Varesano; Pierre Fabre; Danielle Bassiak.

## Easy Rider

U.S.A.; 1969; 94 minutes;
released by Columbia.

**Directed by** Dennis Hopper.
**Produced by** Peter Fonda.
**Screenplay by** Peter Fonda, Dennis Hopper and Terry Southern.
**Photographed by** Laszlo Kovacs.
**Art direction by** Jerry Kay.
**Edited by** Donn Cambern.
**Music by** Numerous pop artists.
**Cast:** Peter Fonda; Dennis Hopper; Jack Nicholson; Luana Anders; Luke Askew; Toni Basil; Karen Black; Warren Finnerty; Sabrina Scharf; Robert Walker.

# Films About Films

# 8

Just as novelists have written novels about novelists, and playwrights have written backstage plays, so filmmakers have made films about films. These are partly the products of their desires to clarify their lives and their relationship with their industry, to express their rage at the system in which they work, to savor the sweetness of vengeance against prototypal enemies, and to make personal statements, to describe the world they know best, and to create self-portraits on celluloid. The motion-picture business is notorious for being cruel, and these films about films are often visions of that cruelty, reflecting with varying degrees of intensity the filmmaker's dilemma.

What, exactly, is that dilemma? One finds it described often by filmmakers interviewed in freewheeling and bitter moods. It is first the constant struggle for financing, and then the struggles with philistine studio chiefs, stupid and overbearing producers, difficult and temperamental stars, and the corrupt and vicious practices of a corrupt and vicious industry. Throughout the short history of the cinema, the filmmaker has been confronted with the problems of having his work altered, reshot or re-edited without his consent, being cheated out of a fair share of the money earned from his successes, and, when his films have failed with the public, being ignored and driven to exhaustion and collapse. The horror stories are endless and when filmmakers get together tales of double crosses, abuses of power, and various mutilations are exchanged.

Why has Elia Kazan turned to writing novels? Why do so many people speak of Orson Welles' career as "tragic"? Why was Francis Ford Coppola fired five times during the shooting of THE GODFATHER? Why was Fred Zinnemann's MAN'S FATE cancelled? What has happened to the announced projects of Richard Lester? What about the struggles of Sam Peckinpah? Why was Dennis Hopper's second film "dumped"? Why was George Cukor fired from GONE WITH THE WIND? Why did John Huston resign from A FAREWELL TO ARMS? What happened to Erich von Stroheim and David Wark Griffith? What about blacklisted screenwriters, actors who commit suicide, multimillion-dollar litigations, works massacred for television? Why so many feuds, embargoes, scandals? Why have so many fine talents been degraded? What is the process that so softens filmmakers of promise that corruption actually seems to ooze out of works made only a few years after their promising early efforts? One could go on forever with the questions, and, of course, in each case there is a specific answer. But the general answer to all of them may reside in the peculiarities of the movie industry, engaged in the manufacture of products that have no saleable value beyond their ability to entertain, and thus dependent for survival on the unpredictable force of public taste. Unlike the steel or coal or automobile industries, the movie industry is, by its very nature, subject to economic extremes, and these extremes create vicissitudes and pressures that tear at people, turn them into monsters, and sometimes destroy them.

The movie business is corrupt, capricious, and ruthless because, among other things, all the problems inherent in any sort of show business (and movies are just an extension of the carnival and circus businesses) are combined with the problems inherent in big-money speculation. When big money is at stake artists always suffer. The demands of box office success and artistic self-fulfillment are nearly impossible to reconcile. One could examine the relative positions of filmmakers in the American cinema solely in terms of the ways each has tried to reconcile his artistic aspirations with the demands of his backers that his pictures make money. In short, American filmmakers have always been stretched on a rack, pulled from one side by money and from the other by art.

From time to time, when the opportunity arises, filmmakers have made films about the filmmaking process and depicted their dilemma. Such films are widely scattered through the years, but they have themes in common, and when examined together and treated as a genre one may discern in them a streak of cynicism, and, particularly in American films about films, a large quotient of self-hatred. Hollywood loves to lacerate itself, and the proof of that much-repeated axiom is to be found in the Hollywood films about the Hollywood filmmaking milieu. A sociologist from another galaxy would deduce from an examination of these films about films that Hollywood is one of the most terrible places on earth, not, like the American West, a territory for contending forces of good and evil, but a place where viciousness and cruelty are to be found at exalted heights.

A few words about the pictures chosen for this chapter. The word "great" has been expanded in this book to embrace pictures ranging from "great works of art" to "great masterpieces of entertainment," "great personal visions," and even impaired works which have "great emotional intensity" or which are "great" by reason of some technical or stylistic innovation, or on account of their prophetic power. When it comes to choosing films about films this word "great" must be stretched even more. THE BAD AND THE BEAUTIFUL, for example, discussed here with several other films of which it is an outstanding example, can only be construed as great if one accepts the



Preceding pages: The wages of stardom — Norma Desmond, brilliantly played by Gloria Swanson, makes her last entrance in Billy Wilder's SUNSET BOULEVARD. For all its pathos, this may be the cruelest scene in the history of Hollywood films about films.

proposition that there can be such a thing as a "great piece of trash." THE BAD AND THE BEAUTIFUL is a film that revels in and insists upon its trashiness, and therein lies its fascination.

As for Godard's CONTEMPT, not many people have seen it, but of those who have many despise it greatly. CONTEMPT is one of the few films that actually encourages its audiences to walk out. Aside from the fact that it has something important to say and says it interestingly, CONTEMPT is a nadir of entertainment, and for this reason, and because it is one of the most alienated and alienating films ever made, one can choose to call it great, too.

# Billy Wilder's **Sunset Boulevard** 1950

Of all the films about films, none exhibits so much self-hatred and cynicism as Billy Wilder's SUNSET BOULEVARD:

1. This story about an aging silent-movie queen, her former director/husband-now-butler, and their grotesque existence, is told against a background of the then (1950) alive, youthful Hollywood. Yet this background ambience, used as a contrast to the grotesqueries in the mansion on Sunset, is a disgusting, vile world of arrogant producers (Sheldrake cannot remember his story editor's name), ruthless agents (Morino never returns William Holden's calls; when cornered on the golf course he refuses to loan him $300, and threatens him with a softly muttered, "Maybe you'd better get yourself another agent"), and a hierarchy of fools (when Norma Desmond arrives at Paramount to visit Cecil B. De Mille, word is phoned from the gatehouse, through a series of lackey assistants, until it finally reaches the "great" De Mille, who takes a condescending interest). Not only are the characters vile, but the dialogue of the picture is filled with put-downs and self-disgust. Holden refers to one character as a "yes-man at Metro," to his agent as "the big faker," cringes before the producer Sheldrake, and says of the best script he ever wrote: "It was a beautiful script about Okies in the dust bowl. When it reached the screen it took place on a torpedo boat."

2. When casting the freaks for his "old Hollywood," Wilder comes up with the following cynical ideas: Gloria Swanson, biggest of the real silent-movie stars, will play Norma Desmond, biggest of the fictional silent-movie stars, who wants to make her comeback. In fact, Swanson's appearance in SUNSET BOULEVARD did represent a comeback, but unlike Norma Desmond's it was not a fiasco. It was brilliant. This grotesque, Norma Desmond, is to be served by a butler who is to be her former husband and director, Max von Meyerling. Who does Wilder cast? Erich von Stroheim, the most famous of the early directors broken by the Hollywood system. At one point Stroheim says: "In the early days there were three directors of great promise: D. W. Griffith, C. B. De Mille, and Max von Meyerling." True, perhaps, if one thinks of Meyerling as Stroheim, who is here forced, in effect, to play out his own degradation. And whom does Wilder dig up for his "waxworks," the has-beens with whom Norma Desmond plays bridge? H. B. Warner, Anna Q. Nilsson, and Buster Keaton! (Keaton gets applause in the theatres now when SUNSET BOULEVARD is re-run. In 1950, however, he was in such decline that his appearance as a "waxwork" was something of a sick joke.)

3. Against this weird typecasting of the "old Hollywood" Wilder creates a character with whom he, presumably, identifies. This is the hack writer Joe Gillis (William Holden), a man with a certain small amount of integrity and a huge amount of self-disgust. Though Gillis speaks wistfully of returning to his profession of newsman in Dayton, Ohio, he is too far gone, too deep into the Hollywood money trap, performing hack work, but too lethargic to give up the rat race. This may well have been the collective dilemma of Billy Wilder, Charles Brackett, and D. M. Marshman, Jr., the writers of SUNSET BOULEVARD. Although they were highly successful, big-time screenwriters, there is in their creation of Gillis the idea that movie writing is a phony profession and that "real" writing takes place in newsrooms in Dayton.

4. Are the rats in the empty pool at Norma Desmond's estate any more a proof of decadence than the frantic phoning of the younger characters from booths in Schwab's Drugstore? Are Hedda Hopper and Cecil B. De Mille any better, because they are involved in the phony-real world of Hollywood, than Norma Desmond and Max von Meyerling, living in painful seclusion in the mansion on Sunset? Is the Gloria Swanson film, QUEEN KELLY, actually directed by Stroheim, which Norma projects in her house and which makes William Holden squirm, really any worse than the exploitive "spectacular" that De Mille is making at Paramount? The answer to all these questions is an ambivalent no. SUNSET BOULEVARD is like two

mirrors facing each other, reflecting images of "good" and "bad," the neurosis of recluses and the neurosis of the rat race, back and forth until all values are blurred and the reflection is infinite.

5. Indeed, what could be more cynical than to write a story for a film that will be told as a flashback by a character who is already dead? The suspension of disbelief required is incredible, yet the picture is so involving that we forgive the intentional fallacy of having William Holden, whom we first see as a corpse floating in a swimming pool after being shot by Norma Desmond, narrate the story. Presumably we should be grateful that Wilder didn't use a sequence he actually shot. The film was to open with the camera tracking down a row of corpses stretched out on slabs in the morgue. When it reached Holden's body he was to sit up suddenly and address the audience!

These notes on the cynicism of SUNSET BOULEVARD are by no means meant as an attack on the picture. Like all great films about films it deals with the insanity of the picture business, the difficulty of doing good work in the face of madness, and the cruel cynicism of its scenes and dialogue helps clarify this theme. We will always remember certain scenes from SUNSET BOULEVARD:

Gloria Swanson's marvelous imitation of Chaplin, interrupted by a call from Paramount. "Paramount!" she snarls at Stroheim. "Let 'em wait! *I've* waited long enough!"

When Holden recognizes her for the first time and mentions that she used to be "big," she replies, "I *am* big. It's the pictures that got small!"

When she stands up in the cone of light thrown by the projector in her living room, places her hands on her face, and says, "They don't make faces like that anymore!" Or when she visits De Mille at the studio and an old-time grip turns a brute arc on her, making her cringe before its blinding glare, we are moved and disgusted, filled with pity and terror.

The monkey burial by candlelight is one of the more grotesque scenes ever filmed, and it provided Wilder with the opportunity to make one of his most famous *bons mots*. An assistant approached him and asked him how he planned to stage the scene. Wilder is alleged to have shrugged and answered: "You know—the usual monkey-funeral sequence."

The last scene of SUNSET BOULEVARD is unforgettable. As Gloria Swanson comes down the stairs to face the newsreel cameras, she is urged on by Stroheim, whom in her madness she mistakes for De Mille. The final close-up of her face, and her fingers twisted like fangs, is as cruel a comment as has ever been made on what the movie business is all about.

From SUNSET BOULEVARD: Swanson (opposite) to William Holden: "They don't make faces like that anymore!" Erich von Stroheim (l.) plays out his degradation as Norma Desmond's butler. Swanson and Cecil B. De Mille. The monkey funeral. Swanson and captive Holden dance in mouldering mansion on Sunset.

# Joseph L. Mankiewicz's **All About Eve** 1950

ALL ABOUT EVE was released in the same year as SUNSET BOULEVARD. Although strictly speaking not a film about films, since it deals with the world of the Broadway stage, and is therefore not really fair game for exhaustive analysis or even inclusion in this chapter, ALL ABOUT EVE nevertheless is worth at least cursory examination, for it is a magnificently entertaining work that says more about the mythical ruthlessness and temperament of performers, and says it better than movies set in Hollywood that deal with these same themes.

Like SUNSET BOULEVARD, ALL ABOUT EVE is structured as a flashback. It is even better written than SUNSET BOULEVARD, employing biting and witty dialogue. The story, told almost exclusively in set-piece interiors, shows how Anne Baxter's sneaky Eve uses Bette Davis' bigger-than-life Margo Channing to achieve stardom. It ends on a flamboyant image of narcissism that rivals the flamboyant ending of SUNSET BOULEVARD. A new "Eve," who has slipped into Anne Baxter's suite, postures before the star's full-length dressing mirrors with Baxter's "Sarah Siddons" award in her hands. She falls into a dynamic reverie in which she dreams of great fame and savors the sweetness of imaginary applause. What we know (and she does not, as she admires her endlessly reflected self) is that her destiny is monstrous, that she will be just another in a long line of stars to whom fame has brought loneliness and for whom old age brings the kind of grotesquerie-on-a-staircase that ends the life of Gloria Swanson's Norma Desmond.

Between them, Mankiewicz and Wilder spent the year 1950 carving up the theatrical worlds of the East and West coasts, each creating a legend about the unscrupulous female star who will do anything to advance her career and whose talent is great enough to justify her temperament. SUNSET BOULEVARD tells us that old forgotten stars are bundles of megalomaniacal nerves; ALL

ABOUT EVE tells us how they get that way.

Bette Davis as Margo Channing may even surpass Gloria Swanson as Norma Desmond; George Sanders plays his trademark role as the cad; Marilyn Monroe stands out in a small part as the dumb blonde at a party—a role she spent her life trying to overcome; and Thelma Ritter epitomizes the personal maid-confidante. Though ALL ABOUT EVE has about as much relation to the actual ways of the New York theatre as ON THE WATERFRONT has to what really happens on the New York waterfront, it is nevertheless a lively fiction, true unto itself, reveling in its artificiality and gloating over the unscrupulousness of the world it so magnificently depicts.

Four years after he completed ALL ABOUT EVE, Mankiewicz offered up his film about films, THE BAREFOOT CONTESSA. The two pictures together constitute his best work. THE BAREFOOT CONTESSA expands upon the myth of the female star, in this case Ava Gardner, who ascends to stardom from the gutter, presumably the place from which all stars, including Anne Baxter's Eve, come. It includes many of the stock characters of the genre, the ruthless buys-and-sells-human-beings producer, the boot-licking and permanently sweating press agent, and the once-great-but-now-discarded director, mournfully played by Humphrey Bogart.

What is interesting about THE BAREFOOT CONTESSA is that it is a funny prophecy-in-reverse of the Grace Kelly movie-star-to-princess story. Gardner's Cinderella story turns black. Lustily waiting in bed on her wedding night, she is approached by her as yet untasted continental husband-count, Rossano Brazzi. "There's something I haven't told you," he says and hands her a medical report that documents his impotence. Just as a star uses people, people use a star.

The wages of stardom, as depicted in SUNSET BOULEVARD, ALL ABOUT EVE, and THE BAREFOOT CONTESSA, are loneliness and sexual frustration. The difference between Anne Baxter and Ava Gardner, however, is that Baxter really wants to be a star and is willing to pay the cost and sit around lonely night after night puffing moodily on cigarettes. Gardner, on the other hand, is willing to give it all up, to satisfy her cravings by sleeping with the servants and, ultimately, to pay for her corruption with her life.



From ALL ABOUT EVE: Gary Merrill (l.) comforts Bette Davis, who plays the star Margo Channing; Anne Baxter as Eve (r.) accepts her "Sarah Siddons Award." Little does she know that another "Eve" is lurking in her apartment, ready to do to her what she did to Margo Channing.

# Vincente Minnelli's **The Bad and the Beautiful** 1952 and Other Things.

THE BAREFOOT CONTESSA is one of a series of films about Hollywood which are perhaps best described in order of trashiness. Of these, Preston Sturges' SULLIVAN'S TRAVELS (1942) is probably the least. The story of a director who runs away from the phony world of Hollywood in order to find "real" material for a "real" movie about "real" people, it is a mildly amusing film combining gentle satire and serious social comment. Its net effect, however, is to tickle Hollywood with a feather. Better (i.e., trashier) pictures of this school lash at Hollywood with a whip.

There is Paul Mazursky's ALEX IN WONDERLAND (1970), a film that failed pitifully at the box office. ALEX IN WONDERLAND is so pretentious that one cannot rightfully call it trash. Sort of a poor man's 8½, it is part homage to Fellini (who appears as himself and in his embarrassment seems to put the whole thing down), part film of social comment (it contains extended fantasies on the three Great Social Issues of the age: ecology, race relations, and the Vietnam war. The last is by far the best: The war is staged on Hollywood Boulevard), and partly it is the story of a successful director going through a personal crisis. This portrait of the artist on celluloid is rather tiresome, but it contains an interesting twist that makes it an important film in the subgenre. Mazursky casts himself as one of the new breed of producers whose hipness is merely a façade covering that monstrousness so essential in a producer character in a Hollywood film about films.

William Wellman's A STAR IS BORN (1937) may have been the first and most famous picture in the subgenre. The story of a marriage between stars, which fails when the career of one ascends and the career of the other declines, was evidently considered strong stuff in its day, though in retrospect it looks more like the sort of fantasy about Hollywood harbored in the hearts of the readers of 1930s fan magazines. (When remade into a musical in 1954, George Cukor's filmmaking and Judy Garland's performance transcended the material, and the story seemed altogether extraordinary.)

One truly enters the universe of trash with John Cromwell's THE GODDESS (1958). Cromwell's gift for working with actresses shows in Kim Stanley's remarkable performance as the neurotic and unhappy sex goddess, Rita Shawn, incapable of giving or receiving love. Stanley is married to Lloyd Bridges, a prizefighter and television addict, and the whole thing looks a lot like Marilyn Monroe and Joe DiMaggio though, naturally, everyone concerned denies it. THE GODDESS is clearly another attempt to portray those miseries of stardom suffered by the heroines of SUNSET BOULEVARD, ALL ABOUT EVE, and THE BAREFOOT CONTESSA.

THE OSCAR (1966) is probably Hollywood's most horrible exercise in self-laceration, for in this film the town's most precious icon, which cannot be depicted on the screen without the permission of the Academy of Motion Picture Arts and Sciences, is made the butt of an enormous joke. An Oscar, says THE OSCAR, can be "arranged." Horror of horrors! One wonders how the producers got away with it, how they got Burt Lancaster, Richard Burton, Frank Sinatra, Hedda Hopper, and even the costume designer, Edith Head (who has won just about as many Oscars as anyone else), to play themselves in this delicious monstrosity. THE OSCAR is notable for its heightened use of cliché Hollywood types, as well as for two immortal lines: "The Oscar is a symbol and we don't like it tarnished," and "When you sleep with pigs you come up stinking of garbage."

There are many other devastating films about films: Stuart Heisler's THE STAR (1953), starring Bette Davis; Gordon Douglas' HARLOW (1965), starring Carroll Baker; Robert Mulligan's INSIDE DAISY CLOVER (1966), starring Natalie Wood; Edward Dmytryk's THE CARPETBAGGERS (1964), from the same company that brought us HARLOW and THE OSCAR, etc. But the biggest and the best are the two pairs of masterpieces by Robert Aldrich and Vincente Minnelli, which do for Hollywood in trash what SUNSET BOULEVARD did for Hollywood in quality.

Robert Aldrich is primarily known as the master of *film noir*, and his first film about film, THE BIG KNIFE (1955), is very much in that style. THE BIG KNIFE was knocked off by Aldrich in a mere sixteen days of shooting. The result is an austere, tough, cruel, electric, and highly theatrical charcoal-sketch of Clifford Odets' play. This is the film that enraged Harry Cohn and brought tears to the eyes of Louis B. Mayer, each of whom thought he was the model for the odious movie mogul so brilliantly played by Rod Steiger.

In 1968, Aldrich made THE LEGEND OF LYLAH CLARE, a lavish, florid, self-indulgent, and magnificently trashy film about film that represents a departure from the tough

style of his earlier work and is in keeping with the decadence of his THE DIRTY DOZEN. In THE LEGEND OF LYLAH CLARE, one finds such familiar types as the has-been director (Peter Finch), the starlet who is discovered and turned into a star (Kim Novak), the two-bit agent (Milton Selzer), the brutal producer (this time played by Ernest Borgnine), and all sorts of lesbians and gossip columnists, and Sidney Skolsky playing himself. In the tradition of Ava Gardner in THE BAREFOOT CONTESSA, Kim Novak sleeps with the gardener. The most interesting thing about this picture is the aspect that reflects its total trashiness. It is a film about film in which a character is making a film about film.

To Vincente Minnelli, however, must go the crown. His infamous pair of films about films, THE BAD AND THE BEAUTIFUL (1952) and TWO WEEKS IN ANOTHER TOWN (1962), are unmatched in the entire history of the sub-genre, as well as in the history of the cinema of trash.

Minnelli, of course, is best known for his musicals, which include the very fine MEET ME IN ST. LOUIS and the much-admired but incredibly pretentious AN AMERICAN IN PARIS. But his later films—stylish, melodramatic, decadent, and lavish—are of equal interest, and THE BAD AND THE BEAUTIFUL and TWO WEEKS IN ANOTHER TOWN are of this type.

THE BAD AND THE BEAUTIFUL trashes CITIZEN KANE. There are flashbacks as characters narrate different versions of the same series of events. (It is interesting that Minnelli's producer was John Houseman, who had worked on the script of CITIZEN KANE until he and Welles had a falling out.) Kirk Douglas plays the monster-producer Jonathan Shields, who, among other fiendish things, double-crosses directors, dumps a big alcoholic star (Lana Turner—"tossed on the ash heap by this town"), and entices a Pulitzer Prize-winning novelist (Dick Powell) to Hollywood, where his wife is lured into an affair with an actor, so Powell will be able to give his full attention to screen writing.

Jonathan Shields, it seems, was the son of a movie tycoon who died poor and despised, and by this his ruthless character is psychologically explained. Of course, some people think that Charles Foster Kane's character is explained by the fact that as a child he was separated from his beloved sled, but the difference here is that Minnelli offers his explanation as a camp effect which his audiences accept as a convention, while Welles uses Rosebud as an ironic reminder that human character is impenetrable and mysterious.

THE BAD AND THE BEAUTIFUL is filled with magnificent characters and set-pieces. Two-bit agents, directors, stars, and moguls abound—and there is an institutional Hollywood cocktail party, a quintessential Hollywood funeral, lots of movie lingo, and scenes set in famous places on Hollywood Boulevard and in Beverly Hills.

Ten years later Minnelli, Kirk Douglas, John Houseman, and the screenwriter Charles Schnee got together and cooked up another film about film based on Irwin Shaw's novel, TWO WEEKS IN ANOTHER TOWN. In this



Kirk Douglas and Lana Turner in Vincente Minnelli's trash masterpiece film about film, THE BAD AND THE BEAUTIFUL. Minnelli later used bits of this film to embellish TWO WEEKS IN ANOTHER TOWN, thus piling trash upon trash to create an infinite resonance.

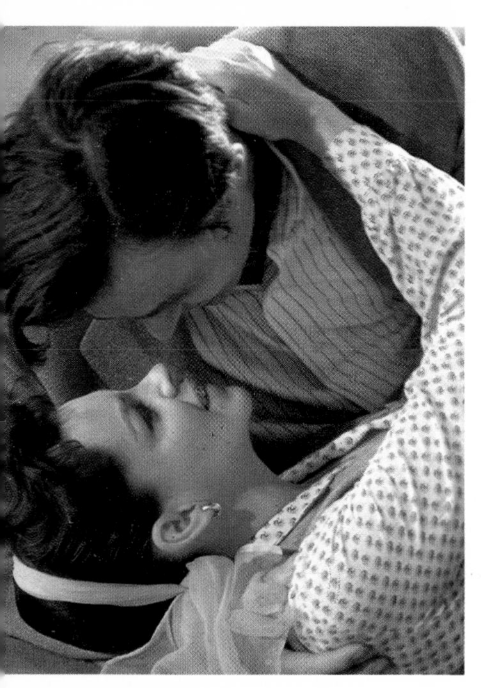

Clockwise, from top left: Kirk Douglas exhibits producer's ire in THE BAD. Gaynor-March A STAR IS BORN (1937). Robinson-Douglas in TWO WEEKS. Kim Stanley, THE GODDESS. Finch-Novak in LYLAH CLAIRE. ALEX IN WONDERLAND. Mason-Garland A STAR IS BORN (1954). Opposite: Jack Palance embraces Brigitte Bardot in CONTEMPT.

to the point of a breakdown, he decided to make a film about film that would be, in his own words, "more than a confession—my testament."

8½ is the greatest of all films about films, and it is also the first great filmed self-portrait. It is as rich, complex, endlessly analyzable, and endlessly seeable as CITIZEN KANE, with which it must stand as one of the summit works in cinema, a picture that expands the possibilities of the form.

8½, like CITIZEN KANE, is one of those few films that makes people want to become filmmakers. And also, like Welles' masterpiece, it deals with a huge number of subjects in a comprehensive way, entwining them with the story of a single dominating character. 8½ is not merely a film about film. It is about power, art, corruption, manners, morals, money, love, marriage, friendship, failed ambitions, disillusionment, religion, childhood, and how a man should live. But unlike many self-portraits by artists in various media it is totally without self-pity, and in this way, too, it is unlike the films about films that have poured out of Hollywood. 8½ has the charm, exuberance, and life force that one has come to expect in a Fellini film, and that one so rarely finds in this age of existential melancholy, self-disgust, and creative ennui.

In a way, all of Fellini's pictures have been about entertainers: carnival performers, journalists, prostitutes, etc. When Fellini decided to make a picture about the subject he knew the best, filmmaking, the motif of the performer could at last be resolved in the form of a filmmaker-protagonist who could only be himself.

8½ is, first of all, a film about the making of 8½. By telling the story of its own production (not the shooting, but the psychic process by which the film was conceived), 8½ becomes a film about itself. It is a measure of the complexity of this work and the skill of its inventor that this idea, already complicated, is allowed to resonate with a self-portrait on celluloid in which scenes of reality, fantasy, and memory are mixed, and the resulting mosaic used to illuminate the character of a filmmaker pondering his next picture (in fact, this picture) while immersed in a personal and professional crisis. Fellini has often been compared to a conjurer, and has himself said that he would like nothing better than to be a magician (though at times, surely, he has given the impression that he would prefer to be a clown). With 8½ he realizes this ambition. In it he conjures up memories of great

warmth, such as the La Seraghina sequence, in which Guido observes the fat whore dancing on the beach, and the wine-making in the farmhouse sequence which, in many ways, is the ultimate Fellini scene. He creates fantasies of delicious intensity, such as the orgy scene, the interview with the cardinal in the subterranean baths, the hanging of his despicable screenwriter collaborator, etc. And he constructs an imaginary world, building, for example, a useless and incredibly expensive space-platform tower which, in effect, he then uses as a throw-away prop, an example of his alter ego's directorial wastefulness. Like Welles in CITIZEN KANE, Fellini provides us with an enormously entertaining circus in which numerous acts take place in numerous rings, with the end result that our heads spin even as we are being moved.

Within the circus that is 8½, the world of film-making is depicted in all its cruelty, made even more unbearable than it actually is by Fellini-Guido's good-natured acceptance. When Guido's producer appears with his entourage in the lobby of the hotel, Guido runs to him, salaaming—an ironic expression of his awe in the presence of an omnipotent force. His relationships with his collaborators are full of strain. He must endure the chatter of the intellectual writer who anticipates almost every criticism that one can make of 8½, and the tired whines and annoying reproaches of his production manager Conocchia. People thrust scripts into his face, laugh at him as they pronounce the collapse of his career, demand explanations of his latest film, accuse him of this, threaten to break him on account of that, behaving with either exaggerated sycophancy or unbearable hostility, pushing him until he is about to crack. Never has the world of a famous film director been so truthfully presented. In no other film about film has the chaos and almost psychotic anarchy that surrounds motion-picture work been so accurately described. In this sense 8½ is a study of the problems of making a film like 8½, and, for that matter, the problems of making any film at all. If one were to sum up 8½ as a film about film (and, of course, it is much more than that), one would have to say that it depicts the insanity of its own enterprise, yet justifies that insanity on the ground that out of it can come a masterpiece. 8½ is the sort of picture that gives film-makers hope. Even as it describes all the horrors they must endure, which they speak of so often and describe in their films about films, it demonstrates the potentials of the medium on such an inspiring level that it justifies their endurance and proves that their profession is worthwhile.

# Credits

## All About Eve

U.S.A.; 1950; 138 minutes;
released by 20th Century-Fox.

**Directed by** Joseph L. Mankiewicz.
**Produced by** Darryl S. Zanuck.
**Screenplay by** Joseph L. Mankiewicz, adapted from the story and radio play, "The Wisdom of Eve," by Mary Orr.
**Photographed by** Milton Krasner.
**Art direction by** Lyle Wheeler and George Davis.
**Edited by** Barbara McLean.
**Music by** Alfred Newman.
**Cast:** Bette Davis; Anne Baxter; George Sanders; Celeste Holm; Gary Merrill; Hugh Marlowe; Thelma Ritter; Marilyn Monroe; Gregory Ratoff; Barbara Bates; Walter Hampden.

## Contempt (Le Mépris)

French-Italian Co-production; 1963;
100 minutes.
Released in the U.S. by Embassy Pictures.

**Directed by** Jean-Luc Godard.
**Produced by** Georges de Beauregard, Carlo Ponti, and Joseph E. Levine.
**Screenplay by** Jean-Luc Godard, from the novel, "Il Disprezzo," by Alberto Moravia.
**Photographed by** Raoul Coutard.
**Edited by** Agnès Guillemot and Lila Lakshmanan.
**Music by** Georges Delerue.
**Cast:** Brigitte Bardot; Michel Piccoli; Jack Palance; Fritz Lang; Giorgia Moll; Jean-Luc Godard; Linda Veras.

## Sunset Boulevard

U.S.A.; 1950; 111 minutes;
released by Paramount.

**Directed by** Billy Wilder.
**Produced by** Charles Brackett.
**Screenplay by** Charles Brackett, Billy Wilder and D. M. Marshman, Jr.
**Photographed by** John F. Seitz.
**Art direction by** Hans Dreier and John Meehan.
**Edited by** Arthur Schmidt.
**Music by** Franz Waxman.
**Cast:** William Holden; Gloria Swanson; Erich von Stroheim; Nancy Olson; Fred Clark; Lloyd Gough; Jack Webb; Franklyn Barnum; Larry Blake; Charles Dayton; Cecil B. De Mille; Hedda Hopper; Buster Keaton; Anna Q. Nilsson; H. B. Warner; Ray Evans.

## The Bad and the Beautiful

U.S.A.; 1952; 118 minutes;
released by MGM.

**Directed by** Vincente Minnelli.
**Produced by** John Houseman.
**Screenplay by** Charles Schnee, based on the story by George Bradshaw.
**Photographed by** Robert Surtees.
**Art direction by** Al Ybarra.
**Edited by** Tony Martinelli.
**Music by** David Raksin.
**Cast:** Kirk Douglas; Lana Turner; Walter Pidgeon; Dick Powell; Barry Sullivan; Gloria Grahame; Gilbert Roland; Leo G. Carroll; Vanessa Brown; Paul Stewart; Sammy White; Elaine Stewart.

## 8½ (Otto e Mezzo)

Italy; 1963; 138 minutes;
released in the U.S. by Embassy Pictures.

**Directed by** Federico Fellini.
**Produced by** Angelo Rizzoli.
**Screenplay by** Federico Fellini, Ennio Flaiano, Tullio Pinelli and Brunello Rondi from a story by Federico Fellini and Ennio Flaiano.
**Photographed by** Gianni Di Venanzo.
**Art direction by** Piero Gherardi.
**Edited by** Leo Cattozzo.
**Music by** Nino Rota.
**Cast:** Marcello Mastroianni; Anouk Aimée; Sandra Milo; Claudia Cardinale; Rossella Falk; Barbara Steele; Guido Alberti; Madeleine Lebeau; Jean Rougeul; Caterina Boratto; Annibale Nichi; Giuditta Risson.



Frolicking schoolboys enjoy La Seraghina's lascivious dance in 8½. The fat, bittersweet whore is a recurring character in Fellini films, coloring the sexual attitudes of his protagonists who never forget their initiations at her hands.

# Cinema of Personal Expression

9

A great film, by definition, expresses the world view of its maker and is an artistic expression of his personality. Sometimes, however, it is difficult to locate this directorial personality, to isolate it from the restrictive conventions of motion-picture genres. For example, when a man makes a western he usually deals with the terrain of the American West, the period and costumes of the 1880s and 1890s, and such conventions as the showdown gunfight, the ambience of the saloon, the role of the sheriff in the frontier town, etc. If he is to express himself, his personal vision must be squeezed through these conventions.

In the cinema of personal expression there are no such problems. The personal vision of the filmmaker is the raison d'être of his film. He does not have to impose himself upon his material. His vision, his personality, are his picture's subjects.

The trouble with personal films—films that are conscious expressions of a filmmaker's self—is that they constitute a luxury few people can afford. Attempts to make the screen serve art often lead to bankruptcy. Such pictures are called "art-house films" or "chamber films," which is another way of saying that their appeal is to a relatively small segment of the audience. Because film production is very expensive a mass audience is usually necessary in order to recoup an investment and turn a profit. The personal film is only possible in countries where production costs are relatively low, or where there exists some form of government subsidy.

It would have been inconceivable for a John Ford or a Howard Hawks or an Alfred Hitchcock to go to the head of a Hollywood studio and demand production funds because, "I want to make a picture that will express me as an artist." These men have obtained financing by saying, "I want to make a western [or an adventure film, or a thriller]. Here's the story. We can star so-and-so, bring it in for a million seven and project profits at four million eight." The head of the studio could then make a business decision without any meaningless talk about art and self-expression. Yet Ford and Hawks and Hitchcock, being artists, put so much of themselves into their pictures that their personal signatures are always evident, even if they have to be deciphered from what Peter Wollen, in *Signs and Meaning in the Cinema*, calls the

Preceding pages: Giulietta Masina as Gelsomina in Federico Fellini's great filmic poem, LA STRADA. Above: With Anthony Quinn as the strong man Zampano, performing their circus act for villagers. Masina's performance has been compared to best of Keaton and Chaplin.

"noise" of the star, the studio, the story, or the genre.

In the cinema of personal expression there is no "noise." The filmmaker is up front and on the line. His picture is presented for what it is: a work of art expressing his vision of the world.

Much has been written in recent years about the emergence of the personal film. Actually, the personal film has been a part of cinema since the beginning. What could be more personal, for example, than the early works of Fritz Lang, Carl Dreyer, F. W. Murnau, Griffith's INTOLERANCE, Jean Vigo's ZÉRO DE CONDUITE, and every thing made by Charles Chaplin? No, the personal film is not new. What is new is a self-conscious approach to it, possible only because in recent years the economies of the film industry have been favorable in a few places.

The five pictures discussed here all were made by European directors. They were all, in addition, austerely produced. (Only one, BLOW-UP, is in color.) Bergman, Buñuel, and Bresson are inconceivable in Hollywood. The pictures they make are incompatible with the financial realities of the American film industry. Fellini, though probably the most famous living director, has difficulty obtaining financing because, although some of his pictures have become hits, he is not dependably commercial. Antonioni's flirtation with Hollywood resulted in ZABRISKIE POINT, a financial and artistic failure. The point is that although these five men are among the dozen most interesting directors around, their collective fame is less than one hundredth of John Wayne's, and their bankability is resultingly limited.

Do not look, then, in their work for spectacle, lavishness, an exciting story, or escapist entertainment. Be prepared for seriousness, self-revelation, and even obscurity. The artists of the American cinema necessarily had to produce popular works in order to survive. In Europe it has been possible for artists to use the screen without giving their highest consideration to popular taste. Nothing is more useless than to set up hierarchies in which a man like Robert Bresson is placed above or below John Ford; or Luis Buñuel, at his most alienated and eccentric, is said to be greater than or inferior to Alfred Hitchcock. The wonder of the cinema is that it is flexible enough to embrace all who can use it well, including the man who uses it directly to express his inner self.

# Federico Fellini's **La Strada** 1956

The career of Federico Fellini is one of the most remarkable in the history of the cinema. He is and has for some years been the most famous filmmaker in the world, with movie audiences in Europe and America at his feet. In this way he bears a resemblance to Pablo Picasso, the most famous painter in the world, and in another and very important way, too: both men have recreated themselves many times. Each has had a tendency to adopt a style, carry it to heights of accomplishment, and then abandon it for something new. In fifteen years Fellini has made at least five great films (three of them discussed in this book), a personal accomplishment that no other filmmaker can claim. I VITELLONI is a surpassing autobiographical film; LA STRADA is a lyrical film, a great personal poem; LA DOLCE VITA is an influential film of social comment; 8½ is probably the greatest self-portrait of an artist on celluloid; and SATYRICON is an extraordinary film of fantasy, an incredible fictional vision. Fellini is now in his early fifties, at the height of his powers. We can only wonder what he will do next, what new territory he will explore and dominate.

LA STRADA won the Academy Award for Best Foreign Film in 1956, and has collected a good fifty more prizes besides. It is the favorite movie of many people, including filmmakers as diverse as Sam Peckinpah (whose "tough" outlook is about as far as one can get from Fellini) and the documentarian Albert Maysles (who doesn't like fiction films much at all).

LA STRADA is a film with an uncanny power to move people to tears. It is simple and modestly produced, and it haunts members of the toughest audiences. It is a poem about marginal people living on the fringes of society. It takes place, literally, "on the road," in deserted lots, on beaches between highways and the sea. Its message—that everyone needs someone; that loneliness and solitude are unbearable—is almost simple-minded, yet it is exquisitely expressed. LA STRADA is episodic, unpredictable, spontaneous. It is filled with seemingly gratuitous scenes linked together in the most casual way, yet they add up to a rich and powerful vision of life, an offering from a filmmaker to a public that adores his every crumb.

One has the feeling about the Fellini of LA STRADA (and of the other pictures of the same early period, IL BIDONE and NIGHTS OF CABIRIA) that his films are bear hugs, that he is grasping his public to him in a powerful and warm embrace, rubbing his rough whiskers against the smooth cheeks of his audiences as if to say: "I give you a world from my heart; may it move you and may you taste in it the rough-warm flavor of life."

The story of LA STRADA is so simple that one feels certain that in screenplay form it would have been rejected by every studio in the United States, just as it nearly was by Carlo Ponti and Dino de Laurentiis. They agreed to produce it only when Fellini told them he would employ the American actor, Anthony Quinn.

A strange, half-mad girl is "bought" from her mother by a second-rate carnival strongman, and the two go on the road. Zampano (Anthony Quinn) brutalizes Gelsomina (played by Fellini's wife, Giulietta Masina, in a weird pantomimist style that has been compared to the styles of Keaton, Chaplin, and Marcel Marceau). When they join a provincial circus, Gelsomina meets the tightrope walker, Matto the Fool (Richard Basehart). Zampano hates Matto, who taunts him mercilessly, and when, after provocation, he pulls a knife, he is arrested and sent to jail for the night. Gelsomina wants to leave Zampano, but Matto convinces her to stay with him. With a pebble in his hand he tells her: "All in this world serves some purpose... even this little stone." So Gelsomina stays with Zampano. Later, when they meet up again with Matto on the highway, Zampano beats him up and accidentally kills him. Gelsomina goes mad and Zampano abandons her on a roadside. Years after, Zampano hears a girl hum the tune that Gelsomina used to sing. He discovers that Gelsomina has died, he goes out on a drunk, and that night he falls to his knees on a beach and weeps over the loss of her warmth and the misery of his own solitude.

This little story is enriched by a series of extraordinary episodes having to do with the experiences of Gelsomina as she discovers and marvels at the world:

When Zampano abandons her in front of a trattoria and goes off to sleep with a whore, she spends the night weeping. In the morning she is amazed when a riderless horse strolls by her down the street.

At a country wedding, where she and Zampano have done their act, she is taken by some children to an attic room to see a deformed child named Oswaldo, who peers strangely at her from his bed.

When Gelsomina runs away from Zampano and is sitting by a roadside wondering what to do, three musicians surrealistically appear in a single file and lead her to a village where she sees a religious procession. She watches it with awe, and later that night sees the aerial ballet of Matto the Fool for the first time.

With such apparently gratuitous scenes Fellini suffuses us with his rough warmth. In a context of clowns, carnivals and circuses—a continuing motif in his movies, derived, we are told, from his own adolescent experiences as a member of a carnival troupe—he sings us an exquisite poem about an innocent girl, a brutal man, and an artist-fool. It is a poem that haunts.

## Luis Buñuel's **Viridiana** 1961

Nothing could be further from the warm humanism of Federico Fellini than the ironic misanthropy of Luis Buñuel. The differences between them are compounded by the fact that the world of Fellini is accessible to everyone (even children), while the world of Buñuel is the delight of a small, devoted cult which must constantly defend him against self-appointed guardians of the public morality. For Luis Buñuel has been accused of almost every sin, every sort of political extremism, every variety of sexual perversion. He has been accused of being the Marquis de Sade of cinema, even of being a man who dines upon live ants. His films, filled with paranoia, anticlericalism, foot-fetishism, and cruelty, are presented with the rage and passion of a man who seems set upon the alienation of the public. Call him bizarre, violent, scandalous, outrageous, he remains one of the tremendous personal voices of the cinema, a hurricane that howls from the normally vacuous screen, a man who clearly does not give a damn for anyone, who is thoroughly committed to nothing but the violent expression of his tormented self. Buñuel with a camera is an iconoclast with a blowtorch.

He has been making scandals since 1928, when he collaborated with Salvador Dali on UN CHIEN ANDALOU, and shocked the public with a shot of a razor blade slicing through a woman's eyeball. In 1930, he established himself as the master of the surrealist cinema with L'AGE D'OR, a picture that so enraged audiences that they tore its first-run theatre apart. There followed various odd jobs: producer of antifascist films in Spain, resident docu-

mentarian at the Museum of Modern Art in New York, dubbing director in Hollywood, and then a long period as a filmmaker in Mexico, where he created more than fifteen works, some brilliant, some mediocre, all stamped with the brand of his unique sensibility.

Since UN CHIEN ANDALOU and L'AGE D'OR, the highpoints of his career have been the socially committed LOS OLVIDADOS (1950); a paranoic fantasy on jealousy, EL (1952); a satanic farce, THE LIFE OF CRIME OF ARCHIBALD DE LA CRUZ (1955); and the cryptoreligious masterpiece, NAZARIN (1958). In 1961 Buñuel created his greatest film, the masterpiece in which every sin and outrage of which he had been accused was exhibited in its fullest development. VIRIDIANA, like other Buñuel films, was an enormous scandal. He had returned to Spain for the first time in twenty-five years in order to make it, and had worked under the supervision of Spanish censors. When it won the grand prize at the Cannes Film Festival, the Spanish government was forced to ban and disown it. Somehow, by some route of deviousness too complex to trace, Buñuel had sneaked by his censors a picture that was an abomination to the Fascists he despised and whose regime his work officially represented.

It is impossible to describe the visual texture of this film and its extraordinary force. VIRIDIANA is a picture that must be seen. Certainly the orgy of the beggars (destruction, copulation, and sacrilege) is a stunning sequence, shattering, violent, as perverse as anything that has ever been rendered on the screen. (It makes brilliant contrast with the now-standard "decadent party" sequence, inevitable in films about alienation, and usually so boring.) It climaxes when the beggars form a tableau, in imitation of Leonardo's painting of the Last Supper. Christ is played by an evil blind man, a scratched recording of Handel's "Messiah" plays on an antique Victrola, and the moment is "photographed" by a demented whore, who snaps it with her "box camera"—revealed when she abruptly lifts her skirts.

VIRIDIANA is an indictment of charity, mercy, all Christian virtues, and all the paraphernalia of the Catholic church. (Viridiana travels with certain personal props: a cross, a hammer and nails, and a crown of thorns, which she burns when she renounces Catholicism for sensualism.) It is filled with seemingly gratuitous shots of feet, insects, cruelty, and other Buñuelian obsessions, including a particular emphasis on the maid's daughter's jump rope, an instrument used alternately for play, strangulation, and bondage. The decaying estate and the perverse happenings on it are probably symbolic of Buñuel's vision of the condition of his native Spain. And the whole picture is shot through with Buñuel's cruel irony, perhaps no place better illustrated than in the famous sequence of the dog and the cart.

Jorge takes pity on a wretched dog tied to the undercarriage of a peasant cart, which he rescues by buying from its owner. As he walks away, Buñuel shows us another dog, even more wretched, trotting tiredly along under another cart coming down the road from the other direction. This scene illuminates the ethos of Buñuel's universe: the innate cruelty of the world, and the stupidity and hypocrisy of performing good deeds. It is a devastating indictment of liberalism, with revolutionary implications: The world cannot be changed by a fine gesture. If it can be changed at all, which is doubtful, it will be by a total destruction of every existing system. Buñuel's message, if one can call it that, seems to be that since everything is awful, and nothing anyone does can make any difference, an amusing solution is to laugh at life's cruelties. This is an extremely unpopular notion, calculated to alienate almost everyone. But Buñuel's hatred is immense, and in VIRIDIANA, at the age of sixty-one, it is as stone-hard and knife-sharp as in any of his outrages.



Ultimate in anticlericalism, as dwarfs, whores, and half-wits re-enact the Last Supper in an orgy of destruction, copulation, and sacrilege at climax of Luis Buñuel's VIRIDIANA. Even after forty-five years of filmmaking, Buñuel's hatred of the church has not softened.

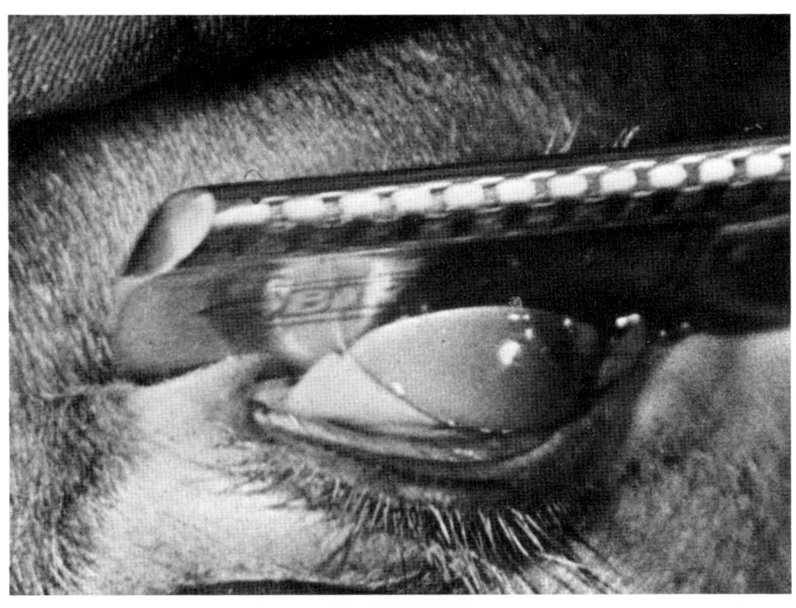

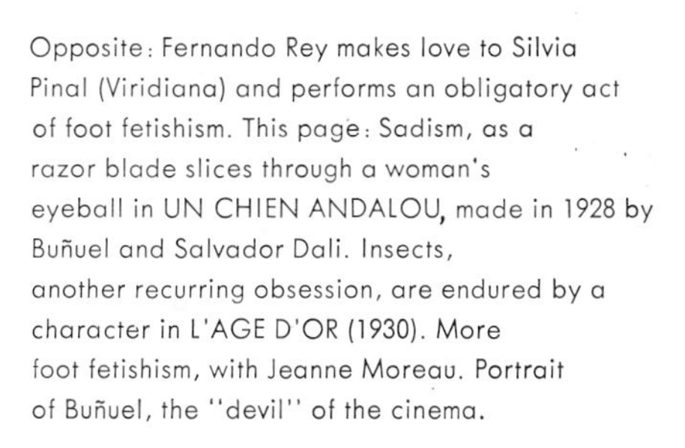

Opposite: Fernando Rey makes love to Silvia Pinal (Viridiana) and performs an obligatory act of foot fetishism. This page: Sadism, as a razor blade slices through a woman's eyeball in UN CHIEN ANDALOU, made in 1928 by Buñuel and Salvador Dali. Insects, another recurring obsession, are endured by a character in L'AGE D'OR (1930). More foot fetishism, with Jeanne Moreau. Portrait of Buñuel, the "devil" of the cinema.

# Ingmar Bergman's **Persona** 1966

If Buñuel is the Spanish Director—the only one of international repute, and typically Spanish on account of his fascination with the grotesque, reminiscent, in ways, of the vision of Goya—Ingmar Bergman is the Swedish Director, and, for that matter, the most famous living Swede. Though Buñuel is sometimes slipshod in his work, Bergman is fastidious, a perfectionist with a supreme command of the film medium. And while Buñuel brandishes a blowtorch and throws acid on the conventions of society, Bergman explores the dark recesses of his psyche, and there fabricates fantasies that illuminate his personal anguish.

The Bergman freaks, or Bergmaniacs, as they are sometimes called, believe their man to be the greatest filmmaker of all time. If ever a Nobel Prize is given for cinema they will holler if it is not given to him. Bergman

Left: Bibi Andersson (foreground) and Liv Ullmann in scene from Ingmar Bergman's PERSONA. Note resemblance to each other. Below, Andersson as nurse, Ullmann as mute stage actress. Scene from a dream sequence. Bottom, right: Bergman conferring with his actresses (Ullmann facing).

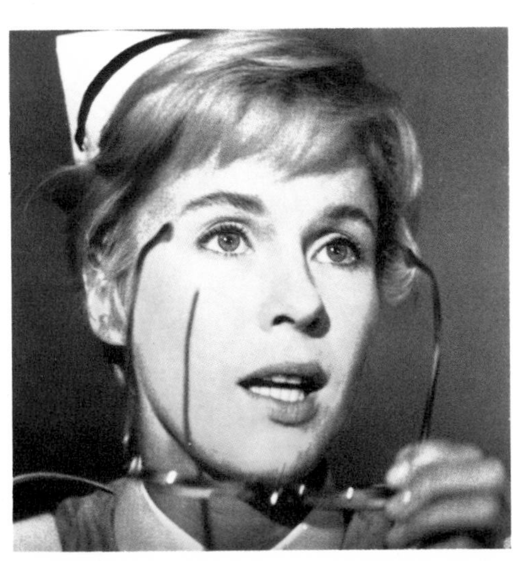

has his detractors, too, people who are bored by his obscurity, and irritated by his heavy symbolism and his austere, icy, Scandinavian melancholy. Both admirers and detractors have their points. Bergman is one of the very few filmmakers who has consistently treated the cinema as a fine art, and has expanded its possibilities as a medium of personal expression. On the other hand, he is just as certainly uncompromising when it comes to providing entertainment. Bergman may be an artist, but he is not a showman; the audience at a Bergman film is forced to work very hard without much certainty that its hard work will provide much penetration into the fog.

Unlike Fellini, Bergman does not give up much warmth to the public. His is a pure blue flame. He makes his films, they get better and better, and his personal odyssey, his search for meaning in life, is there for anyone who wants to observe it, but in the end Bergman doesn't much care what people think. Each of his pictures is a part of a long dialogue with himself.

PERSONA may be his masterpiece, though there are people who are devoted to SMILES OF A SUMMER NIGHT, THE SEVENTH SEAL, WILD STRAWBERRIES, THROUGH A GLASS DARKLY, WINTER LIGHT, THE SILENCE, and THE PASSION OF ANNA. His pictures can be arranged into trilogies, and his development traced and measured in phases. In his later work the intrusion of himself—interrupting action while actors speak about their parts, allowing equipment to be seen along the fringes of the frame, leaving in clap-sticks, using deliberately shoddy and transparent special effects, and repeating takes so as to suspend progression of action —suggests an interest in establishing the artificial "made" quality of his films, in stating very clearly that he is not presenting reality in a manner that requires suspension of disbelief, but is rendering experience in the form of art. The fact that PERSONA opens with shots of the lighting up of an arc lamp in a projector and of film leader being fed onto sprockets, and closes with the film running out and the arc lamp dying, suggests a deliberate attempt to say: This is a film, an artifact, a thing I made and dreamt, not a document of reality I observed. In addition, this opening and closing may represent a definitive statement by Bergman that he is not providing escapist entertainment.

In PERSONA, a stage actress, played by Liv Ullmann, is being treated for catatonia. During a performance of "Electra" she suddenly stopped acting, the next day she fell silent, and she hasn't spoken since. Her doctor sends her to a house by the seashore in a remote area of northern Sweden, accompanied by a nurse-companion (Bibi Andersson). The faces of the two women are strikingly similar, and as the film progresses their clothes, their gestures, even their expressions begin to merge. The actress, the artist, is totally silent; her behavior could be conventionally described as mentally diseased. The nurse is talkative, unmiserable, effusive, an equally conventional projection of a normal young woman. In the house by the sea the relationship between them develops in a strange and fascinating way. As the nurse babbles and reveals herself, and the actress listens, there comes a point where the normality of the nurse becomes questionable and the silence of the actress explicable. It is as if the actress is infecting the nurse, and some process of reversal is taking place; as if the talkative nurse is becoming hysterical, and the silent actress is becoming eloquent.

The turning point comes when the actress gives the nurse an unsealed letter to mail. The nurse reads it and discovers that the actress has been toying with her. Hostility erupts. The nurse leaves a shard of glass on the terrace of the house and is pleased when the actress cuts herself on it. There are fights between them, unexpected outbreaks of physical violence, intimate caresses, even a bloodsucking episode suggesting lesbianism and also a complete merging of identities. At last, after a terrifying nightmare in which the nurse dreams of making love to the actress' husband while the actress stands by like a voyeuse, the two women part, the actress still silent, still uncured, the nurse apparently returning to the normal world.

What does it mean? Impossible to say. Bergman gives very little in PERSONA, not enough to clarify its many obscure points. However, it seems clear that this story, realized so perfectly, rendered with enormous skill and acted and photographed with astonishing brilliance, constitutes some sort of speculation about the role of the artist and the meaning of art. The symbiotic relationship between artist and audience, the way life and art feed upon one another, fight, merge, exchange and separate, the madness that is at the core of art—these seem to be the abstract themes symbolized by the relationship between the actress and the nurse, whose faces Bergman actually combines, at one point, in a strange, surreal superimposition. In another sense, one could say that PERSONA is a justification for the personal film. If the artist does not discharge his agony in the constructive form of art, his silence will destructively infect the public. Art, then, thrives upon disease, and Bergman's films are the product of his neurosis.

It is not his obscurity that is so frightening about Bergman. It is his intensity. There is such tension in PERSONA that it comes at times to be an almost unbearable experience. One senses a man revealing his anguish at the furthest extremes of cold fire, compelling attention by the blazing sting of total chill. In PERSONA the faces of Liv Ullmann and Bibi Andersson are incandescent with this intensity. Their interchange is so intimate that at times we want to avert our eyes.

The mystery surrounding Bergman is whether he himself knows what his pictures are about. In PERSONA one has the feeling that something very personal is being revealed, wrenched out of himself and placed with great creative agony upon celluloid. Bergman seems to be hovering very close to some momentous revelation, or to some irreversible fall into an abyss of obscurity and unresolved symbolism. His future work will reveal whether he can fully communicate his anguish, or whether his attempts to communicate it are burning him out.

Whether one likes him or not, Bergman cannot be dismissed. His craftsmanship is impeccable, his skills with actors and camera enormous. In his films he offers himself up as few men ever have. In each succeeding work there is a sense of a man straining against the limits of his abilities and the limits of his art, using the screen as a diary, not of his exterior life, but of the life of his tormented soul.

# Robert Bresson's **Au Hasard, Balthazar** 1966

Robert Bresson has been called the Ingmar Bergman of France, a description that is much too facile and that prevents real understanding of a unique directorial personality. Both filmmakers are intensely austere, Bresson perhaps even more so than Bergman. His pictures are severe in the manner of a Jansenist Catholic, redeemed from utter coldness by an innate Gallic warmth. But while Bergman's films are saturated with symbolism, Bresson's films are more realistic, and while the struggles of Bergman's characters mirror struggles within Bergman's own soul, the struggles of Bresson's characters are the struggles of real people whose humanity is never denied. Bergman exhibits great inner anguish; Bresson, in his films, exudes a composure, a self-containment that suggests a man at peace with himself.

Robert Bresson is a master of total control in the cinema. His every shot is precise and his spare images are indelible. Every move, every gesture, every utterance of his players (usually nonprofessional actors) is dictated with precision. Bresson is a puppeteer and his players are marionettes. It is said that he gives precise line-readings and enforces his will by making innumerable takes, wearing down anyone who contradicts him until all resistance is dissolved. The famous downward glances of his people, their avoidance of eye contact, and the famous Bresson monotone in which all the characters speak in more or less the same rigid, styleless way, are evidences of the very special sensibility he imposes.

Like Bergman, Bresson is utterly uncompromising when it comes to matters of public taste. He decidedly does not produce works of escapist entertainment, nor cater in any way to current fashions. But unlike Bergman he is not well known—a national monument, even a national treasure in France, perhaps, but virtually unrecognized in the rest of the world. AU HASARD, BALTHAZAR, his greatest film, has received only the most cursory distribution in the United States. Bresson, who has made no more than ten films in forty years, is perhaps the most obscure great filmmaker around, content to be the darling of film festivals and the object of a small, devoted cult, totally uninterested in personal fame or mass adulation.

It is not easy to gain access to the world of Bresson. His films require an audience to work. He leaves many things unsaid, removing everything from his stories that is not essential. His characters are usually revealed only in moments that illuminate their natures. These people are often vile, sometimes evil, always sinful, yet they are depicted with compassion, for they are human and are therefore blessed with grace. In this sense Bresson is very much a Catholic filmmaker, a man interested in truth-



Balthazar the donkey dies amid a flock of sheep at end of Robert Bresson's AU HASARD, BALTHAZAR. Among other enormous accomplishments of this film is the fact that it is nearly impossible not to feel moved; after all that happens this death seems a final outrage.

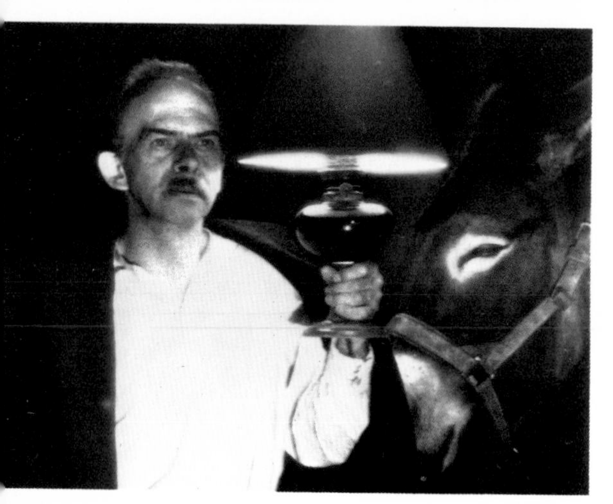

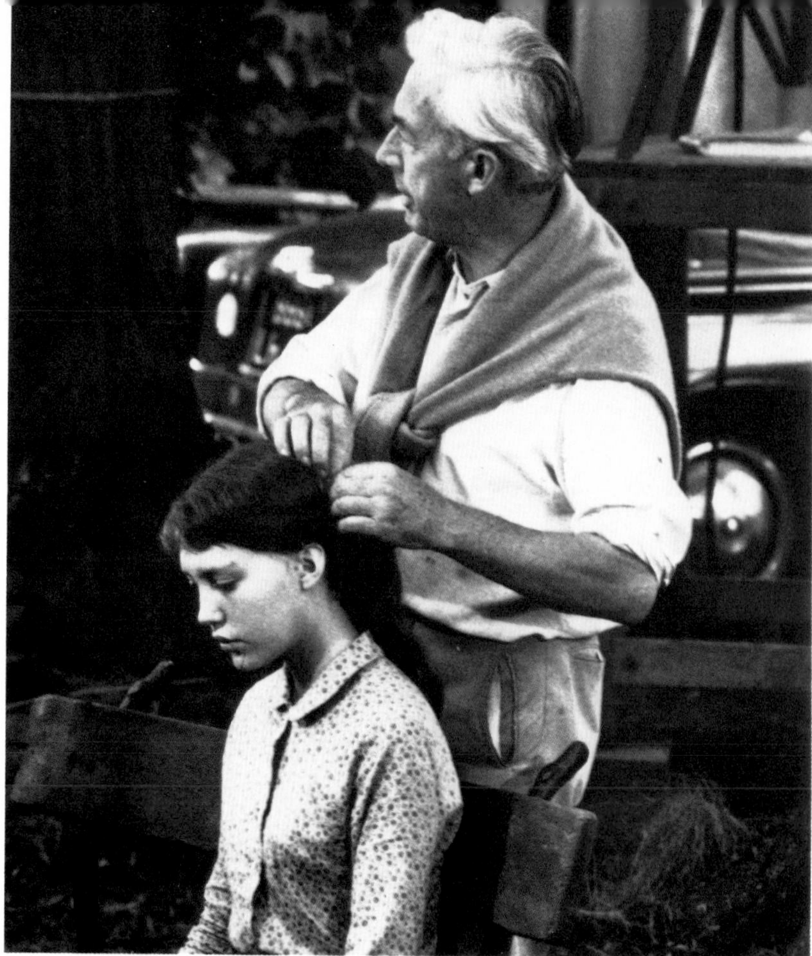

fully illuminating the predicament of people of whose eventual salvation he has little doubt. A Bresson film is spare and episodic, characterized by short, intense scenes linked together by dissolves. The narrative voice is staccato, and the special quality of the performances, from which every attempt at "acting" has been removed, endows his characters with an aura of spirituality that the makers of Biblical epics never seem to obtain.

AU HASARD, BALTHAZAR is set in rural France, a brooding frontier region, where human life is mostly taken up by toil. A donkey, Balthazar, is the central character. His life intersects with the lives of humans who either own him or use him at various times. The lives of these human characters also intersect, and thus through the device of the donkey a complicated story of human entanglements and struggles is told. The principal characters are Marie, a sullen girl who first adopts and names Balthazar (she is torn between spirituality and sensuality, sensuality wins out, and at the end she is gang-raped and dies); Gérard, a young sadist, leader of a motorcycle gang, a sinister youth who is the first seducer of Marie, and who torments Balthazar by setting fire to his tail; and Arnold, a half-witted drunken tramp, who owns Balthazar for a while, is alternately cruel to and solicitous of him, and who also dies in the course of the film.

When Balthazar is young he is loved and caressed by children. Later, turned into a beast of burden, he is tormented by men. In his middle age he becomes a stunt donkey in a circus and is applauded for his brilliance. And in his old age he is regarded by his final owner as a saint. Gérard is ultimately responsible for his death. He steals Balthazar, uses him on a smuggling expedition, and then deserts him when he is shot by a border guard.

It is difficult to convey the intensity of this film and its ability to evoke emotion. When Balthazar dies in a high meadow, amidst a flock of sheep, slowly sinking to the ground, the depth of one's feelings for him is remarkable. There have been many pictures about animals, and most of them have been sentimental. AU HASARD, BALTHAZAR is not one of these. It is a hard, tough picture about suffering and cruelty, human vice and human struggle. The fact that one can come out of a theatre unashamedly moved by the death of a donkey suggests some special power in Robert Bresson. He brings off an almost impossible feat, a picture in which the agony of the human race is convincingly illustrated by the life story of an animal which, by its end, becomes the bearer of the enormous weight of all unexpiated human guilt.

AU HASARD, BALTHAZAR, as Jean-Luc Godard has said, "is really the world in an hour and a half."



From AU HASARD, BALTHAZAR: Downward glance of Anne Wiazemsky (Marie) is typical of Bresson's style. Pierre Klossowski as the corn merchant, with Balthazar. Right: Robert Bresson tends Marie's hair. His relationship with his actors is that of puppeteer to his marionettes.

# Michelangelo Antonioni's **Blow-Up** 1966

The warm embrace of Federico Fellini is opposed by the cool elusiveness of his fellow countryman, Michelangelo Antonioni. Antonioni is not misanthropic like Buñuel, or heavily symbolic like Bergman, or severe like Robert Bresson. His universe is fashionably existential, peopled by characters embroiled in crises of despair. The Antonioni hero is a man or a woman who has acquired all the possessions that society regards as the accouterments of success, but whose inner life is empty, whose spirit is voided, and whose ability to alter his predicament is curtailed by ennui. The world of Antonioni is the world of T. S. Eliot's "The Wasteland": Love is illusory and the meaning of life is elusive. Modern urban society is a wasted landscape through which he wanders, unsatisfied by money, sex, relationships, a strange place where all conversations are elliptical, contact with other humans is strained, matters arise that are never resolved, and life is bounded by boredom and meaninglessness.

For many years Antonioni was obscure. He filmed his existential tales, mastering motion-picture technique and evolving a personal style, and the public yawned. Eventually, in 1960, his L'AVVENTURA became a *succès de scandale* when it was booed and hissed at the Cannes Film Festival. An excruciatingly slow but perfectly told story of modern despair, it enraged audiences by neglecting to explain the disappearance of a girl on a deserted island. A backlash against those who had booed swiftly developed. "But of course he doesn't explain it! That's just the point! That's how life is! Nothing can be explained!" Those who had hissed were relegated to the category of philistines. Suddenly the public was ready for a filmmaker who raised questions and then refused to answer them. LA NOTTE in 1961 and ECLIPSE a year later completed Antonioni's trilogy about alienation, and established one of the contemporary cinema's most characteristic and easily satirized motifs: the long, meditative walk through an urban wasteland, interrupted by unlinked and random events that evoke futility and despair. By the time of the release of Antonioni's first color film, RED DESERT, in 1964, he had established himself as the master of alienation—perhaps not so financially rewarding a position as Hitchcock's master of suspense, but infinitely more chic.

With BLOW-UP (1966), Antonioni created a genuine hit. The sort of picture that would normally have been seen only on the art-house circuit a few years before, it was widely played, even in small towns, and became a compulsory conversation piece in its year of release. The public was finally ready for Antonioni; his particular brand of avant-gardism had finally become fashionable. Perhaps it was the picture's milieu—"swinging" London, youth pop culture, a few then-daring scenes of erotic sex—but Antonioni had at last surmounted the barrier that had always lain in the personal filmmaker's path: He became a commercial success.

BLOW-UP concerns a successful mod photographer in London whose world is bounded by fashion, pop music, marijuana, and easy sex. His inner life is as bored and despairing as that of any classic Antonioni hero, but in the course of a single day he stumbles upon an event that challenges his ennui, evokes for a few moments the possibility that he may overcome it, but leaves him in the end much as he was before.

While snapping photographs in a park he accidentally captures on film the commission of a murder. The fact that he has photographed a murder does not occur to him until he studies and then blows up his negatives, uncovering details, blowing up smaller and smaller elements, and finally putting the puzzle together in a masterful sequence which in visual strength and suspense would be a credit to Alfred Hitchcock. Whether out of moral weakness, or something in modern life beyond his control, the photographer cannot follow through on his discovery. In the end his photographs are stolen, all evidence of the crime disappears, and he himself begins to question the truth of what he thinks he has seen.

Antonioni's telling of this story is perfection. He is said to have screened every print of BLOW-UP before release to assure himself that the quality of the color met the standards he brought to the production. Many of the scenes, including the simplest, were shot over and over again. The backgrounds—left by many filmmakers to chance or to uncaring assistants—are meticulously controlled. (Note the turbaned Hindu and the foursome of Nigerians who appear in two of the street scenes.) Background buildings were painted in hues that Antonioni believed would evoke specific emotional responses. The behavior of the actors is characteristically Antonioniesque: They move languorously, deliver their dialogue in carefully arranged tableaux of alienation, faces averted, stances opposed, lines left incomplete. Their faces are often suddenly distracted by unexplained noises or random events outside, and they play their sex scenes with chilly intensity. The sound track, too, is a marvel of perfection. Antonioni listened to hundreds of recordings of wind blowing through trees before settling on the mixture that produces the special texture of the scenes set in the park.

The meaning of BLOW-UP has been widely debated, and an entire book of speculations about it has been assembled. Though most critics are convinced that a real murder was committed, there are some who believe the murder was only an illusion of the photographer. Interpretations have been suggested ranging from the thesis that the more one looks at something the less one knows about it (the very process of blowing-up a photograph renders it increasingly abstract); that life is an illusion while art is substantial; that the interaction between life and art is ambiguous and ungraspable; to the idea that it is impossible to know the difference between what is true and what is false in the contemporary world.

Whatever the precise meaning of BLOW-UP, its effect upon audiences was intense. For the first time an extremely personal and difficult film was bought as entertainment. One wonders, however, how long Antonioni will remain in vogue. It is possible that for a brief time his personal obsessions coincided with public taste, but that the public, forever in pursuit of the novel, has moved on to new areas—extreme violence, perhaps, or the "wholesome" escapism of "family" pictures.

Antonioni may be left, like Bergman, Bresson, and Buñuel, with a small, devoted audience. This is the dilemma of the personal filmmaker. While he may spend a lifetime working out his personal themes, refining them, working toward an ultimate film that fully expresses them, the public is constantly on the lookout for new forms of escapism, and the personal fantasies of a single man are not of popular interest for very long. This is the main reason that the personal film is a great luxury, almost unknown in America except, perhaps, immediately after a director has made an enormous commercial hit. Film is just too expensive to be a fine art. The personal film is one of the side shows of cinema. The mainstream lies elsewhere, in the popular genres.

From BLOW-UP: Intimacy without passion as David Hemmings (Thomas) photographs high-fashion model Verushka in balletic sequence of opening reel. With Vanessa Redgrave. Michelangelo Antonioni at work. Opposite: Seemingly split Thomas contemplates studio setting for photograph.

# Credits

## La Strada (The Road)

Italy; 1956; 108 minutes;
originally released in the U.S. by
Trans-Lux.

**Directed by** Federico Fellini.
**Produced by** Dino de Laurentiis and Carlo Ponti.
**Screenplay by** Federico Fellini,
Tullio Pinelli, and Ennio Flaiano.
**Photographed by** Otello Martelli.
**Edited by** Leo Cattozzo and Lina Caterini.
**Music by** Nino Rota.
**Cast:** Anthony Quinn; Giulietta Masina;
Richard Basehart; Aldo Silvani; Marcella Rovere;
Livia Venturini.

## Persona

Sweden; 1966; 81 minutes;
released in the U.S. by
Lopert Pictures Corp.

**Directed by** Ingmar Bergman.
**Produced by** Ingmar Bergman.
**Screenplay by** Ingmar Bergman.
**Photographed by** Sven Nykvist.
**Art direction by** Bibi Lindström.
**Edited by** Ulla Ryghe.
**Music by** Lars Johan Werle.
**Cast:** Bibi Andersson; Liv Ullmann;
Gunnar Björnstrand; Margaretha Krook.

## Viridiana

Spain; 1961; 91 minutes;
originally released in the U.S. by
Kingsley International.

**Directed by** Luis Buñuel.
**Produced by** Gustavo Alatriste.
**Screenplay by** Luis Buñuel and Julio Alejandro.
**Photographed by** José Aguayo.
**Art direction by** Francisco Canet.
**Edited by** Pedro del Rey.
**Music:** Handel's "Messiah."
**Cast:** Silvia Pinal; Francisco Rabal;
Fernando Rey; Margarita Lozano; Victoria Zinny;
Teresa Rabal; José Calvo; Joaquín Roa.

## Au Hasard, Balthazar (Look out, Balthazar)

France; 1966; 95 minutes;
released in the U.S. by
New Line Cinema.

**Directed by** Robert Bresson.
**Produced by** Mag Bodard.
**Screenplay by** Robert Bresson.
**Photographed by** Ghislain Cloquet.
**Art direction by** Pierre Charbonnier.
**Edited by** Raymond Lamy.
**Music by** Franz Schubert Piano Sonata No. 20.
**Cast:** Anne Wiazemsky; François Lafarge;
Philippe Asselin; Nathalie Joyaut; Walter Green;
J.-C. Guilbert; François Sullerot;
M. C. Frémont; Pierre Klossowski; Jean Remignard;
Jacques Sorbets; Tord Paag; Sven Frostenson;
Roger Fjellstrom.

## Blow-Up

Great Britain; 1966;
111 minutes; released by MGM.

**Directed by** Michelangelo Antonioni.
**Produced by** Carlo Ponti.
**Screenplay by** Michelangelo Antonioni and Tonino Guerra;
English dialogue in collaboration with
Edward Bond; inspired by a short story by
Julio Cortázar.
**Photographed by** Carlo di Palma.
**Art direction by** Assheton Gorton.
**Edited by** Frank Clarke.
**Music by** Herbert Hancock.
**Cast:** David Hemmings; Vanessa Redgrave;
Sarah Miles; John Castle; Peter Bowles;
Jane Birkin; Gillian Hills; Harry Hutchinson;
Verushka.

# Fantasy & Horror

10

Because the photographic process makes it possible to simulate reality, realism has been the mainstream of the cinema. But fantasy has been a subterranean stream since the earliest days of the medium, since the late nineteenth century, when Georges Méliès made L'EVENTAIL MAGIQUE. Méliès was a magician, and his interest in cinematography was in its potential to create magic through special effects. This magical aspect of filmmaking has been basic to the cinema of fantasy down to our own time and the greatest masterpiece of the genre, Stanley Kubrick's 2001: A SPACE ODYSSEY.

The great horror film overlaps the great film of fantasy. Neither, in this discussion, concerns mad scientists (except, of course, for the inescapable Rotwang), Frankenstein monsters, and evil beings with fangs dripping blood, staples of the enormous category of exploitation films that frighten children, amuse adults, and quickly desert the memory. The best horror pictures, the ones made by master filmmakers, extrapolate from the horror that coexists with normality in everyday life, and fantasize worlds which inspire terror because they are so plausible. The macabre characterizations of Lon Chaney are an interesting phenomenon, but Godard's vision in WEEKEND is ten times more terrifying than THE HUNCHBACK OF NOTRE DAME or THE PHANTOM OF THE OPERA. It is a fantasy that cannot be disregarded because it could come true.

In this same sense, 2001: A SPACE ODYSSEY is a horror film. The magic of its technology and its matter-of-fact tone are infinitely more terrifying than all the devices of menace in ROSEMARY'S BABY. 2001 is truly frightening because an amoral universe is more plausible than a cabal of witches, and an unseen manipulative intelligence is scarier than a flesh-and-blood demonic doctor.

Hitchcock's PSYCHO is the cinema's greatest horror-murder film, though it includes only two murders and most pictures of the genre usually deal with many more. It doesn't take decapitations and gore, a leering paranoid with a reverberating chuckle, or Vincent Price in a wax museum, to make people scream. All it takes is a sympathetic character in an ordinary situation, suddenly confronted by the violence that resides just beneath the surface of everyday life. In a Transylvanian castle, committed by a wolf man or an anthropomorphic vampire, a knife murder would be merely hokum. In the shower cubicle of a shabby motel it is a stroke of genius.

Great horror is not to be seen on the Japanese monster-insect-King Kong-Dracula circuit, but in the subtler films that have a basis in real life. The cheapie horror pictures of the quick-kill commercial cinema wear the tawdry trappings of the carnival freak show. The great horror films, the fantasies of great filmmakers, are gripping and powerful because even their components of magic are personal and visionary.

Fantasy is a realm which fascinates every filmmaker, even those who are not true fantasists at heart. Fellini's SATYRICON, Welles' THE TRIAL, Bergman's THE MAGICIAN, and Charles Laughton's NIGHT OF THE HUNTER are just a few of many phantasmagoric creations which are not included here. Works have been included which are peaks of achievement in various subcategories of the genre: METROPOLIS, a futuristic fantasy produced on an epic scale; PSYCHO, the absolute summit of screen terror, perhaps the most manipulative film ever made; THE MANCHURIAN CANDIDATE, a prophetic work of political science-fiction; WEEKEND, a vision of horror so personal that it may constitute the first nervous breakdown ever recorded on celluloid; and 2001: A SPACE ODYSSEY, a great magic show, a frightening horror story, and a distinguished work of motion-picture art.

## Fritz Lang's **Metropolis** 1926

METROPOLIS has been called absurd, a work of insanity, and, by H. G. Wells, "quite the silliest film I have seen." It is all of these things, and also a strikingly visual, monumental production, and an important landmark in the history of motion pictures.

Charges of absurdity are usually leveled against the story of METROPOLIS—its tyrant master, its mad scientist Rotwang, Freder, Maria, revolution and floods and a final reconciliation between capital and labor, with love in the end conquering all. Not a very promising story, perhaps, but this tale of a mechanical world in which men are enslaved by machines, becomes the excuse for Fritz Lang to build enormous sets, employ all sorts of screen magic, and visualize an incredible future with all the technical and financial resources of the German cinema at his command.

Lang is said to have received the inspiration for METROPOLIS when he first came to New York in 1924 and



Preceding pages: One of the vast, mechanistic sets used in METROPOLIS (1926). Robot-like class of worker-slaves tends the underground machines that supply energy to the city of Metropolis. Opposite: Director Fritz Lang (r.) and cameraman Karl Freund carried by assistants in gag shot on flood set.

beheld the Manhattan skyline from the deck of his ship. His wife, Thea von Harbou, wrote *Metropolis* as a novel, and then developed it into a screenplay. Lang turned the paper story into a vast celluloid monument of personal excess.

Everything about METROPOLIS is big. It even rivals Griffith's INTOLERANCE in volume of spectacle. The picture cost more than $1.5 million, an enormous sum in 1926. Nearly two million feet of film were exposed; twenty-five thousand men (eleven thousand with shaven heads), eleven thousand women, seven hundred and fifty children and twenty-five Chinese played the extras; the shooting time was three hundred and ten days and sixty nights. During the course of the production rumors were widespread: Lang was doing something monstrous, the UFA Company (Germany's largest motion-picture firm) was going bankrupt, the wild director had even discovered a way to achieve epic grandeur by some sort of magical process that combined miniature sets with real actors. (This was a reference to Lang's use of the Shuftan Process, a special-effects technique invented by the same Eugene Shuftan who, years later, won the Academy Award for Cinematography for THE HUSTLER.)

Lang was the director originally assigned to the now legendary film, THE CABINET OF DR. CALIGARI, ultimately directed by Robert Wiene. CALIGARI, so famous and so fundamental to the whole German Expressionist Movement, is something of a disappointment today because, though its motifs are rather interesting, it contains very little that could not have been done on a theatrical stage. METROPOLIS, on the other hand, is a cinematic miracle, reflecting Lang's special ability to create an atmosphere by visual means, and to propel a story by using a moving camera and by staging scenes in strong geometric patterns. Among its more brilliant and purely visual sequences is the scene in which Maria struggles against Rotwang's power, an unrelenting beam of light in which she is imprisoned and which forces her to make a long, terrifying run through a dark labyrinth of catacombs beneath the city.

The production excesses of METROPOLIS were matched by its excessive length: seventeen reels in the original version. Many of these reels are taken up by long, tormenting shots of workers arranged in architectural tableaux, or marching in ornamental unison, like dancers in a Busby Berkeley musical.

As a fantasy METROPOLIS has been called prophetic. The choreography of its geometrically arranged people is to be seen in Leni Riefenstahl's Nazi documentary, TRIUMPH OF THE WILL. It is as if Lang prophesied the manipulative, mechanistic world of National Socialism. (It is also interesting that Goebbels told Lang that he and Hitler had seen METROPOLIS years before they came to power, in a small provincial theatre. Hitler had turned to Goebbels and said: "Lang is the man to make our films" —which Lang, of course, refused to do when Goebbels offered him the job in the course of the same conversation.) The prophetic power of METROPOLIS may not yet have been spent. There are those who believe human society is headed toward an ultimate split between masses of toiling have-nots and an elite of decadent pleasure-seekers. Lang's "absurd" vision may yet prove valid.

METROPOLIS employs many of the themes which Lang worked out later in his suspense-thriller M. There is his characteristic mood of oppression, his favorite device of contending forces and an enclosing trap, individuals struggling with omnipotent mobs, and a prosaic ending to a bizarre situation, which is usually a disappointment to contemporary audiences.

METROPOLIS, quite unlike THE CABINET OF DR. CALIGARI, is not a cul-de-sac. It began a tradition of great personal screen fantasies displaying the excesses of directors making incredible demands upon studios, usually because these directors had recently achieved commercial success and the studios involved were afraid to say no. 2001: A SPACE ODYSSEY is very much a part of this tradition. Like METROPOLIS, it is a highly personal, utterly fantastic futuristic vision, produced on a gigantic scale, in which machines rule humans, implacable forces contend, robotism is a leit-motif, and the location in time is almost the same. (METROPOLIS is set in the year 2000.)

Fantasy and horror expressed on a vast scale are the essence of METROPOLIS. Above: Freder (Gustav Frölich) grapples with evil inventor Rotwang (Rudolf Klein-Rogge), while Maria (Brigitte Helm) hangs precariously from cathedral roof. Right: Shooting the flood sequence. Though Lang worked with miniature models and employed trick photography, much of METROPOLIS was shot on huge sets. Opposite: Wedge of workers at cathedral doors in final reconciliation scene. Rotwang with rig for transferring Maria's form and substance to robot. Freder's agony at inhuman conditions of workers. False Maria burns at stake.

PARUFAMET

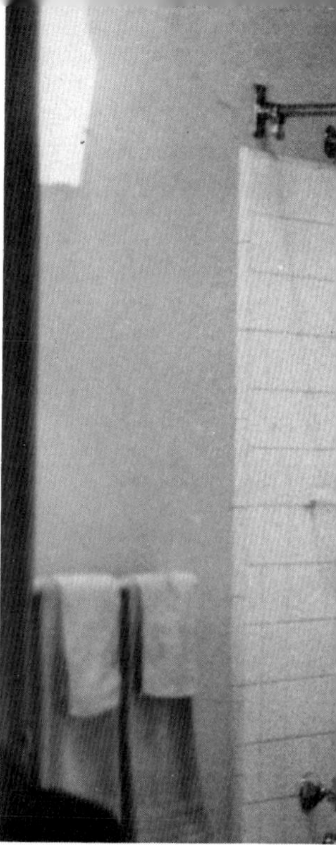

# Alfred Hitchcock's **Psycho** 1960

PSYCHO is the most astounding, audacious, and successful horror film ever made. There are films which contain more killings, more bloodshed, and more frightening and ludicrous characters, but no film has ever gripped an audience and induced it to scream with quite the same force as this most expertly crafted masterpiece of murder and psychosis.

Hitchcock is very clear about his motives. "It was rather exciting to use the camera to deceive the audience," he says to Truffaut, in the latter's famous study of his favorite American director. "The game with the audience was fascinating. I was directing the viewers. You might say I was playing them, like an organ." And later: "I didn't start off to make an important movie. I thought I could have fun with this subject and this situation.... PSYCHO cost us no more than $800,000 to make. It has grossed some $15 million."

"My main satisfaction," he says, "is that the film had an effect on the audiences; ... [it] made the audience scream. I feel it's tremendously satisfying for us to be able to use the cinematic art to achieve something of a mass emotion. And with PSYCHO we most definitely achieved this. It wasn't a message that stirred the audiences, nor was it a great performance or their enjoyment of the novel. They were aroused by pure film. That's why I take pride in the fact that PSYCHO, more than any of my other pictures, is a film that belongs to filmmakers."

And then Hitchcock turns to Truffaut, a young man famous for his films of high culture, though of perhaps limited appeal, and says: "That's what I'd like you to do—a picture that would gross millions of dollars throughout the world. It's an area of filmmaking in which it's more important for you to be pleased with the technique than with the content... it won't necessarily get you the best notices, but you have to design your film just as Shakespeare did his plays—for an audience."

Ah, ha! At last the secret is out. Alfred Hitchcock, who for years has denied that he is an artist, who has claimed over and over again that he considers himself merely an entertainer, who confesses to having taken enormous pleasure in manipulating an audience and milking it for millions of dollars, now speaks of his most manipulative and successful picture as a "filmmaker's film," and equates himself by inference with the greatest artist of all time. Well, he may be right, on every count.

Never in the history of the cinema has a filmmaker so audaciously played his viewers "like an organ." For the first forty-five minutes of PSYCHO, Hitchcock carefully, meticulously builds up sympathy and audience identification with Janet Leigh. She is young, attractive, in love, and has problems that money can solve. She cannot resist when tempted by the possibility of stealing $40,000 from a disgusting and dishonest old man. Will she get away with it? Will she be caught? Or will she come to



Left to right: Tony Perkins brooding beside house in PSYCHO. Notice his posture, indicative of his unique mincing walk. Perkins terrorized by bloody sight on bathroom floor. One of the images from the shower-murder sequence that took seven days to shoot.

her senses, return the money, and salvage her life? We cringe as she blunders. We pity her for her naïveté when she draws herself to the attention of the police. When she stops at the Bates Motel and has the sort of intimate conversation with Anthony Perkins that is only possible with a sympathetic stranger, we are relieved that she sees the error of her ways and decides to return the money, making up for what she's spent out of her own meager savings. She has redeemed herself, and when she returns to her room and takes a shower, we feel as though the dirt of her crime is being washed away.

And then, after caring for her and identifying with her for three quarters of an hour, we watch with amazement as she is brutally slain, knifed to death in the shower by a maniacal woman who slashes at her again and again. Her blood mixes with the water and swirls down the drain, and when that shot is matched to a spiraling pullback from an extreme closeup of one of her dead eyes, her world, so carefully and lavishly built for us, is gone. The center has dropped away. Every convention of storytelling has been defied. Our heroine is dead and the film is only half done. We are horrified by her death, and even more horrified by the breakdown of narrative. We know we are in a nightmare world where anything is possible. What Hitchcock has done has been outrageous. Now he has us completely in his hands. (Hitchcock experimented with killing off a heroine in VERTIGO, where we see Kim Novak killed twice! But because our main identification is with Jimmy Stewart, the effect is not so strong as in PSYCHO, where our total attention is on Janet Leigh.)

With Janet Leigh gone, we must transfer our loyalties to Anthony Perkins, the pleasant, modest, charming young man, who gains our sympathy, Truffaut insists, by the way he cleans up the bathroom and protects his mother. Yes, incredible as it may seem, when Perkins mops up the shower stall we begin to root for him.

This is another Hitchcock trick, of course, because we have no reason to suspect that Perkins' mother does not exist. We are certain we have seen her murder Arbogast, the detective, and Hitchcock confesses with delight that the high-angle shot he uses for her mad, knife-brandishing rush from her bedroom, and the similar shot when Perkins carries her to the cellar, are ingeniously designed so that we will never ask ourselves why we have not been allowed to see her face. It never occurs to us that she is a mummy, preserved by her friendly young taxidermist son, the matricidal maniac. And when he is revealed as the killer, our world is shattered again. It's all tricks, yes, and manipulation, yes, and yes, indeed, Hitchcock does play us "like an organ."

PSYCHO is one of the most strangely constructed films ever made. It goes against every expectation of the audience, and thus reduces it to a trembling, fearful, screaming mass. It is a demagogic work by a master craftsman of the film medium, who knows precisely what he is doing and why he is doing it. To gross $15 million, to have "fun" with the camera (he spent seven days shooting from seventy camera set-ups to make the shower-murder montage), to demonstrate the power of the screen, and, like Shakespeare, to please an audience—these are the things that Hitchcock is all about.

# John Frankenheimer's **The Manchurian Candidate** 1962

THE MANCHURIAN CANDIDATE is a political fantasy, a warped extension of conditions inherent in the American political scene. Its horror resides in its relation to events that have occurred since its release: a series of political assassinations, the Vietnam War, the emergence of extreme violence in everyday life, an expansion of political extremism, and the interchangeability of the far Right and the far Left. Its much-criticized perversity—that Joe McCarthy could have been a Communist agent; that a Presidential candidate could be assassinated; that a captured soldier could be brainwashed and turned into a walking time bomb—unfortunately no longer seems so farfetched. When John Kennedy was assassinated many people believed that Lee Harvey Oswald was some sort of "Manchurian candidate." His sojourn in the USSR suggested that perhaps, in his case, life was imitating art.

The fantasy is the creation of the novelist Richard Condon. It is his vision, one of a series of fascinating speculations he has made in novels with the common themes that anything is possible, that peoples' motives are usually the opposite of what one might suppose, and that social facts can be the basis of outrageous possibilities. But the visualization of THE MANCHURIAN CANDIDATE must be credited to John Frankenheimer, who brought to it superb élan, created many dazzling sequences, and piled his own embellishments upon the excesses of Condon, and the screen-writer George Axelrod.

Frankenheimer has contributed brilliant touches to this fiendish and paranoid story of the brainwashed Raymond Shaw, used by his mother as a tool to gain control of the United States. When Shaw kills Senator Jordan he uses a silenced pistol. The bullet enters Jordan through a carton of milk he happens to be carrying. The milk that runs out is a grotesque and satirical symbol of the proverbial milquetoast liberal.

Another fine sequence is the press conference held by the Secretary of the Army, who has been accused by the demagogic Senator Iselin of harboring Communists in his department. The scene is covered partly through the monitoring screens of television cameras, a device that not only supplies verisimilitude—being similar to scenes set in Senate hearing rooms that one sees on evening news shows—but also brings the faces of the protagonists into striking juxtapositions.

The Madison Square Garden sequence is brilliant, filled with political hoopla, mass hysteria, and the terror of assassination. (When Iselin is shot, one cannot help but be reminded of portions of the Zapruder film of the Kennedy assassination in Dallas.) The political drama combined with the subjective vision of the assassin through the cross hairs of his telescopic sight is worthy of Hitchcock and makes for a tense dramatic finale.

But by far Frankenheimer's best sequence is the brainwashing. Here he dollies his camera around and around as the scene shifts back and forth between the brainwashing as it actually took place, and the woman's garden-club milieu in which the brainwashees believe themselves to be.

It is interesting that Frankenheimer has not surpassed THE MANCHURIAN CANDIDATE, which came fairly early in his career. He seems to have given up a pyrotechnical approach and attempts at dazzling sequences in favor of a solemn and sometimes heavy-handed narrative style which is certainly more pure, but just as certainly more tiresome. The sort of material that seems to attract him now is less commercial and more arty than THE MANCHURIAN CANDIDATE, less dazzling and more profound in an academic sense. Since he evidently was close to Robert Kennedy, who spent the last day of his life at Frankenheimer's house in Malibu, it is possible that his recent austerity represents a reaction against the razzle-dazzle associated with that particular tragedy. Then again such a speculation may be unfair to a man who continues to make worthy films within a difficult commercial system, and from whom the credit for THE MANCHURIAN CANDIDATE, a great work of political fiction, cannot be taken away.

John Frankenheimer (above) at work.
Opposite: Sergeant Raymond Shaw (Laurence Harvey) kills a comrade during brainwashing sequence of THE MANCHURIAN CANDIDATE, while Major Bennett Marco (Frank Sinatra) sits in a daze. Both victim and chair are knocked across the room.

# Jean-Luc Godard's **Weekend** 1967

Like the other films of horror being considered here, Jean-Luc Godard's WEEKEND is a fantasy extrapolated from the real world. It reflects a personal view of existence, a view of the roles of art and politics in life, and, in addition, a special, deeply felt, highly personal hatred of the bourgeoisie. WEEKEND is passionate, chaotic, a marred work of genius by a man who made more innovations and affected the cinema more deeply in the eight years prior to this work than any other filmmaker of his time. With WEEKEND we have the impression that Godard may have burned himself out, so incandescent, so passionate, so intense is the vision and so hellish is the horror.

WEEKEND begins with a long, casual description of a sex orgy that is so disorienting and so obscene that one is tempted to leave the theatre. It observes the adventures of a young couple evidently out to murder the wife's rich mother for an inheritance, and proceeds through a long series of satirical sequences in which life is seen in terms of a weekend, a hell of rape, murder, traffic jams, automobile accidents, blood, and carnage. It then offers a mystical sequence in which a pile of smashed-up cars is transformed into a herd of sheep, a pastoral interlude in which we watch a man playing a Mozart sonata in a farmyard, on-camera interviews with a Negro and an Algerian who drive a garbage truck filled with the refuse of western civilization, and ultimately it plunges into a milieu of hippie-guerrillas who kill and literally eat the flesh of the bourgeoisie. There are appalling scenes along the way: a pig having its throat cut, a goose being decapitated, a fish being inserted into the vagina of the antiheroine, and at the end a scene in which she eats pieces of her husband's chopped-up body. WEEKEND is excessive. Among other things it is a vision of life as horror, a premonition of the youth revolution, a dissertation concerning the contending views of Mao Tse-tung and Lyndon Johnson, a stylized reference to the Vietnam War, a social satire, a poem of hatred, and the ultimate in audience alienation.

What is one to make of all this bloodshed, butchery, carnage, this satire on the aspirations of the middle class (when the antihero and antiheroine are asked to make three wishes, they respond: "A better car, naturally blond hair, a weekend with James Bond!"), this finale of anarchy and cannibalism? There is only one thing to make of it: A filmmaker has carried his obsessions so far, and expressed his rage with such intensity, that filmmaking for him may afterward be impossible. Although Godard has made other films since WEEKEND, they have mostly been political diatribes, agitprop pictures in the service of what he calls "the Revolution." The real clue to the personal meaning of WEEKEND may be the title on its final frame. "End of Film" the caption reads, and then, "End of Cinema." For Jean-Luc Godard, most influential filmmaker of the 1960s, most innovative groundbreaker of the French New Wave, WEEKEND is perhaps "the end of cinema." His view of existence is so horrible that cinema—film in the service of art—may no longer be possible for him. With WEEKEND Godard destroys everything he hates in a bloody massacre, and very possibly he also destroys himself. WEEKEND is a brilliant psychopathic work, a horror story containing strong evidences of a filmmaker's self-destruction.

Above: Butchery in the woods and carnage on the highway – scenes from Godard's WEEKEND. Opposite: The "Starchild" of Stanley Kubrick's 2001: A SPACE ODYSSEY. Inscrutable to some, deeply meaningful to many, the Starchild is one of the memorable screen images of the 1960s.

## Stanley Kubrick's **2001: A Space Odyssey** 1968

2001: A SPACE ODYSSEY was the most controversial and misunderstood film of the 1960s. When it opened it "disappointed" many reviewers who found it slow and tedious, and who felt that its resolution was phony-profound. Actually, the real deception concerning 2001 was not the result of Kubrick's lightweight metaphysics, but the critical establishment's inability to deal with a new kind of picture in a new kind of way. The backlash against this initial hostility was quick to come: first, when the "youth audience" discovered that 2001 was a great "trip," and then when younger critics used it as an excuse to flog the "liberal-arts mentalities" of their older rivals. As a result, an enormous amount of nonsense has been written about 2001 on both sides of the generation gap.

By now the controversy has passed and 2001 has been more or less accepted as one of the very few great films of our time. As a science-fiction fantasy it remains unexcelled. No other picture in the genre even comes close. As a horror story, too, it is a towering achievement, not on the same scream-inducing level as Hitchcock's PSYCHO, but in a subtler and far more haunting way. There are many elements of horror in 2001, but perhaps the most overwhelming one is the picture's vision of man, a creature that mutates from the spontaneous, frightened, wretched, clumsy, murderous apes of the "Dawn of Man" section into the controlled, unemotional, sterile, competent, dehumanized technologists of the moon visit and the Jupiter mission. Somewhere in between, civilization came and went. In Kubrick's fantasy the Golden Age of man was a negligible instant between an ape's exaltation at discovering the first weapon, and a satellite carrying a nuclear weapon floating in a graceful orbit around the earth. A future containing an astral Howard Johnson's is so horrible that it is enough to make one long for the dissolution and cannibalism of Godard's WEEKEND.

Almost everyone who has seen 2001 has been struck by the fact that the HAL 9000 computer is the most "human" character in the movie, that its preference to commit murder rather than admit an error is less sinister and more "human" than the unfeeling logic of HAL's astronaut-caretakers. When Keir Dullea lobotomizes HAL by unscrewing his higher mental functions, one feels considerably more sympathy for the victim than when HAL discontinues the life functions of the hibernating astronauts.

As a spectacle 2001 is a marvel. There are no great crowd scenes, no massed armies, but millions of dollars' worth of glittering machinery that works. From story to completion the picture took five years to make. The special effects alone occupied a year and a half. The great device that made possible the unusual shots in the spaceship, particularly the phenomenal one of Gary Lockwood jogging and shadow-boxing through 360 degrees, was a $750,000 centrifuge ten feet wide and thirty-eight feet high. Throughout 2001, one is faced with computers and control panels covered with read-out display screens; all of them are active with authentic material, the result of intricate rear-screen projections of numerous specially made animated films. The landing at the Clavius Base on the moon, in which the Aries craft enters an airlock and passes tiers in which tiny human figures can be seen at work, was achieved by a most painstaking and elaborate use of matte processes.

Kubrick was assisted by a huge staff of designers and scientific advisers, and induced hundreds of corporations, government agencies, and research institutions to help work out the technology of the year 2001. All the devices one sees are supported by the finest and most thorough scientific research. The result is that in 2001—as opposed to other science-fiction films—one is surrounded by a totally believable futuristic environment. Its technical perfection gives substance to Kubrick's speculations. The mysterious dimension of the story is backstopped by a sensual dimension in which one can actually feel the texture of the future.

2001: A SPACE ODYSSEY is not a linear film. It is more like a sensory experience which one either rejects or accepts, depending on one's instincts. Kubrick has called it a "mythological documentary." Though its many details are logical, its grand design is not. It is very much a speculation about time, intelligence, and human destiny, and its open ending, into which Kubrick urges viewers to read whatever they like, is but one example of a new film language deliberately opposed to the tight construction of the conventional three-act story. Of course, 2001 is not the first nonlinear film, but the fact that everything is not neatly tied up at its end annoys many people. They demand clarity where there can only be mystery; they insist upon an answer where there can only be a question.

Arthur C. Clarke, who wrote the original story and collaborated on the screenplay, has pointed out that if a fifteenth-century man were transported to our time, he would think of our airplanes and television as feats of magic, because he would not understand the logic of the technology we have devised. By the same token, Clarke points out that an encounter between a man of 2001 and a vastly more advanced technology would result in the same sensation of magic. On this basis alone one can justify the mysterious ending of 2001. When Keir Dullea

encounters a slab—similar to the one which inspired the apes to use weapons, and another which was set up as some sort of sentinel on the moon—everything that happens to him must be magical. For those who can accept this premise, the ending of 2001 is deeply moving. Some have even called it a religious experience. For those who resist it, for whom mysticism is unacceptable, the final powerful and haunting "star-child" image is a source of endless infuriation.

2001 is a film filled with riches—brilliant sequences and extraordinary moments: the stunning first half-hour in which the story of the apes is told visually, without a single line of dialogue (the apes were played by dancers and mime-artists, and two live baby chimpanzees); the restrained satire of the scenes aboard Orion, the space station, and Aries (the zero-gravity toilet, the smiling stewardess); a stewardess on Aries turning upside-down (actually she is on a treadmill, it is the spaceship set and camera that turn); the banality of all human exchanges (the chitchat with the Russians, Gary Lockwood's canned birthday greeting from his family, Dr. Floyd's conversation with his daughter on the picturephone); the terribly frightening moment when we realize that HAL is reading the astronauts' lips; the tension leading to the moment when Dullea must pass through total vacuum, and the actual image of him being sucked toward us (achieved by having him fall upon the camera, his fall broken by wire restraints); HAL singing "Daisy, Daisy" in his death throes; the magical alignments of sun, moon, and earth, and of Jupiter and its moons, that occur whenever the slab appears.

One must view 2001 ultimately as a personal triumph for Stanley Kubrick, who devoted himself to it for five years. At a time of grave economic trouble within the picture industry, when the grandiose projects of equally famous directors were being canceled right and left, and when MGM, the film's sponsor, was passing through near-bankruptcy and debilitating proxy fights, Kubrick held on. Think of him, spending $10.5 million, and sending back tens of thousands of feet of frolicking apes to executives who could not hope to understand how such scenes could be transformed back into money.



Glittering hardware that doesn't look like cardboard is one of the attractions of 2001. Production values of the picture were exemplary. Kubrick induced corporations and scientists to help him create an environment with the texture of the future.

Horror in 2001: Astronaut in the hands of a machine. Below: Humor—space stewardess defies gravity.

Bowman (Keir Dullea) enters "time slot."

Space station orbits moon in Kubrick's cosmic ballet.

# Credits

## Metropolis

Germany; 1926; 94 minutes
(U.S. version); released by UFA.

**Directed by** Fritz Lang.
**Produced by** Erich Pommer.
**Screenplay by** Thea von Harbou from her novel.
**Photographed by** Karl Freund and Gunther Rittau.
**Art direction by** Otto Hunte, Erich Kettelhut and Karl Vollbrecht.
**Cast:** Alfred Abel; Gustav Frölich; Brigitte Helm; Rudolf Klein-Rogge; Fritz Rasp; Theodor Loos; Erwin Biswanger; Heinrich George; Olaf Storm; Hans Leo Reich; Heinrich Gotho.

## The Manchurian Candidate

U.S.A.; 1962; 126 minutes;
released by United Artists.

**Directed by** John Frankenheimer.
**Produced by** George Axelrod and John Frankenheimer.
**Screenplay by** George Axelrod, based on the novel by Richard Condon.
**Photographed by** Lionel Lindon.
**Art direction by** Richard Sylbert.
**Edited by** Ferris Webster.
**Music by** David Amram.
**Cast:** Frank Sinatra; Laurence Harvey; Janet Leigh; Angela Lansbury; Henry Silva; James Gregory; Leslie Parrish; John McGiver; Madame Spivy.

## Psycho

U.S.A.; 1960; 109 minutes;
released by Paramount.

**Directed by** Alfred Hitchcock.
**Produced by** Alfred Hitchcock.
**Screenplay by** Joseph Stefano, from the novel by Robert Bloch.
**Photographed by** John L. Russell.
**Art direction by** Joseph Hurley, Robert Claworthy, and George Milo.
**Edited by** George Tomasini.
**Music by** Bernard Herrmann.
**Cast:** Anthony Perkins; Janet Leigh; Vera Miles; John Gavin; Martin Balsam; John McIntire; Simon Oakland; Frank Albertson; Patricia Hitchcock; Vaughn Taylor.

## Weekend (Le Weekend)

France; 1967; 105 minutes;
released in the U.S. by Grove Press.

**Directed by** Jean-Luc Godard.
**Screenplay by** Jean-Luc Godard.
**Photographed by** Raoul Coutard.
**Edited by** Agnès Guillemot.
**Music by** Antoine Duhamel.
**Cast:** Mireille Darc; Jean Yanne; Jean-Pierre Kalfon; Valerie Lagrange; Paul Gegauff; Virginie Vignon; Jean Eustache; Ernest Menzer; Jean-Pierre Léaud.

## 2001: A Space Odyssey

Great Britain; 1968;
141 minutes; released by MGM.

**Directed by** Stanley Kubrick.
**Produced by** Stanley Kubrick.
**Screenplay by** Stanley Kubrick and Arthur C. Clarke, based on Clarke's story "The Sentinel."
**Photographed by** Geoffrey Unsworth.
**Art direction by** Tony Masters, Harry Lang, and Ernie Archer.
**Edited by** Ray Lovejoy.
**Music by** Richard Strauss, Johann Strauss, Aram Khatchaturian and György Ligeti.
**Cast:** Keir Dullea; Gary Lockwood; William Sylvester; Daniel Richter; Douglas Rain (voice of HAL 9000); Leonard Rossiter; Margaret Tyzack; Robert Beatty; Sean Sullivan; Frank Miller.

# The Concerned Cinema

# 11

The concerned cinema is the cinema of social commitment, the cinema that confronts an issue or a problem, the cinema that speaks for those without a voice.

Its pitfalls are many: political bias; making a statement at the expense of emotional involvement; cardboard characters enunciating ideologies; the notion that good and honorable intentions and a sincere desire to straighten out the world are an excuse for bad art. Among the worst mistakes that a filmmaker can make is to think that because his point of view is just, his nobility of heart will move an audience, or that because an issue is important its form is not. Subject matter will not redeem a bad film. Sincerity of purpose is not sufficient.

The great film of concern is not propagandistic, is not made in the service of a state-owned cinema, or a political party. It does not manipulate the truth in order to convince its audience of the correctness of a political line, nor does it impose an ideology to which its characters and scenes must conform. If it has a bias, it is not intellectual; it is the bias of the filmmaker's soul. If it is concerned, the concern is not applied a priori; it derives from the material, the story, and the characters of the film.

The concerned film serves art, not politics. It produces emotion on account of its story, not its issue. Its antagonists are not depicted as bad merely because they happen to be on the "wrong" side. The great film of concern is, above all else, compassionate. It reveals its characters in their many-sided complexity, not merely as automatons reflecting points of view. In this sense great films of this genre are humanitarian. Their concern is with people. And if they are critical of the social order, their criticism is implicit and not imposed.

Everyone who is sane is against war, poverty, crime, fascism, slavery, lynching, anti-Semitism, and the oppression of minority groups. It's not very difficult to be right about the basic issues of society. What is difficult is to reflect one's rectitude or one's rage in terms that can move an audience. Nothing is more tiresome than the film which tells us what we already know in terms we have seen a hundred times. Originality of expression is very important in this kind of film. The how is more important than the what, the depth of concern is more important than its existence.

Many people are afraid of the cinema because it seems such a powerful medium. Lenin recognized this and spoke of it several times. Hitler turned to Leni Riefenstahl after he had seen and been impressed by THE BATTLESHIP POTEMKIN, because he wanted a filmmaker who would serve him the way he thought that Eisenstein had served the USSR. Because the cinema seems so powerful, there are people who fear the men who have mastered its art. Surely the worst stain on the history of Hollywood is the blacklisting and purges of the 1950s.

It would be vulgar to demean the suffering of people who were deprived of their right to work on political grounds, and that is not the intention here. But aside from the issue of whether such people were guilty or innocent of the biases of which they were accused, the truth is that their power to alter political and social consciousness was vastly overrated. Many men have made films of social concern, but very few have made films that were great. It takes enormous excellence to make a truly moving film, a film that captures a dilemma, crystalizes it in human terms, renders it with compassion. Audiences know a great film when they see one, because audiences have an uncanny ability to recognize the truth. No matter how powerfully a position is expressed—and one thinks of some masterpieces of early Soviet filmmaking in this regard—its concern must be truthful or it will be merely a technical triumph. That is the only thing the opponents of any of the five following films need fear: not the politics of the men who made them, not even the power of their art, but the truth of what they say.

## Vittorio De Sica's **The Bicycle Thief** 1948

In THE BICYCLE THIEF, Vittoria De Sica and his writer/collaborator Cesare Zavattini are concerned with the poor, the anonymous poor for whom a minor incident becomes a personal tragedy and toward whom society is indifferent. "Look at the story of this ordinary man," they seem to be saying. "There are ten million stories like this happening every day. We must be concerned with this man and his story because we are human and so is he."

THE BICYCLE THIEF is the summit work of Italy's Neo-Realist movement, the school of documentary-style fiction filmmaking that flourished there after the fall of Mussolini. Neo-Realism was characterized by the use of real locations, usually the streets of Italy's war-wrecked cities, of nonactors whose lives resembled the lives of the



Preceding pages: Antonio (Lamberto Maggiorani, r.) and son Bruno (Enzo Staiola) drive through streets of Rome in search of stolen bicycle in Vittorio De Sica's Neo-Realistic masterpiece, THE BICYCLE THIEF. Note use of grainy photography to convey documentary "look."

characters they portrayed, and of a certain gritty, documentary look that proclaimed the authenticity of the material. (When one tries to imagine a Neo-Realist film in color, one understands immediately that it is impossible. The drabness of unlit documentary black-and-white photography is essential to the Neo-Realist "look.")

In addition to elements of style, subject matter of a certain type was central to the Neo-Realist film. These pictures told stories about poor people, forgotten people, stories about the passions of the forgotten. They represented an attempt to remove everything that was false, all feelings that were fake. The objective was to peer into the world and find the simple and the true, the unusual that resided, hidden, within the ordinary, and to relate a small, personal story to the problems of society at large. Such an approach may seem naïve from the vantage point of the 1970s, but in the context of more than a quarter century of Fascist rule, in which pompous rhetoric and false emotion were the signature of the head of state, and escapist trash was ground out by the studios, the poignancy of Neo-Realism can be understood. In reaction to the past, amid the ruins of postwar Italy, it was inevitable.

The principal works of the Neo-Realist movement are Rossellini's OPEN CITY (1944) and PAISAN (1946), Zampa's TO LIVE IN PEACE (1946), De Sica's SHOESHINE (1946), De Santis' TRAGIC CHASE (1947), Lattuada's WITHOUT PITY (1947), and Visconti's LA TERRA TREMA (1948). The one authentic masterpiece of the era, the film which represented all that was best in Neo-Realism, and that outlives the movement, is De Sica's THE BICYCLE THIEF, a highly structured, self-consciously simple, deeply concerned, and intensely warm picture that gives the impression of being a social documentary, but which is really, in the best sense of the word, artfully contrived for maximum emotional impact.

The story of THE BICYCLE THIEF develops like a chase, and as a result the audience is kept in suspense. Will Antonio Ricci find his stolen bicycle and keep his job, or will he fall back into unemployment and despair? There is the relationship between Antonio and his son Bruno, slowly, subtly revealed through their day of misery in all of its unspoken tenderness, loving, even in the final moments, when Bruno learns a harsh lesson. In this sense, the film is a story of a boy coming of age. Finally, because of the way the search for the bicycle is structured, the film is a virtual encyclopedia of social comment, revealing the sullen indifference of the police, the tough hypocrisy of the church, and the dehumanization of urban society, illustrated by the way a vast spectrum of people reacts to the problem of a single desperate man. What seems at first to be a simple, linear story is really a story of suspense, a story of relationships, and an exposé of the inadequacy of social institutions, all three interwoven with such skill that audience involvement is total.

De Sica's film reveals certain of the flaws of Neo-Realism. While appearing to be random it is actually contrived, while appearing to be a documentary it is actually theatrical, while appearing to depict the reality of an incident in the life of a poor man, it actually pits him against a stacked deck. THE BICYCLE THIEF also shows the cul-de-sac of Neo-Realism. It is a picture which says, "This is the way things are," and that is as far as it goes. The next step was for a film to say, "This is how things must be changed," to depict class struggle and revolution. Thus, the hard-core Left dislikes THE BICYCLE THIEF, seeing it as a bourgeois film bemoaning the faults in society without showing how they can be cured.

But just as THE BICYCLE THIEF reveals flaws in Neo-Realism, as the ultimate Neo-Realist film it also reveals what was best in the movement: conviction, compassion, humanity, and concern. The performances are rich, radiant, luminous. This apparently was De Sica's special gift: an ability to bring out the nonactors' great authenticity of expression. The relationships between Antonio and Bruno, and Antonio and his wife Maria, are informed by deep and radiant love. No dialogue expresses this—just the looks between these people, the way they act together, their gestures toward one another, their concern. If the long, smooth dolly shots of BICYCLE THIEF look artificial now because *cinéma-vérité* documentaries have reformed our notion of what is truth on film, the truthfulness of these performances nonetheless cancels out any contrivances of production or script.

There is a famous story about THE BICYCLE THIEF. When De Sica was looking for financing, the American producer, David Selznick, offered it on condition that Cary Grant play the role of Antonio Ricci. De Sica refused, and of course he was right on every aesthetic ground. But the story is significant beyond its interest as an amusing anecdote. Great films of the concerned cinema possess an integrity that a commercial producer can never comprehend. One has only to compare THE BICYCLE THIEF to any of the "socially conscious" films of Stanley Kramer, filled with self-congratulation and movie stars (Curtis and Poitier in THE DEFIANT ONES; Peck, Gardner, and Astaire in ON THE BEACH; Tracy and Hepburn in GUESS WHO'S COMING TO DINNER?) to understand the differences between authenticity and fakery, art and product, concern and chic.

From THE BICYCLE THIEF: Neo-Realist Italian cinema – a reaction against pomposity of Fascist era – uses real locations, nonactors, and characters caught up in social problems. Director De Sica (fist raised, below r.) was aided by honest and sympathetic script by Cesare Zavattini.

# François Truffaut's **The Four Hundred Blows** 1959

In THE FOUR HUNDRED BLOWS, François Truffaut is concerned with a child and the injustices he endures. The child, Antoine Doinel, is vulnerable, like Antonio Ricci in THE BICYCLE THIEF, and like Antonio Ricci he wages a futile war against the indifference of society. THE FOUR HUNDRED BLOWS is a film about brutalization. Implicit within the picture is a stern indictment of social institutions, but the film is completely different from THE BICYCLE THIEF in aura, mood, and intention. De Sica places Antonio Ricci in a drab, closed, forbidding Rome. The Paris in which Truffaut places Antoine Doinel is also drab, but in addition it is various, open-ended, rich in possibilities. Ricci is a prisoner of his economic situation; Doinel is only a prisoner of his age. De Sica's film is focused on the outside forces that crush an individual; Truffaut's film is about the inner life of a child who resists. The differences between these films are also, in an interesting way, the differences between Italian Neo-Realism and the French New Wave: social comment versus autobiography; broad concern for humanity versus specific concern for the individual; melancholy versus *joie de vivre*; the abstract versus the subjective; the predestined versus the spontaneous; realism versus expressionism.

Along with ANTOINE AND COLETTE, STOLEN KISSES, and BED AND BOARD, THE FOUR HUNDRED BLOWS represents a phenomenon unprecedented in the history of cinema: a series (which might be called *The Life and Times of Antoine Doinel*) of strongly autobiographical pictures by the same director, made over a period of years with the same actor, Jean-Pierre Léaud, enacting various stages in the life of this fictional character while he, the actor, grows up.

In THE FOUR HUNDRED BLOWS, as in the other films of this series, Truffaut creates richly delineated characters who do not represent points of view or philosophies of life, but who simply exist as mysterious and unfathomable human beings. Even the minor characters are revealed as three-dimensional people whom we, through Truffaut's eyes, understand with compassion. Although there are samples of atrocious human behavior in THE FOUR HUNDRED BLOWS, the perpetrators of these atrocious acts are never really villainous. Truffaut shows their good and bad sides without condemnation, and if there is a villain in the picture it is that side of human society that is hard and blind and insensitive, that would crush the spontaneity of youth and destroy the joy of life.

This is the theme of THE FOUR HUNDRED BLOWS, a film about fifteen-year-old Antoine Doinel, free and spontaneous, neither brilliant nor dull-witted, but acutely sensitive to the richness of living. And, too, it is a film about a world of parents, teachers, police, janitors, and psychiatrists who would make him less than a free spirit, who would make him conform to a narrow vision.

THE FOUR HUNDRED BLOWS is permeated by warmth, a love of man even at his worst. It is a film that may have more painful and yet understated moments than any other, and its subject matter—the pain and joy of childhood—is universal.

One thinks particularly of certain scenes: Antoine reciting to himself from Balzac; Antoine taking down the garbage at night, performing the distasteful task with an awareness of the mystery that lies behind every door; Antoine, awake in his bed, listening to his parents' quarrelling; the two occasions when Antoine is slapped, once by his father in front of his fellows at school, and the second time at the reformatory where he has been sent for observation (both times we wince with the pain); and Antoine's disturbing view of the dark streets of Paris as he is hauled away in a police wagon after being caught stealing a typewriter from his father's firm.

There are marvelous scenes in this film which upon first viewing may seem too long. What is one to make of the long series of shots of the boy who keeps smudging the ink in his exercise book? Or of Antoine in the centrifuge staring at the world upside-down? Or of the children reacting to the puppet show? Or of the comic episode of the school gym teacher leading the students on an exercise run through a dingy quarter of Paris and being deserted by them until he is left running alone? These scenes are very much to the point in this sort of filmmaking, for they form the rich tapestry, the humanistic background of the story of Antoine's brutalization.

As we watch this strange boy, this alter ego of Truffaut, stealing a bottle of milk in the cold dawn after he has run from home, breaking the ice in a fountain to find water to wash his face, and, finally, trapped between pursuers and the sea after a long run, turning to us and having his perplexed face suddenly and unexpectedly frozen, our deepest compassion is aroused. A filmmaker has made a work of art out of his own life, has moved us with his concern for the defenseless, the vulnerable,

the young, without for a single instant descending into sentimentality.

THE FOUR HUNDRED BLOWS is usually defined as a great autobiographical film, or a great personal film. It is, of course, both of these, but it is also a great film of concern, not in any strict political sense, but in the broad sense that the genre has been defined here. In THE FOUR HUNDRED BLOWS the social comment is implicit, never stated outright. How can one watch this film about the battering of a child and not read into it an indictment of everything in bourgeois culture, everything that is heavy, routine, heartless, stifling, without compassion? In THE BICYCLE THIEF society has merely deprived Antonio Ricci of his right to the dignity of work. In THE FOUR HUNDRED BLOWS society may have deprived Antoine Doinel of a portion of his soul. Which deprivation constitutes a more serious crime? Which picture, in the end, is more revolutionary?



From THE FOUR HUNDRED BLOWS (clockwise from top l.): "Little Quiz" (teacher) singles out Antoine Doinel (Jean-Pierre Léaud). Antoine in holding cell at police station. Truffaut with alter ego Léaud. Antoine admonished by parents after his "homage to Balzac" starts a fire.

# Elia Kazan's **On the Waterfront** 1954

It is difficult to come to grips with ON THE WATERFRONT. On the one hand it has enormous strengths, indisputable elements of greatness, and on the other it is surrounded by ambiguities which cannot be wished away.

The surface concern of ON THE WATERFRONT is gangsterism in the trade-union movement. The film appears to be concerned with the exploitation of working men by the mob, and thus presents itself as a reformist picture, one that demonstrates a social ill and apparently hopes that it will inspire its cure. However, on inspection, this surface concern seems little more than a gloss, covering up a story whose real concern is the problem of whether or not a man should be an informer. The question of informing, of course, is a valid issue, a worthwhile subject for a psychomoral drama. Why, then, surround it with a reformist cocoon? This is one of the ambiguities that tends to blur the greatness of ON THE WATERFRONT.

Terry Malloy (Marlon Brando) agonizes over this problem of informing, but in the end he testifies before the crime commission investigating gangsterism on the waterfront. Everything in his past militates against his becoming a "stool pigeon," a "cheese eater," or a "canary," but he informs nevertheless because events make clear to him that by so doing he will improve conditions on the docks and liberate his fellow longshoremen from the gangster bosses who exploit them. The moral dilemma of Terry Malloy is well drawn in the film. The crucial question of whether or not to "squawk"—which provides the film's suspense—is only resolved after incidents of considerable dramatic intensity: the murder of Kayo Dugan, Terry's terrible confession to the girl he loves that he inadvertently helped kill her brother, the high-pressure moralizing of a very tough priest, the witnessing of various forms of violent and ruthless behavior, and finally the murder of his own brother, Charley, knocked off because he would not betray Terry to the mob. ON THE WATERFRONT not only justifies Terry as an informer, presenting his problem in such a way that his integrity can only be legitimized by his act of betrayal. It elevates it with something close to religious exaltation.

All of this has a curious parallel in the life story of Elia Kazan. Kazan and Arthur Miller, who worked together so successfully on two of Miller's famous plays, *All My Sons* and *Death of A Salesman*, wanted to do a picture together about life on the New York waterfront. But when Kazan testified as a "friendly witness" before the House Un-American Activities Committee, Miller was appalled and collaboration became impossible. Kazan then turned to the writer Budd Schulberg, who had also been a friendly witness, and another friendly witness, Lee J. Cobb, was hired to play Johnny Friendly, the mobster heavy in the story. This triumvirate was involved with a picture that views informing, under certain circumstances, as a noble act, in direct contrast to John Ford's THE INFORMER, where it is viewed as unforgivable, and Arthur Miller's own waterfront play, *View from the Bridge*, which views it as so heinous and ignominious a thing that it can be expunged only by suicide. Although everything was more or less forgiven between Miller and Kazan some years later, it is possible to argue—and many have—that ON THE WATERFRONT is not the film it seems because it is really a self-serving effort used by Kazan to justify his own actions. Whether this interpretation is valid or not, it does provide an explanation of the first of the two areas of ambiguity that surround the picture, the problem of where its concern truly lies.

The second area of ambiguity is an artistic one, known, in some circles, as "the Kazan Problem." Succinctly stated, "the Kazan Problem" revolves around the paradox that Kazan achieves both sublime truthfulness in his films, and moments of mannered hysteria and falseness.

The scene in ON THE WATERFRONT between Rod Steiger and Brando in the taxicab—one of the famous scenes of American film—is an example of Kazan at his best. He himself takes little credit for it, insisting that the special way Brando says "Oh, Charley" is the key to its success. But the conviction of both actors, and the total truthfulness of their performances must be credited to a fine director working at the height of his powers. The same could be said for the scene between Brando and Eva Marie Saint, when Brando confesses his role in her brother's death. It is a love scene of enormous power. Brando's love for Edie Doyle, his anguish at what he must say, and her reactions to both, make it one of the truly exquisite moments in film acting.

On the other hand, Kazan is quite capable of the overblown pretentiousness and total falsity of the scene in the hold of the ship when Karl Malden, as the blue-collar priest, Father Barry, tells the men that Christ is on the waterfront, and the body of Kayo Dugan is then raised as if he were a martyred saint. Suddenly, Kazan and Schulberg seem to be telling us that we are viewing a Catholic

allegory, a sort of Passion Play performed in T-shirts. It is a wretched moment, embarrassing and empty, similar to some of the trashier scenes that ruin Kazan's other concerned film, VIVA ZAPATA. He is also capable of grouping his extras, playing longshoremen, into false, stylized configurations, herding them about, in this supposedly documentary-style film, like the background people in an Italian sword-and-sandals epic.

How can one reconcile this paradox: Kazan the evocator of truth and Kazan the purveyor of phoniness, the artist who controls and the pyrotechnician who supercharges? One cannot, and that is precisely the problem. ON THE WATERFRONT is like a symphony by Mozart with occasional passages by Rimsky-Korsakov thrown in.

As a film of concern, ON THE WATERFRONT is about the best the American cinema has to offer. The classic choice is Ford's THE GRAPES OF WRATH, but this picture is so inferior to the novel, and so dated by its style—lacking the formal contemplation that makes Ford such a master of the western—and suffers from being so tiresomely predictable, that it is best forgotten.

ON THE WATERFRONT offers the required amount of social comment: on the exploitation of the working class, on the toughness of life at the bottom, on the dehumanization of meaningless labor. Whether its overt concern with a specific social ill, gangsterism in the unions, is really its subject, must remain a moot point. One may accept ON THE WATERFRONT at its face value, for, like all great concerned films, its concern is ultimately with the problems of people.



From ON THE WATERFRONT: Rod Steiger and Marlon Brando in famous taxicab scene. Karl Malden as Father Barry. Brando with Eva Marie Saint. Lee J. Cobb fights Brando. Far right: Brando as Terry Molloy, one of his great roles, not equalled until his appearance eighteen years later in Bernardo Bertolucci's LAST TANGO IN PARIS.

# Alain Resnais' **Hiroshima, Mon Amour** 1959

When HIROSHIMA, MON AMOUR opened in New York in 1960, it was received with the hushed reverence reserved by the public and the critics for a "film of the year." Months later backlash developed in certain critical and political circles. Alain Resnais, it was said, had trivialized the horror of Hiroshima by equating it with a banal story about lost love and had made a "woman's picture." He was also accused of palming off staged footage from a Japanese propaganda film as newsreel footage of Hiroshima after the bomb.

Why such reverence and such damnation? Perhaps the controversy proves, in a way, the greatness of this picture, which is audacious in subject matter as well as style, and whose concern is so vast, so all-encompassing, as to be invisible to a viewer looking only for a film committed to a specific program of social justice, or to some particular act of struggle and revolution. HIROSHIMA, MON AMOUR is concerned with man, in the fullest sense, and must be considered among the most powerful films of social commitment ever made.

Alain Resnais, and his writer-collaborator Marguerite Duras, combined a love story with an antibomb story; they made a film that delves both into the horror of Hiroshima and the sorrow of a lost first love. In Resnais' own words: "[in the film] we oppose the immense, fantastically enormous quality of Hiroshima and the little story of Nevers, reflected through Hiroshima as the light of a candle is magnified and reversed by a lens. The explosion of the bomb over Hiroshima is a gigantic event and it cannot be measured in relation to the case of this woman and her love affair. That is the whole point." On another occasion Resnais acknowledges that the Nevers story is a "threepenny romance."

When Resnais was asked to make a feature-length documentary about the atomic bomb, he brooded over the subject and then went to Marguerite Duras with an extraordinary idea: a love story set in Hiroshima, a love story "within a framework of other people's suffering." Duras explains the reasoning when she points out that in dealing with such an enormous subject as Hiroshima, "All one can do is talk about the impossibility of talking about Hiroshima." Hiroshima is a place, she says, where "every gesture, every word, takes on an aura of meaning that transcends its literal meaning."

Thus, a love story in Hiroshima, which might seem at first to be a vulgar and impossible contradiction, becomes instead a brilliant concept for a film. No matter the horror of the exhibitions in the Hiroshima Museum, and of the footage of the city in the days after it was bombed, Hiroshima is a tragedy that numbs us, while the "threepenny" story of love in Nevers makes us cry. But, if the two stories are entwined, allowed to resonate, we can begin to understand the true relationship between our personal tragedies and the tragedy of mankind as revealed in the bombed ruins of Hiroshima, or, for that matter, if Resnais had chosen to set it where he made his famous documentary, NUIT ET BROUILLARD, in the gas chambers at Auschwitz.

The story of Nevers does not trivialize the story of Hiroshima. Rather, on account of this audacious counterpoint, all our emotions are engaged in a most extraordinary and powerful way. We gasp at the tragedy of Hiroshima as we weep over the tragedy at Nevers; we contemplate a cosmic and a personal problem at the same time.

The sheer daring of this film might be enough to justify calling it great, but HIROSHIMA, MON AMOUR is also great on account of the virtuosity of its technique and the invention by its director of a new film language. Its experimental style, which so annoyed those who think a film cannot be socially committed unless it appeals to the stupidest member of the audience, is as audacious as the juxtaposition of subject matter.

Near the end of the first reel we see a closeup of Emmanuèle Riva, who has just glanced at Eiji Okada, asleep. Suddenly there is a brief flash-cut of the body of a wounded young man lying in approximately the same position in another place. Resnais cuts back to Riva's face, and then back to Okada asleep, and in that split second the technique of the subliminal flash cut, used to describe



Emmanuèle Riva and Eiji Okada in HIROSHIMA, MON AMOUR. Shots of their lovemaking (opposite) are intercut with images of destruction in famous opening in which Resnais explores the sensuality of death, and counterpoises personal drama and cosmic tragedy.

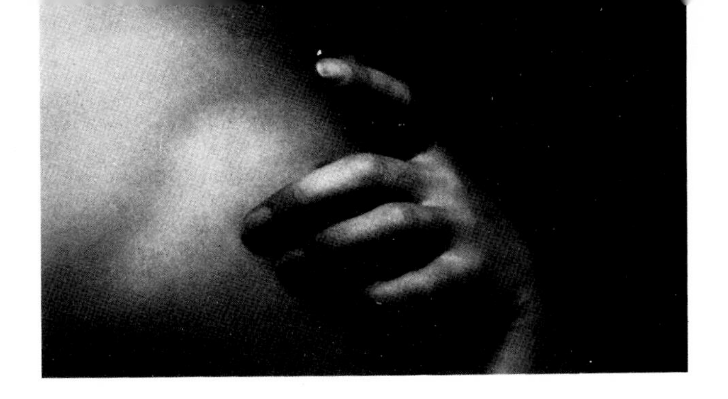

a character's state of mind, is born.

This cut is the key to the film, for it is the man whom she calls "Hiroshima" who reminds her of her lover at Nevers. It is the tragedy of his race that reminds her of the small tragedy of her life. This identification is carried through in the most neurotic moments of her recitative, when she looks at the Japanese and speaks to him as if he were her German lover of fourteen years before.

The whole Nevers story is told in a mosaic of images, out of sequence if one is concerned with chronology, in sequence in terms of emotional importance to the girl who is remembering. This Proustian technique of examining the past, remembering through triggering events in the present, was a startling and powerful innovation. Unfortunately, it has since been imitated endlessly by lesser directors, used by them to say, in effect, "Look, everybody, I can do it, too!" and has become so familiar as to seem, at times, tawdry.

The interlocking of Riva's narration of her story with fragments from her memory is ingenious. The camera moves flow together. We are drawn from present to past and back to present. The shots are designed to fit together perfectly. The sound track of the present always covers the images from the past, so that we know that what we are seeing at Nevers is in her mind.

HIROSHIMA, MON AMOUR is not plotted with a beginning-middle-and-end. Rather, it is structured like a piece of music, with themes and variations that entwine, and movements paced at different tempos. It is filled with slow traveling shots, dollies forward, pullbacks, and pans. (Resnais says: "I love the street. I love to walk in streets. That, too, is traveling, and then I often ride my bicycle through the streets. . . .") The sound track and the picture fit together with equality, neither one dominating the other, the two synthesized with classical restraint. The picture, finally, has an unforced flow which is extraordinary when one analyzes its intricate structure. It is a film of complements: image and sound; past and present; the actual and the remembered; Hiroshima (a city of neon) and Nevers (a city of gray stone); the personal and the cosmic; a man and a woman; concern for the individual and concern for mankind.

## Gillo Pontecorvo's **Battle of Algiers** 1967

If in the genre of concerned films THE BICYCLE THIEF is concerned with the poor, THE FOUR HUNDRED BLOWS with the brutalization of children, ON THE WATERFRONT with exploitation and the morality of informing, and HIROSHIMA, MON AMOUR with human destiny, BATTLE OF ALGIERS finally gets down to the core subject of socially-oriented filmmaking. It is concerned with the people who make a revolution.

The film has become famous, sort of a cinematic parallel to Frantz Fanon's *The Wretched of the Earth.* There are some people who think it should be banned because they view it as a movie textbook of urban guerrilla warfare. It is the sort of picture that frightens the middle class. They note the parallels between the Algerian Casbah and the black ghettos of America, and comprehend their vulnerability if these ghettos should ever explode. The film Z, on the other hand, which is far less compassionate and much more a work of tendentious propaganda, is a picture the middle class can appreciate. They can enjoy the luxury of feeling a liberal distaste for a distant Greek fascism without having to think about any possible echoes in their own political milieu.

BATTLE OF ALGIERS is frightening—so much so that it was banned in France for years, and when it finally did open the Paris theatre that showed it was threatened with bombing. What is interesting about all this is that the picture was not made by the Algerian government or any other third-world force, but by an Italian director, Gillo Pontecorvo, working in the tradition of Italian Neo-Realism. Though Pontecorvo is clearly sympathetic to the struggle of the Algerian people for independence, he is understanding of French colonialism, too. BATTLE OF ALGIERS does not make torture palatable, but it makes the French use of torture in Algeria explicable. It is a human document, not a propaganda piece, and in this way it can be considered a direct descendant of Rossellini's OPEN CITY, and the two "concerned" warm pictures of De Sica, SHOESHINE and THE BICYCLE THIEF. Its debt to these earlier works can also be seen in its documentary style and its use of nonactors in primary roles. (The only professional actor in the picture is Jean Martin, who plays the French Colonel Mathieu. The FLN leader, Kadar, is played by Yacef Saadi, who actually held a high position in the National Liberation Front apparatus, and who was instrumental in organizing resistance in the Casbah.)

There is a note on the screen at the beginning of BATTLE OF ALGIERS saying that the picture contains "*not one foot* of newsreel or documentary film." This disclaimer is neither boastful nor gratuitous. In some countries the effect of the film was so real that audiences believed they were watching a documentary compilation with some fictional episodes thrown in. Though every single frame has been staged, many scenes look like newsreel coverage. This verisimilitude is the result of a documentary style of camerawork—a simulation of *cinéma-vérité* by using a hand-held camera—and the use of high-contrast, high-grain lab processes. Above all, it is a credit to the expertise of Gillo Pontecorvo, who spent more than a year researching the subject, poring over photographs and newsreels and talking with eyewitnesses, and then five painstaking months shooting the story as accurately as he could. The major strength of BATTLE OF ALGIERS is its overpowering sense of truth.

There is something inexorable about the progress of the story and its punctuation by subtitles representing FLN communiques and news headlines in the Algerian papers. Each act of violence on one side is countered by an act of violence on the other. As the film progresses this violence escalates to crueler and more frantic heights.

It begins with random incidents of terror, FLN assassinations of French police. The French close off the Casbah, which plays into the hands of the FLN by polarizing the two races. FLN terrorism continues and is countered by right-wing French vigilantism. Some Frenchmen bomb the house of an innocent Arab worker, and the Arabs retaliate by dispatching three women to blow up mobs in the French quarter of the city. Paratroops arrive from France. They use torture and provocation to smoke out the insurgents. The FLN calls a general strike, the paratroops raid the Casbah, the FLN orders even wilder and more random terrorism, and the French engage in more torture and killing. At the end the French seem to win; they succeed in tracking down all the FLN leaders. But revolutionary fervor cannot be stifled. Two years later the Casbah erupts again. The people pour out in an orgy of celebration. French rule in Algeria is doomed.

Pontecorvo sees revolution as something sublime, something like a holy rite. When men are tortured he gives us organ music, and when Ali La Pointe and his friends are blown up we hear it again. The Arabs are not cardboard puppets; they are human, but also obsessed with gaining their liberty. Nothing can stop them because they are prepared to die. The French, for all their cruelty, are human too. Colonel Mathieu, leader of the paratroopers, is a complicated and ambiguous man. He is paid by the French government to do a very dirty job, and there is a harsh logic in the situation, as he points out at a press conference: "If you want France to stay, you must accept the consequences."

The film is Marxist, perhaps even Maoist. It is concerned with people who are colonized and oppressed by foreign masters. It has implications for Vietnam, Rhodesia, South Africa, Latin America. It is a human document about the twentieth century—about throwing off the imperialist yoke—and though committed to revolution it is also tempered with compassion. At the end of the picture when the Arab masses break out of the Casbah and dance wildly in the squares of the French quarter, waving FLN flags they have secreted for years, it is impossible not to be stirred by this image of men coming out of a dark maze of oppression, bursting into sunlit plazas of liberty.

# Credits

## The Bicycle Thief (Ladri di Biciclette)

Italy; 1948; 90 minutes;
originally released in the U.S.
by Mayer-Burstyn.

| | |
|---|---|
| **Directed by** | Vittorio De Sica. |
| **Produced by** | Vittorio De Sica. |
| **Screenplay by** | Cesare Zavattini from the novel by Luigi Bartolini. |
| **Photographed by** | Carlo Montuori. |
| **Edited by** | Eraldo da Roma. |
| **Music by** | Alessandro Cicognini. |
| **Cast:** | Lamberto Maggiorani; Enzo Staiola; Lianella Carell; Elena Altieri; Gino Saltamerenda. |

## On the Waterfront

U.S.A.; 1954; 108 minutes;
released by Columbia.

| | |
|---|---|
| **Directed by** | Elia Kazan. |
| **Produced by** | Sam Spiegel. |
| **Screenplay by** | Budd Schulberg, based on a story by Schulberg suggested by articles by Malcolm Johnson. |
| **Photographed by** | Boris Kaufman. |
| **Art direction by** | Richard Day. |
| **Edited by** | Gene Milford. |
| **Music by** | Leonard Bernstein. |
| **Cast:** | Marlon Brando; Karl Malden; Lee J. Cobb; Rod Steiger; Pat Henning; Eva Marie Saint; Leif Erickson; James Westerfield; Tony Galento; Tami Mauriello; John Hamilton; John Heldabrand; Abe Simon; Mike O'Dowd; Martin Balsam; Fred Gwynne. |

## The Four Hundred Blows (Les Quatres Cents Coups)

France; 1959; 94 minutes;
released in the U.S. by Janus.

| | |
|---|---|
| **Directed by** | François Truffaut. |
| **Produced by** | François Truffaut. |
| **Screenplay by** | François Truffaut, with dialogue by Marcel Moussy, based on a story by François Truffaut. |
| **Photographed by** | Henri Decae. |
| **Art direction by** | Bernard Evein. |
| **Edited by** | Marie-Josèphe Yoyotte. |
| **Music by** | Jean Constantin. |
| **Cast:** | Jean-Pierre Léaud; Claire Maurier; Albert Rémy; Guy Decomble; Patrick Auffay. |

## Hiroshima, Mon Amour

France; 1959; 91 minutes;
originally released in the U.S. by
Zenith International.

| | |
|---|---|
| **Directed by** | Alain Resnais. |
| **Produced by** | Samy Halfon. |
| **Screenplay by** | Marguerite Duras. |
| **Photographed by** | Sacha Vierny and Michio Takahashi. |
| **Edited by** | Henri Colpi, Jasmine Chasney, Anne Sarraute. |
| **Music by** | Georges Delerue and Giovanni Fusco. |
| **Cast:** | Emmanuèle Riva; Eiji Okada; Bernard Fresson; Stella Dassas; Pierre Barbaud. |

## Battle of Algiers

Italy; 1967; 118 minutes;
released in the U.S. by
Allied Artists Pictures.

| | |
|---|---|
| **Directed by** | Gillo Pontecorvo. |
| **Produced by** | Antonio Musu. |
| **Screenplay by** | Franco Solinas and Gillo Pontecorvo. |
| **Photographed by** | Marcello Gatti. |
| **Art direction by** | Sergio Canevari. |
| **Music by** | Ennio Morriscone and Gillo Pontecorvo. |
| **Cast:** | Yacef Saadi; Jean Martin; Brahim Haggiag; Tommaso Neri; Samia Kerbash. |

Gillo Pontecorvo (l.) in Neo-Realist tradition works with nonactors during shooting of BATTLE OF ALGIERS. His skill in simulating newsreel "look" of mass action, and his sympathy for his characters, no matter their politics, gives his film an extraordinary quality rare in the genre.

# Period Films

12

The period film—or the historical film, or costume film—is not a genre in the strict sense of the western, the suspense thriller, or the musical. There are no strict criteria that a period film must meet other, of course, than that it be made in period. Many pictures that fall into other genres—westerns, war films, adventure films, etc.—can be produced in period. Furthermore, one can argue that the five pictures discussed here as great period movies could just as easily be placed in other genres. BONNIE AND CLYDE could be classified as a gangster picture, or even as a comedy, THE MAGNIFICENT AMBERSONS as a film of social comment, LES ENFANTS DU PARADIS and GONE WITH THE WIND as romances, and HENRY V either as a war film, or as one of that special breed, a screen adaptation of a famous play. Because of all this overlap and ambiguity, the question arises: Why create a category which is, in some respects, a catchall?

The answer is that although a filmmaker need not fulfill specific requirements when making a period film, there are a certain number of great pictures made in period which have certain elements in common when viewed from the outside. If the period film is not a genre in the commercial sense, in that producers do not sit down and say, "Let's make a film in period to appeal to the segment of the audience that goes for things like that," it is a genre that has been created by critics and moviegoers who have set its standards by deduction.

What, then, are these deduced standards?

First of all, a picture produced in period has in common with other pictures produced in period the problem of historical authenticity, which is not so obvious as it may sound. Anthony Mann's EL CID, for instance, doesn't even try to recapture its period. Its costumes look Venetian, and Charlton Heston, six feet tall and clean-shaven, plays the part of an historical personage who was known for his small stature and enormous beard. In a great period film costumes and decor must be correct, art direction and production design must be informed by authenticity. Richard Sylbert's master set for Sidney Lumet's LONG DAY'S JOURNEY INTO NIGHT is impeccable, but in some early exteriors we see out-of-period motorboats in the background—a minor flaw, not sufficient to destroy the illusion, but indicative of the sort of problem that must be met. There are one hundred thousand pairs of eyes searching the background of period films for just such errors. The connoisseur of period films cannot resist

## Marcel Carné's **Les Enfants Du Paradis** 1945

LES ENFANTS DU PARADIS is old-fashioned and this quality may be its greatest strength as a period movie. It is old-fashioned in the sense that it has a complicated plot filled with chance encounters between strong characters whose lives are traced over a period of years. It is old-fashioned, too, in that it is a story with a grand encompassing theme, in this case the Shakespearean idea that "all the world's a stage, and all the men and women merely players." It is a story that makes comparisons between the behavior of people in different social strata, between different forms of theatre, and between different types of love. It is long, complex, and highly structured, very much like a nineteenth-century French novel by Balzac or Dumas père. Since it is set in the Paris of the 1840s, the time and place in which these authors lived and wrote, one can say that it not only recaptures a specific period, but also a specific literary style.

In this sense it is different from the other period films considered here. It does not use its period as a means of distancing the past and then interpreting it through a modern sensibility, like BONNIE AND CLYDE. It does not attempt to recapture and interpret a poignant historical moment, like THE MAGNIFICENT AMBERSONS. It does not fabricate a lush romantic style for the purpose of creating escapist entertainment, like GONE WITH THE WIND, or poeticize the past to encourage those in the present, like HENRY V. Instead, LES ENFANTS DU PARADIS immerses itself in its period in a deliberate effort to find a cinematic equivalent for a literary style. It does not attempt so much to recreate the reality of the past, as the reality of its fiction.

The story is the sort that is laughed at now, an involved series of encounters between several different men, and the evolution of their relationships with a single dominating female presence. At times LES ENFANTS DU PARADIS approaches the brink of sentimentality; sometimes it even teeters at that brink. But it never falls because of the good taste of its authors, the poet Jacques Prévert and the director Marcel Carné, and a cast of actors as great as has ever been assembled in any French film: Jean-Louis Barrault, who plays the mime-actor Deburau; Pierre Brasseur, certainly the Laurence Olivier



Preceding pages: Clark Gable and Vivien Leigh as Rhett Butler and Scarlett O'Hara in Victor Fleming's GONE WITH THE WIND. Opposite: Balconies of a mid-nineteenth century Parisian theater. At top are the cheap seats where sit "the children of paradise" in Marcel Carné's film of that title.

rising from his seat and pointing his finger at the television aerial on the house in the picture set during Prohibition, or the 1970 Chevrolet in the picture set in 1964. It is said that Erich von Stroheim carried period realism too far when he insisted that extras playing Austrian cavalrymen had to have Hapsburg double eagles sewn into their underwear. Be that as it may, Stroheim understood the first essential requirement of a great period film: Its period must be authentically reproduced.

Secondly, a great period film must do more than use its period setting as a backdrop for a story. It must also provide an interpretation of the past. When a novel set in the past is to be adapted for the screen, the first question that arises is whether or not the story should be updated. If the answer is no—that the story should be kept in period—it is incumbent on the filmmaker to put that period to some specific use, either to comment on the past, or to evoke nostalgia, or to draw some analogy or contrast with the present, or to provide a sense that the story being told could only have happened in a certain time and place, or even, if necessary, to pervert the past, to alter its sensibility (but not its costumes and decor!) in order to make a point. On this ground alone, most Biblical spectacles, mythological epics, and sword-and-sandal dramas (including Stanley Kubrick's bizarre if interesting SPARTACUS) can be dismissed. Not only are such pictures usually abysmally unauthentic, but for all their historical references, they could as easily have been set in the year 2001.

Ultimately, and this is the most important standard that must be met, the director of a great period film must go beyond authenticity. He must convey period by a directorial concept that leads to stylization. It is not sufficient to dress an actor in a suit of armor and then tell him to act like G. I. Joe, because, the director says, "all soldiers act alike." The director of a great period film imposes a sense of period upon his picture by employing a style that conveys a point of view. He may get his ideas from scholarly research, or he may invent them in his own mind; it doesn't matter. In the end the picture must have a sense of itself, a photographic style, a camera style, an acting style that tells us, rightly or wrongly, that this is what this period was like. Two pictures by Ken Russell may illuminate this point: WOMEN IN LOVE has a comprehensive style that conveys a sense of period; THE MUSIC LOVERS employs a dozen styles which make useful dramatic points but destroy the period entirely.

of France, who plays the tragedian Lemaître; Marcel Herrand, who plays the failed playwright and ruthless gangster Lacenaire; Louis Salou, who plays the cold and hypocritical Count de Montray; and finally the actress who calls herself, simply, Arletty, who plays Garance, the mellow, mysterious, self-contained *femme fatale*, with whom the four men, each in his own way, is in love.

Deburau loves Garance with the idealizing passion sometimes known as sacred love; Lemaître loves her carnally, profanely; the selfish and self-hating Lacenaire loves her as much as he is able, with a sort of skeptical friendship; and the Count de Montray loves her in the agonizing, possessive way of a man who owns a woman but suffers because he knows his passion is not returned.

These characters interact, and circle Garance, against a lavishly presented background of the world of show business in mid-nineteenth-century Paris, the carnival atmosphere of the "Boulevard of Crime," and the mobs called by the actors "the children of paradise"—those who sit in the cheap seats in the high balconies of the theatres where they hoot or applaud the performances taking place on the stage. The story and the film are stylized and artificial, and yet also great, in the same way that Balzac and Victor Hugo are great: They are irresistible. The acting and the dialogue are so good, and the camera work and editing so unobtrusive, that the viewer is drawn into and then absorbed by a fictional world. LES ENFANTS DU PARADIS is a splendid theatrical experience, a three-hour immersion in history and art, an archetypal escapist film.

This element of escapism was very much to the point when the picture was made, during the German occupation of France, and under the supervision of Gestapo censors. One can imagine the difficulties, and also the incongruities, of mounting so lavish a production (the Boulevard of Crime set, built in Nice, was more than five hundred feet long, and involved the manipulation of hundreds of costumed extras) in a time of severe shortages and national anguish. Many of the scenes were shot secretly, and several people who worked on the production did so while being hunted by the Nazis. The electricity often failed and it is said that the food provided as props for the banquet scenes was eaten by starving extras before these scenes were filmed. Somehow under these conditions Carné was able to make the picture without ever succumbing to pressures which would unnerve lesser directors. The film does not contain a moment that is not in keeping with its overall design. Its high style is maintained throughout, and there is no evidence of compromise in its many vast and complicated scenes. From the time Deburau encounters a "blind man" (who turns out to be a jewelry estimator for the underworld), goes with him to a crowded dance hall, encounters Garance, dances with her, fights off one of Lacenaire's henchmen, and takes her to his hotel, we are fascinated beyond our expectations. Barrault's mime scenes must rank with the finest mime work ever filmed, and the finale, when he fights his way through the teaming masses on the Boulevard of Crime, searching for Garance, is surely a superb example of personal passion counterpoised against a joyful celebration—a favorite formulation of the Soviet cinema. It is an ending strong enough to make one reel as one walks out of the theatre, onto streets which seem mundane compared to the Boulevard of Crime.

From LES ENFANTS DU PARADIS: The great Pierre Brasseur playing the great nineteenth-century actor Lemaître playing Othello carries out theme of Carné and screenwriter Jacques Prévert that "all the world's a stage." Right: Brasseur with Marcel Herrand as the failed playwright and gangster Lacenaire.

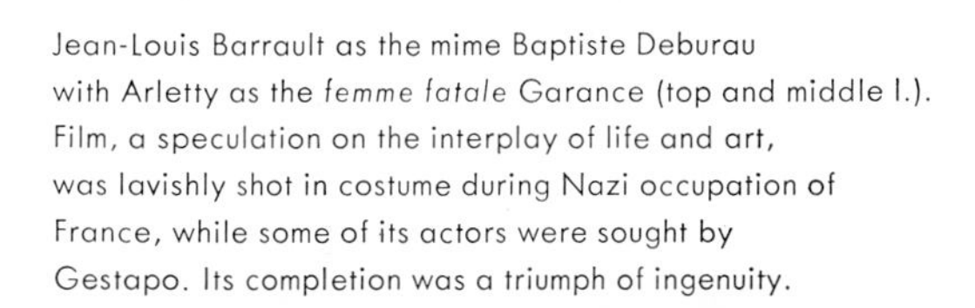

Jean-Louis Barrault as the mime Baptiste Deburau with Arletty as the *femme fatale* Garance (top and middle l.). Film, a speculation on the interplay of life and art, was lavishly shot in costume during Nazi occupation of France, while some of its actors were sought by Gestapo. Its completion was a triumph of ingenuity.

# Victor Fleming's **Gone With the Wind** 1939

A world apart from LES ENFANTS DU PARADIS is GONE WITH THE WIND, a picture that is a masterpiece of mass entertainment and decidedly not a work of art. Here the period is conceived in lush and romantic terms, stylized to serve the purposes of escapism. There is little doubt that the Old South wasn't much like the milieu of GONE WITH THE WIND, but it doesn't make any difference. A concept, derived from the style of Margaret Mitchell's long, complex, best-selling historical novel has been imposed, and the result is a picture that has very much a sense of itself.

At the time of writing, GONE WITH THE WIND has earned more than $75,000,000 in rentals in the domestic market alone and the end is not in sight. This phenomenal success is not difficult to understand. The picture was based on the most popular book of its day, set in the most turbulent and romantic era of American history, the years during and after the Civil War. It was well produced by a top-rank showman, David O. Selznick, stars Clark Gable, the most dashing male actor of his time, and runs three-and-a-half hours, thus providing the viewer with a vast, epic world of fantasy.

But more important, and perhaps the true key to the picture's success, is that its story is built around the adventures of a character named Scarlett O'Hara (played by Vivien Leigh), whose actions, motives, whims, joys, and sufferings make her the perfect centerpiece for a lush, romantic film. Her obsession—to rebuild her plantation, Tara, to "never be hungry again," to restore the majesty and romance of a "land of cavaliers and cotton fields in the Old South"—is calculated to stimulate the audience to heights of sympathy and identification.

GONE WITH THE WIND is not only King, it is also King Corn—King of Soap Opera, King of Schlock, tear-jerker of tear-jerkers—produced on a mighty scale with a sense of itself, a vibrating aliveness, that sets it apart from other screen soap operas. GONE WITH THE WIND is King Corn with a difference, with a certain something that continues to move people, and reap in the millions each time it is released, an artifact of universal fantasy fulfillment that is worthy of serious consideration.

1. Certainly Vivien Leigh must be credited with a good deal of the success of this picture. She was an obscure British actress when introduced to Selznick at MGM the night he supervised the shooting of the Burning of Atlanta sequence—really a conflagration of old movie sets on the back lot. A debate had raged through the nation over who should play Scarlett O'Hara. Something about Miss Leigh appealed to Mr. Selznick. He chose her by instinct and thus performed one of the inspired pieces of casting in movie history. Vivien Leigh is magnificent. She carries the picture, she dominates it, and reproduces the character of Scarlett in all its mercurial complexity.

2. The film is deceptive in a strange and interesting way. Many people who have seen it long ago recall it as an epic of the Civil War. They think they remember seeing many vast scenes containing thousands of extras, and including scenes of battle. In fact, their recollections are faulty. GONE WITH THE WIND is not really a "spectacular" except in terms of its length. It is basically a film of interiors and medium shots. It contains no battles, although it gives an impression, quite powerfully, of the Civil War by its one really grand scene, the thousands of wounded lying about the Atlanta railroad station. As for the famous Burning of Atlanta sequence, there are a couple of shots of collapsing buildings, but the whole flight-through-the-fire sequence is highly stylized, with action taking place against a red sky. In GONE WITH THE WIND we see very little in the way of big scenes, certainly a lot less than in Griffith's INTOLERANCE, and yet we feel as though we have seen a lot. In the obligatory nightrider and KKK sequence, for example, we are shown nothing except a group of women sitting around worrying, while men come in to tell them what has happened outside. The fact that this scene works extremely well, and that we are deceived into recalling the picture as a spectacle, is proof of the power of its technique. In short, GONE WITH THE WIND is good cinema.

3. Rhett Butler is a first-class bastard, Scarlett O'Hara is a first-class scheming bitch, and both characters are fascinating. The goody-goodys on the other hand, Ashley Wilkes and Melanie Hamilton, are bores. Considering the prevailing moral standards at the time this picture was made, this use of a couple of hustlers to give the picture life must be considered a daring stroke, and one that keeps the picture alive today.

4. The bleeding sunsets and the wallowing sentimentality of the picture are good fun. One can enjoy them because GONE WITH THE WIND does not pretend to be anything but an impossible romantic fiction, and, thank God, does not attempt to make an Important Social Statement.

5. When one sees the picture in a theatre today, the Negro characters, Mammy (Hattie MacDaniel), Pork



Clark Gable, leading male star of the era, was the inevitable choice to play gambler and lady-killer Rhett Butler, but debate raged over who should get role of Scarlett. Gable, evidently displeased by George Cukor's direction, asked Producer David Selznick to replace him. Victor Fleming got the job.

ATLANTA EXAMINER

TENNESSEE HOU
GEORGIA R. R. & BANKING Co AGENCY

(Oscar Polk), and Prissy (Butterfly McQueen), produce about as much laughter as they produced when the film was first released. The difference is that in 1939 audiences were laughing at the quaint childishness of these slave characters; today they are laughing at the patronizing sensibility that thought black characters acted that way.

6. The screenplay of GONE WITH THE WIND is extraordinarily fine. It is credited to Sidney Howard, who did the original treatment for Selznick before he died. Selznick hired other writers to produce other drafts, and on one occasion suspended shooting while Ben Hecht completely rewrote the first nine reels in seven days. Hecht's account of this experience in his autobiography, *A Child of the Century*, is hilarious, and most revealing of the outrageous methods by which Hollywood films were then made.

7. The director of GONE WITH THE WIND was Victor Fleming, brought in after George Cukor was fired at Clark Gable's request. The final version of the film contains scenes shot by Cukor, and though we cannot be sure exactly which ones they are, we can be certain that they are among the picture's very best. Cukor was a first-class director, while Fleming was an erratic director-for-hire. The irony is that Fleming ended up directing two of the most entertaining films ever made, GONE WITH THE WIND and THE WIZARD OF OZ, while Cukor, who directed many fine pictures, never made anything quite so popular.

8. Much credit must go to Selznick and the expert production designer William Cameron Menzies. Menzies, who had originally been an illustrator of children's books, was legendary for his sketches, which were not simply drawings of costumes and sets, but also of characters, their entrances, exits, the camera angles from which they should be shot, and instructions on how they should be lit. He drew more than 2,500 sketches for GONE WITH THE WIND, one for each and every camera set-up.

As for Selznick, he never got over the enormous success of GONE WITH THE WIND, which came relatively early in his career. For years afterward he would interrupt a meeting on another picture, or begin the dictation of one of his long and infamous memoranda, with the phrase: "This is how we did it when we shot GONE WITH THE WIND. . . ."

9. As a period film, GONE WITH THE WIND is a perfect example of a case where a specific period has been thoroughly used—in this case milked—for everything it has to offer. A fortune was spent on costumes, props, and decor, and it shows. GONE WITH THE WIND is full of authenticity, even, in some of the period war scenes, resembling the ambience of photographs by Mathew Brady. The people are not authentic. They are fictitious, impossible. Yet placed in this special period, surrounded by authentic props and locales, with a consistent, polished, and highly artificial romantic style imposed upon them, they come to life. The incredible thing about GONE WITH THE WIND is that it is possible to believe in Rhett Butler and Scarlett O'Hara—not only to believe in them but to care about them, to suffer and rejoice with them, to feel that their lives are bound up with one's own.

## Laurence Olivier's **Henry V** 1944

The background of HENRY V is well known. During World War II, when England was under siege as never before, Laurence Olivier was persuaded to mount an extravagant and expensive production of Shakespeare's *Henry V.* It was believed that this play, filled with so much heroism and chauvinism, would in the form of a film be helpful in raising British morale. It seemed a brilliant idea: to use the greatest English writer to rouse the English people, to use the past as propaganda, to make an historical film that would serve the same purpose as Winston Churchill's inspiring speeches.

But if this were all there is to HENRY V, the movie would only make an interesting footnote to film history. HENRY V achieves greatness on its own artistic merits, apart from any of the intentions surrounding its production. It is a brilliant transposition of a play to the screen, brilliant in its handling of period reality, and enriched by a brilliant Olivier performance.

The problem that comes up whenever a play is to be filmed is: "How are we going to 'open it up'?" The reasoning goes that since theatre is the art form of writers, and cinema the art form of directors, it is not sufficient to merely photograph a stage play—even if it is only a musical comedy. Something must be added, and that "something," whether the play is *Cyrano de Bergerac* or *Who's Afraid of Virginia Woolf*, is usually the pitfall of the filmmaker concerned.

Shakespeare presents more problems than most



Preceding pages: Scarlett walks among the wounded in Atlanta railyard. Many people recall spectacular Civil War battles in GWTW, but there are none. This traveling shot of Confederate casualties is the picture's biggest crowd scene. Opposite: Ashley Wilkes (Leslie Howard) embraces Scarlett, but is loved by Melanie Hamilton (Olivia de Haviland).

A.B.W.P.R.R.
8142

Above: Scarlett and her beloved Tara Hall in "a land of cavaliers and cotton fields." Actual location was Westchester County, N.Y. Far left: Ashley, Rhett, and Yankee captain (Ward Bond) at Melanie's door. Left: Atlanta burns. Scene was shot on back lot of MGM even before production of main part of film began.

playwrights, since his language is so much more sublime than the vision of even the most talented directors. Orson Welles has stumbled against him several times, his falls barely broken by his high cinematic ambition. Perhaps the one man who has been lucky with Shakespeare has been Laurence Olivier, an outstanding actor and a shrewd and intelligent director, who has brought Shakespeare to the screen successfully three times. His HAMLET is played in a dark, moody Elsinore, shot in black and white and lit with powerful arc lamps, so that the depth of field is immense. His RICHARD III is played almost like a German Expressionist horror film, filled with violence and neurosis. And his HENRY V invents a new way of bringing Shakespeare to the screen by, in effect, spitting in the face of the convention of suspension of disbelief.

Olivier's solution is to begin his film in Elizabethan London, then move his camera to the Globe Theatre, where Shakespeare's *Henry V* is being played. By showing us the audience, and activities backstage, he gives us the impression that we are going to see an historical film set in Shakespeare's own time.

But then, little by little, the play itself begins to take over the film. Somewhere (and we are never precisely certain where) the proscenium arch disappears. Though we are still, clearly, watching a play, the fourth wall has slowly closed. Now we are inside the play, amidst painted sets and theatrical props, but out of the Globe, perhaps in a movie studio. And then, as we become accustomed to this new situation, we are quite suddenly thrust into real exteriors, in the year 1415, when the action of Shakespeare's play (as opposed to its presentation in a sixteenth-century theatre) took place. A great and realistically bloody battle scene, the Battle of Agincourt, is played as if it were really happening. We have been drawn through the conventions of the theatre into the reality of the cinema, from the stylized world of Shakespearean poetry into a real world without dialogue or artifice. When the battle is over Olivier slowly leads us back from the real exteriors, through the three-dimensional sets, to the Globe Theatre in time for the finale.

The effect is something like a dream, as if we have become so wrapped up in the performance of a play upon the stage that our minds have been stolen into a world where fantasy becomes reality; and then, as the dream recedes, Olivier gently leads us back to our seats. It is an amazing accomplishment, something never quite done before, in which cinematic realism and theatrical illusion are subtly mixed, and three levels of the past are reproduced in period.

HENRY V is an exemplary period film, but something must be added about Laurence Olivier. Even in roles beneath his talent—Max De Winter in REBECCA or Archie Rice in THE ENTERTAINER—he is phenomenal. Playing Shakespeare he has been at his best, and deserves the accolades he has received as the world's superlative living actor. In HENRY V he brings such energy to his heroic role that he makes the swashbuckling of Douglas Fairbanks and Errol Flynn look tame. And as a filmmaker his invention of what the aesthetician Erwin Panofsky called the "oblique close-up"—when we watch his face in repose listening to his own off-stage voice pronouncing a soliloquy—is one of the few startling visual innovations since the days of D. W. Griffith and Sergei Eisenstein.



From HENRY V: Laurence Olivier as the king in most successful film yet made from a Shakespearean play. Spectacular Battle of Agincourt. Victorious Henry woos French princess (Renée Asherson). Olivier studies script on wartime set. Grandeur shrinks within confines of Globe Theater's "wooden O." Felix Aylmer between player king and queen, Leslie Banks (Chorus) at left.

Comedy mixes with blood, crime with social comment, romance with death in BONNIE AND CLYDE. Above: Gene Hackman, Warren Beatty, and Faye Dunaway pull a bank caper. Right: Clyde is wounded in gun battle with cops. Film was loosely based on adventures of Barrow gang, whose robberies in Southwest were a brief sensation during the 1930s.

# Arthur Penn's **Bonnie and Clyde** 1967

We know from the credit sequence of Arthur Penn's BONNIE AND CLYDE that the film will be in period. The titles are interspersed with sepia photographs of the real Bonnie Parker and Clyde Barrow, and our nostalgia is stimulated by the sound of a pop tune of the 1930s that emerges quietly on the sound track.

Of the several films made about the Barrow gang, none comes close to the level of BONNIE AND CLYDE, whose superiority was barely acknowledged at the time the picture opened. One highbrow critic referred to it as "a bunch of decayed cabbage leaves smeared with catsup"; another called it "clever trash," ending his review with the comment that "slop is slop, even served with a silver ladle." *The New York Times* said the picture was corrupt, accused it of making violence palatable, and a critic for a major newsweekly called it "a squalid shoot-em-up for the moron trade"—a statement he retracted a few weeks later. The tide began to turn, the audience began to swell, and BONNIE AND CLYDE became a *cause célèbre.* It stirred and moved young people, stimulated a trend toward 1930s fashions, and earned more than $22 million in rentals in the domestic market alone.

Speaking of the authenticity to the period of the film, Arthur Penn has said: "We stripped away almost all the extraneous details we could. . . . I didn't think that for a minute we were creating any kind of real world or society. . . . The movie is an abstraction rather than a genuine reportage." Penn created a mood in BONNIE AND CLYDE, an evocation of the 1930s filtered through his 1960s sensibility. Though he says that "the death of Bonnie and Clyde in the film was literally and historically accurate; they did fire a thousand rounds; eighty-seven direct hits were found on their bodies," of course he does not mean that Bonnie Parker and Clyde Barrow died a ritualistic death in slow motion. The sense of period in BONNIE AND CLYDE reflects Penn's vision of how the 1930s seemed, and for all the perfection of the costumes and props, this vision is highly personal.

What is also personal about BONNIE AND CLYDE, and constitutes its unique flavor, is its curious blending of comedy and horror, its romanticization of crime as something that is fun, and that also leads to violent bloody death. BONNIE AND CLYDE is both real and abstract, a gangster movie and a comedy-romance. It is a comedy that turns dark, a romance that ends with death. One could add that the banjo music that covers the interludes are the refrains in Arthur Penn's ballad-like picture.

An alternation between fun and darkness is important to the structure of the film. After their first successful bank stickup, a daring and gay maneuver goes sour when Clyde is forced to shoot a bank guard and real blood gushes from his face—a shot strongly reminiscent of a closeup in the Odessa Steps sequence of POTEMKIN. In the next scene the gang broods in a movie theatre while the gay musical number, "We're in the Money," from a Busby Berkeley picture, plays on the screen.

Bonnie and Clyde take adolescent pleasure posing for photographs with their captive, Texas Ranger Hamer, but when cornered by police in a motel, they turn into vicious outlaws fighting for their lives. C. W. Moss, particularly, evokes Baby Face Nelson, when he blasts at police with a blazing machine gun, his baby face in Cagneyesque repose.

One of the poignant moments in the film occurs when Clyde chases Bonnie through a corn field, while a cloud crosses the sun and slowly shadows the landscape. Here the flavor of the Midwest and the darkening mood of the story are both expressed. The famous reunion scene is distanced and turned into a mood piece with filters, slow motion, and muffled sound. Of this scene Penn has said: "It was supposed to be happening, but in the sense that it was unreclaimable, that it was disappearing like an ancient photograph. That it was there and yet it was all dealing with values that belonged to the past."

This sort of mythic, abstract, nostalgic flavor of the depression is evoked again when C.W. drives his bloodied leaders into an Okie camp and the Okies come around the car to look with awe at the legendary outlaws.

The final "ballet of death," when Bonnie and Clyde are gunned down, has an extraordinary effect upon audiences. (Several cameras were used to shoot this scene, each turning at a different speed; Faye Dunaway's leg was tied to the emergency brake so that she could slump over dead without falling from the car.) Startled birds fly out of trees, we catch a glimpse of weapons shredding shrubbery, and see Bonnie and Clyde grasping for one another in prolonged and exultant agony. There have been premonitions of this throughout, even in the opening titles when their names slowly bled red, but nothing quite prepares us for the reality. Despite the blood they have spilled, our sympathy for them is overwhelming.

A-6

# Orson Welles' **The Magnificent Ambersons** 1942

The distancing of BONNIE AND CLYDE, which gives the film its unique dreamlike quality, is partly a result of nostalgia for the 1930s. World War II is a barrier between now and then, sufficiently high to distance those years, making them an appropriate period for the singing of a ballad or the recounting of a myth. Nostalgia: It is key to certain period films, the overriding emotion that makes them work. BONNIE AND CLYDE uses nostalgia, but another film, Orson Welles' THE MAGNIFICENT AMBERSONS, goes even further. It not only plays upon the nostalgia of its audience, but also deals with the nostalgia of its characters. Furthermore, it takes place over a period of years, so that by its end we are nostalgic for its beginning.

In discussing THE MAGNIFICENT AMBERSONS one may take many points of view. Here, briefly, are a few of them:

1. As a *film maudit:* A cursed, a damned film, like Stroheim's GREED, THE MAGNIFICENT AMBERSONS was massacred, dismembered, thrown away. Certain portions were directed by other people and massive cuts were made without Welles' consent. To add insult to injury it was released in combination with a tawdry comedy, in effect dismissed by its studio as a piece of junk. Welles says that forty-five minutes were cut out and that these sections were the heart of the picture. Despite all this, THE MAGNIFICENT AMBERSONS holds up as a magnificent work. Its



Opposite: Tim Holt and Agnes Moorehead converse on staircase of Amberson mansion in Orson Welles' THE MAGNIFICENT AMBERSONS. Note lighting here and in railway station above. Stanley Cortez' cinematography was as extraordinary in its way as Gregg Toland's in CITIZEN KANE.

flaws, ellipses, and some abruptness in the second half seem minor compared to its enormous strengths. Since it is impossible to know what it might have been, it is fruitless to sigh over its fate.

2. As the other side of Orson: The famous Welles, the legendary Welles, is the Welles of CITIZEN KANE, *Wunderkind,* boy genius, the screamer for attention, the flamboyant artist, the magnificent show-off, the megalomaniacal sleight-of-hand magician. But he has always had another side and it shows most clearly in THE MAGNIFICENT AMBERSONS: Welles the sensitive artist, tranquil, lyrical, and tender, the decent Welles who would credit his collaborators at the expense of his own ego, the quiet, refined, subtle Welles, more interested in making a fine film than in showing the world he can dance circles around his competitors. In public the first Orson dominates the second, but those who know him personally assure us that the second Orson is the true Orson, revealed in unguarded moments. In THE MAGNIFICENT AMBERSONS we face that second Orson, a young man of twenty-six who has made a picture filled with the wisdom, compassion, and refinement that is only supposed to come to an artist in later years. Is it a pose? Decidedly not. THE MAGNIFICENT AMBERSONS radiates sincerity from every frame. One can speculate endlessly about the contradictions in Welles, and attempt to plumb his complicated psychology, but one fact about THE MAGNIFICENT AMBERSONS may provide an important hint. It is the only film he has directed in which he does not appear. This suggests that when Welles' presence is not on the screen, dominating everything around him, his director's eye gives way to something more subtle; that when he no longer needs to use his camera to love himself, his love for others is able to show through.

3. As a technical tour de force: THE MAGNIFICENT AMBERSONS is filled with technical achievements. It is the supreme example of the famous "Welles sound": overlapping dialogue, volume diminishing as characters recede into backgrounds, sound effects and dialogue muffled by architecture, speeches trailing off, voices subdued and hushed by environment and age. As for the camera work, Stanley Cortez may have achieved a greater tour de force than Gregg Toland in CITIZEN KANE. There are long, slow dolly shots through rows of rooms, each one differently lit, sometimes containing mirrors or polished furniture which, only on account of split-second manipulations by the crew, do not reflect the camera; there are extraordinary crane shots; people framed in architectural elements, reflected in mirrors, passing mysteriously through the backgrounds of scenes; and always there is a dark, brooding low-keyed look to everything—the sort of subdued light one finds in photographs of the period. The acting is superb, splendid ensemble playing that shows the hard work of long rehearsals. Agnes Moorehead as Fanny Minafer deserves particular mention; she creates one of the offbeat characterizations for which Welles is so famous. Neurotic, fierce, at times even loathsome, she rises by the end from a mere object of our compassion into a character whom we know will survive.

4. As a film of great sequences: There are enough sequences in THE MAGNIFICENT AMBERSONS for any great film and any one of them alone would make the picture memorable. The spectacular, lush, rich, party sequence at the Amberson mansion is one; the kitchen scenes, in which the camera barely moves, and the early montages, including the breathtaking camera move down main street, are others. But by far the greatest is the unparalleled sleigh-riding sequence shot by Welles over a period of twelve days in a Los Angeles ice factory. It's hard to believe this scene wasn't shot outdoors. The characters' breath steams in the air, the snow is real, and the mood is sublime—lyrical, gay, sensuous, and ultimately sorrowful.

5. As a brilliant period film: THE MAGNIFICENT AMBERSONS is, of course, a story about the vanishing past, of what happens to a town that becomes a city and a rich family that falls when the nineteenth century closes and the industrial twentieth begins. It is a picture steeped with nostalgia for a graceful way of life that disappears before our eyes as characters die and rooms are closed in the great Amberson mansion. The film is compassionate toward Eugene Morgan, who survives and prospers with the change, and George Minafer, who loses everything on account of it. The automobile is the thing that symbolizes the destruction of the past, that kills off the landed gentry and elevates the bourgeoisie, and even the automobile is treated with compassion.

Strangely enough, THE MAGNIFICENT AMBERSONS may be the only Welles film that has anything to do with his own life. As the child of a proud midwestern family, he has obvious sympathy for the Ambersons and the other people of Indianapolis, as well as understanding of a way of life and a region of the country, which comes through with poignant clarity. In the end, THE MAGNIFICENT AMBERSONS is a film about period, about people growing old, people dying, the fall of one way of life and the rise of another. Unlike the other period films discussed here, it does not merely use a period, it is *about* a period. Its period is its subject, and so is nostalgia, which is also its effect.

# Credits

## Les Enfants Du Paradis (The Children of Paradise)

France; 1945; 173 minutes;
originally released in the U.S. by
Tricolore Films, Inc.

**Directed by** Marcel Carné.
**Produced by** S. N. Pathé Cinéma.
**Screenplay by** Jacques Prévert.
**Photographed by** Roger Hubert and Marc Fossard.
**Art direction by** A. Barsacq, R. Cabutti, and Alexandre Trauner.
**Edited by** Henry Rust.
**Music by** Joseph Kosma, Maurice Thierte, and Georges Mouque.
**Cast:** Jean Louis Barrault; Arletty; Pierre Brasseur; Marcel Herrand; Pierre Renoir; Fabien Loris; Louis Salou; Maria Cassares; Etienne Decroux; Jeanne Marken; Gaston Modot; Pierre Palau; Albert Remy; Paul Frankeur.

## Henry V

Great Britain; 1944; 134 minutes;
released in the U.S. by United Artists.

**Directed by** Laurence Olivier.
**Produced by** Laurence Olivier.
**Screenplay by** Laurence Olivier and Alan Dent. Based on "Henry V" by William Shakespeare.
**Edited by** Reginald Beck.
**Photographed by** Robert Krasker and Jack Hildyard.
**Art direction by** Paul Sheriff and Roger Furse.
**Music by** William Walton.
**Cast:** Laurence Olivier; Leslie Banks; Robert Newton; Renée Asherson; Esmond Knight; Leo Genn; Felix Aylmer; Ralph Truman; Harcourt Williams; Ivy St. Heller; Ernest Thesiger; Max Adrian; Francis Lister; Valentine Dyall; Russell Thorndike; Michael Shepley; Morland Graham; Gerald Case; Janet Burnell; Nicholas Hannen; Robert Helpmann; Freda Jackson; Jimmy Hanley; John Laurie; Niall MacGuinnes; George Robey; Roy Emerton; Griffith Jones; Arthur Hambling; Frederick Cooper; Michael Warre.

## Gone With the Wind

U.S.A.; 1939; 220 minutes;
released by MGM.

**Directed by** Victor Fleming.
**Produced by** David O. Selznick.
**Screenplay by** Sidney Howard from the novel by Margaret Mitchell.
**Photographed by** Ernest Haller.
**Production designed by** William Cameron Menzies.
**Edited by** Hal C. Kern.
**Music by** Max Steiner.
**Cast:** Vivien Leigh; Clark Gable; Leslie Howard; Olivia de Havilland; Hattie McDaniel; Thomas Mitchell; Barbara O'Neil; Caroll Nye; Laura Hope Crews; Harry Davenport; Rand Brooks; Ona Munson; Ann Rutherford; George Reeves; Fred Crane; Oscar Polk; Butterfly McQueen; Evelyn Keyes; Victor Jory; Isabel Jewell; Paul Hurst; Jane Darwell; Roscoe Ates; William Bakewell; J. M. Kerrigan; Yakima Canutt; Ward Bond; Lillian Kemble Cooper.

## Bonnie and Clyde

U.S.A.; 1967; 111 minutes;
released by Warner Bros.

**Directed by** Arthur Penn.
**Produced by** Warren Beatty.
**Screenplay by** David Newman and Robert Benton.
**Photographed by** Burnett Guffey.
**Art direction by** Dean Tavoularis.
**Edited by** Dede Allen.
**Music by** Charles Strouse.
**Cast:** Warren Beatty; Faye Dunaway; Michael J. Pollard; Gene Hackman; Estelle Parsons; Denver Pyle; Dub Taylor; Evans Evans; Gene Wilder.

## The Magnificent Ambersons

U.S.A.; 1942; 88 minutes;
released by RKO-Radio Pictures.

**Directed by** Orson Welles.
**Produced by** Orson Welles (a Mercury Production).
**Screenplay by** Orson Welles, from the novel by Booth Tarkington.
**Photographed by** Stanley Cortez.
**Art direction by** Mark Lee Kirk.
**Edited by** Robert Wise and Mark Robson.
**Music by** Bernard Herrmann.
**Cast:** Tim Holt; Joseph Cotten; Dolores Costello; Anne Baxter; Agnes Moorehead; Ray Collins; Erskine Sanford; Richard Bennett; Don Dillaway.

Acknowledgements

The following persons are quoted by the kind permission of their publishers:

Marguerite Duras (page 222), from **Hiroshima, Mon Amour,** copyright 1961 by Grove Press, Inc.; published by Grove Press; reprinted also by permission of Editions Gallimard, and by Calder and Boyars Ltd.

Akira Kurosawa (page 128), from **The Seven Samurai,** copyright 1970 by Lorrimer Publishing Limited; published in the Classic and Modern Film Scripts series by Simon & Schuster, New York, and Lorrimer Publishers, London.

Arthur Penn (page 243), from an interview, copyright 1968 by Robert Edelstein and Martin Rubin, included in **The Director's Event,** copyright 1969 by Eric Sherman and Martin Rubin; published by Atheneum; all rights reserved.

Jean Renoir (page 106), from **Sight and Sound,** vol. 31, no. 2, Spring, 1962. Also (page 104-106), from **Film: Book 2,** copyright 1962 by Robert Hughes; published by Grove Press.

Alain Resnais (page 222 and 223), from **Film: Book 2,** copyright 1962 by Robert Hughes; published by Grove Press.

Andrew Sarris (page 70), from **Interviews With Film Directors,** copyright 1967 by Andrew Sarris; published by the Bobbs-Merrill Company, Inc.

François Truffaut (page 159), from **Cahiers du Cinéma,** no. 138, 1962. Also (page 202), from **Hitchcock,** copyright 1967 by Simon & Schuster, Inc.; published by Simon & Schuster; reprinted also by permission of A. D. Peters and Company for Martin Secker & Warburg Ltd.

# Picture Credits

The editors gratefully acknowledge the studios, collectors, and film archives listed below for their courtesy in providing illustrations.

BB – Brown Brothers
CP – Culver Pictures
Col. – Columbia Pictures
GA – Gene Andrewski
KC – Kobal Collection
MGM – Metro-Goldwyn-Mayer
MOMA – Museum of Modern Art/Film Stills Archive
RKO – RKO Pictures
UA – United Artists
UFA – Universum Film Aktien
WB – Warner Brothers

**8-9:** CP. **10:** (top l. and bot. r.) CP, (others) GA. **11:** (top, l. to r.) CP, GA, CP; (middle, l. to r.) UA, CP, Universal-International, GA; (bottom) GA. **12:** GA. **13:** (top) CP, (l.) William K. Everson, (r.) BB. **14:** (clockwise from top l.) CP (3), GA (2). **15:** CP. **16:** (l.) John Allen; (r., from top) BB, BB, William K. Everson. **17:** (clockwise from top l.) CP, BB, CP, CP, MGM. **18:** (clockwise from top l.) CP, BB, CP, BB, GA, GA. **19:** GA. **20:** (top l.) CP, (top r.) GA, (bot.) Paramount. **21:** (clockwise from top) WB, GA, GA, BB. **22:** Douglas Kirkland. **23:** (l.) GA, (top r.) GA, (bot. r.) UA.

**24-25, 28-29, 30:** UA. **31:** (top) MOMA, (bottom, l. and r.) CP. **33:** CP. **34:** WB. **36-37:** UA. **39:** J. R. Eyerman. **41:** WB. **42:** (l.) WB. **42-43:** James R. Silke. **44:** John Bryson. **45:** William K. Everson.

**46-47:** KC. **49:** (top) Nero Film, (bot. l.) William K. Everson, (bot. r.) MOMA. **51:** Don Ornitz – Globe Photos. **54-55:** CP. **57:** KC/Universal-International. **58:** Universal-International. **59:** CP. **60:** WB. **61:** (top) WB, (bot. l.) MOMA, (bot. r.) CP. **62:** WB.

**64-65:** William K. Everson. **66:** CP. **68:** (top l.) CP, (top r.) John Allen, (bot.) KC/UA. **69:** (top l.) UA, (top r.) CP. (bot.) UA. **71:** (top) Cinemabilia, (bot. l.) CP, (bot. r.) MOMA. **72:** (top, l. and r.) CP, (bot.) The Bettmann Archive. **74:** (clockwise from top) CP (3), Paramount. **77, 78, 79, 80:** Col. **82:** (top) UA, (frames) Marvin E. Newman.

**84-85:** RKO. **86, 87, 88:** CP. **89:** RKO. **90:** KC/MGM. **92, 93:** MGM. **94:** (clockwise from top l.) MGM (4), KC/MGM. **95:** KC/MGM. **98-99:** UA. **100:** (clockwise from top) UA, CP, CP, William K. Everson, UA. **101:** MOMA.

**102-103:** Col. **105, 106:** World Films. **107:** Col. **109, 110, 112:** Bob Willoughby. **113:** Col. **114-115:** (bottom, from l.) CP (3), UA; (top) UA. **116:** UA. **118:** (top l., bot. center, bot. r.) Twentieth Century-Fox, (all others) Norman Snyder.

**120-121:** WB. **123:** Col. **125, 126-127, 128:** Toho. **130:** (left, from top) WB, WB, CP; (top r.) WB; (bot. r.) WB. **131:** (top) KC/WB, (bottom, l. and r.) CP. **133:** CP. **134:** (top and bot.) John Allen, (middle) WB. **135:** CP. **138, 139, 140-141:** Col.

**142-143:** Col. **145, 146, 147:** World Films. **149:** CP. **150-151:** CP. **151:** (from top) RKO (2), CP. **152:** (l.) RKO, (r.) CP. **153:** GA. **155:** Astor Pictures. **156:** (from top) Astor Pictures (2), CP, Astor Pictures. **157:** Astor Pictures. **158, 159:** Les Films du Carrosse/SEDIF. **162:** Col.

**164-165, 168, 169:** Paramount. **170:** CP. **171:** Twentieth Century-Fox. **173:** MGM. **174:** (clockwise from top l.) MGM, UA, MGM, Col., MGM, MGM, Bob Willoughby. **175, 177, 178:** Avco Embassy Corp.

**180-181, 182:** Trans-Lux. **185:** Kingsley International. **186-187:** (clockwise from top l.) Kingsley International, KC, KC, Kingsley International, KC, KC. **188-189:** Lopert Pictures Corp. **191, 192:** New Line Cinema. **194:** (l. and top r.) MGM, (bot. r.) KC/MGM. **195:** MGM.

**196-197, 199:** UFA. **200:** (top) KC/UFA, (bot.) UFA. **201:** (top, middle, bot. r.) UFA, (bot. l.) KC/UFA. **202-203:** Universal Studios. **204:** William K. Everson. **205:** CP. **206:** Gades Films International. **207, 209, 210:** MGM.

**212-213, 216:** Mayer-Burstyn. **218:** Janus Films. **220-221:** Col. **222-223:** Zenith International. **224-225:** Allied Artists.

**226-227:** MGM. **229, 230, 231:** Tricolore Films. **233, 234-235, 236, 238-239:** MGM. **240:** (l.) The Rank Organisation, (r.) CP. **241:** The Rank Organisation. **242:** (top) WB, (bottom, l. and r.) Ron Thal – Globe Photos. **244, 245:** RKO.

# Index

*Caption references in italic numbers*